JAMES JACKSON

Duelist and Militant Statesman

1757-1806

JAMES JACKSON

JAMES JACKSON

Duelist and Militant Statesman

1757-1806

BY WILLIAM OMER FOSTER, SR.

UNIVERSITY OF GEORGIA PRESS • Athens

Paperback edition, 2009
© 1960 by the University of Georgia Press
Athens, Georgia 30602
www.ugapress.org
All rights reserved
Printed digitally in the United States of America

The Library of Congress has cataloged the hardcover edition of this book as follows:
Library of Congress Cataloging-in-Publication Data

Foster, William Omer.
James Jackson, duelist and militant statesman, 1757-1806.
viii, 220 p. 25 cm.
Bibliography: p. 202-212.
1. Jackson, James, 1757-1806. I. Title.
E207.J13 F6
60-16834

Paperback ISBN-13: 978-0-8203-3440-0
ISBN-10: 0-8203-3440-5

CONTENTS

	PREFACE	vii
I	AN ADOPTED PATRIOT	1
II	BLENDING ROMANCE WITH BUSINESS, RELIGION, AND CULTURE	25
III	THE MILITIA GUARDS AGAINST THE TOMAHAWK	36
IV	THE "CHATHAM WOLF" IN THE GEORGIA LEGISLATURE	59
V	A PIONEER IN THE FIRST CONGRESS	69
VI	JACKSON IN THE SENATE	90
VII	THE YAZOO LAND FRAUD	105
VIII	PERSECUTION AND PRAISE	123
IX	PARTY BOSS AND GOVERNOR, 1795-1806	144
X	JACKSON'S SWAN SONG IN THE SENATE, 1801-1806	168
XI	HIS PROPER NICHE IN HISTORY	183
	Notes	193
	Bibliography	202
	Index	213

PREFACE

JAMES JACKSON was an extraordinarily active and useful patriot and citizen, serving as a general in the Revolutionary War and later serving the state of Georgia as governor, congressman, and senator. He was a turbulent personality, with no inhibitions about displaying his militant disposition on the dueling field or in legislative halls. He was a fiery little man, always furiously and fearlessly espousing some cause. Since Jackson has not heretofore been the subject of exhaustive biographical treatment, the author of this work has tried to do him justice, as a citizen and as a personality.

Source material has been plentiful. Jackson was never one to keep quiet on any issue and habitually expressed his views at some length in his numerous letters. Also during most of his public life he was the subject of many personal controversies in the Georgia press, and from 1796 to 1802 he was at the center of the Yazoo controversy in the newspapers of the United States and to a lesser extent of Europe. The manuscript materials are fairly rewarding and the reports of his activities in the First Congress, the governorship, and his numerous duels are adequate.

America's national historians casually assumed and Jackson's enemies openly conceded that he dominated the public life of Georgia from 1796 to 1806, and the records show that in the formative years of the Union he took an active part in the debates of Congress.

Before Jefferson returned from Paris to assume a place in Washington's cabinet and while Madison temporarily lingered in the aristocratic mood of the National Constitutional Convention of 1787, Jackson literally shouted to the House a demand for democratic simplicity in addressing the President and for a moderate centralization of power. When Hamilton induced Jefferson to approve the assumption and funding at par of the state debts, Jackson anticipated Madison in opposing this measure, and hence he deserves the honor of being considered the pioneer Republican or Democrat in the House, Maclay having this honor in the Senate.

The constant bickering between Jackson and his opponents is attributable to his turbulent disposition and the frontier conditions under which he lived. Although it is readily admitted that a spirit of tact would have enlarged his usefulness, it is refreshing to discover a politician who unhesitatingly faced dangerous public issues and who died no richer than when he first entered Congress.

The author takes this opportunity to thank the late Dr. Albert Ray Newsome, Dr. Fletcher M. Green, Dr. Hugh T. Lefler, and Dr. Hugh Holman of the University of North Carolina for their criticisms and encouragement. He also was greatly aided in locating the primary and rare secondary sources by the librarians of the Library of Congress, the universities of North Carolina, South Carolina, and Georgia, Duke and Emory universities, and the Georgia Department of Archives and History, the Georgia Historical Society, the Georgia State Library, and the Carnegie Public Library of Atlanta.

For constructive suggestions in matters of style and composition, the author expresses his gratitude to Mrs. Marjorie Akin of Miami, Florida, and the late Mrs. Emma Humfeld Foster.

I

AN ADOPTED PATRIOT

⋄ · ⋄ · ⋄ · ⋄ · ⋄ · ⋄ · ⋄ · ⋄ · ⋄ · ⋄ · ⋄ · ⋄ · ⋄ · ⋄ · ⋄ · ⋄ · ⋄

THE DUST of battle had still not settled on the cobbled streets of Savannah that July day in 1782 when the British surrendered to the threadbare Americans. Young Lieutenant Colonel James Jackson,[1] who had seen many places and many battles in his twenty-five years, was the officer chosen to accept the keys from the reluctant hands of the British.

Jackson, for whom this was neither the beginning nor the end of fights fought and honors won, had retreated from the same western gate of Savannah through which he now came as a conqueror. Three years, six months, and thirteen days previously, to be exact, the British had taken Savannah and young Jackson, serving under Colonel George Walton in the Georgia militia, had fled his adopted city by swimming a creek and fleeing up the river to Zubly's Ferry where he crossed into South Carolina.

English-born he was, but the country which had adopted him six years earlier, as he had adopted it, claimed his loyalty. In his brief autobiography[2] Jackson boasted, "when scarce sixteen I warmly supported the opposition to British measures and was the first Boy in that state who bore arms against them."

For four generations Jackson's family had lived in Moreton-Hamstead, Devonshire, in the southern part of England. Little is known of how the son, born September 21, 1757, to Mary Webber and James Jackson the elder, came to America. But as young men always want to explore new worlds, so did Jackson. He was eager to come to the new world and chafed restlessly at the family hands which reached out to restrain him. Since some former neighbors in Moreton-Hamstead had found a home in Savannah, Georgia, this was the town the Jackson boy set his sights on.

One of the old stories about him tells us that, unable to get the consent of his mother and maternal grandfather, he once attempted to sail for America by hiding in the hold of a ship but was discovered before sailing time and sent home ignominiously. The family, realizing how determined the boy was and being assured a family friend and former neighbor, John Wereat, would look after him once he reached Savannah, finally relented, and the fifteen-year-old boy boarded a ship for colonial America, this time not as a stowaway.[3] At Wereat's home the boy was received warmly and soon had a job "reading law" in the office of Samuel Farley.

When the break came with Britain a few years later Jackson already had his roots well down into American soil. There was no question where his loyalties lay. His grandfather Webber never forgave him his part in the Revolution and when the old man died he left his grandson James but enough to buy a silver cup.

Georgia was the only one of the thirteen colonies which had received direct aid from the British treasury. It needed the money for defense against the neighboring Indians, Spanish, and French. In addition, its royal governor, Sir James Wright, had served the colony well. Thus it was 1775, a year later than the other twelve colonies, that Georgia broke with Britain. A temporary state government was immediately set up under the Council of Safety and included as its officers Archibald Bulloch, president and acting governor; John Glen, chief justice; William Stephens, attorney-general; and James Jackson, clerk of the Court of Sessions. Later Jackson resigned this post and was named register of probates for Chatham County.[4] In 1777 he helped draw up Georgia's first state constitution. And then he gave up books and legal matters for a long, long time, and became a soldier, a man with gun and sword.

No particulars of James Jackson's military activities are on record until his eighteenth year when in 1775 he took part in the first act of violence done by Georgia to the British. It was one month after the battles of Lexington and Concord and it involved the capture of the Tories' powder magazine in Savannah. The Georgians used a privateer, the first ship of this type to be fitted out by the revolting colonies. Many details of the action are lacking but the name of James Jackson is included in the list of the

An Adopted Patriot

seven known leaders. Joseph Habersham, George Walton, and John Milledge, names well known in Georgia, were some of the others.[5]

Early in 1776, two months after the British evacuated Boston, the harbor of Savannah was host to another violent action of the Georgia revolutionists. Three armed British vessels and two transports, under the command of a Commodore Barclay and a Major Grant, moved up the Savannah River three miles below the city to a point called "Five Fathom Hole." Many years later Fort Jackson was to be built directly across from this point. Two of the ships sailed up Back River, a branch of the Savannah, and one of them, attempting to make a circuit of Hutchinson's Island and sail down the main stream to the city, was grounded at the western end of the island, opposite the plantation of Jonathan Bryan.

During the night the British troops from the *Scarborough*, one of the armed vessels, boarded eleven American rice ships moored at the south end of the island. The patriot Council then ordered that these cargo vessels be burned rather than have them fall into enemy hands. Lieutenant James Jackson was one of the seven men who volunteered for this job of fighting with fire. The first ship attacked, the American *Inverness*, loaded with rice and deer skins, was set afire by the patriots. It drifted across the harbor, setting fire to some of the other rice ships. When the count was taken next day the score added up to three American freighters burned, six dismantled, and two escaped to sea.[6]

The third record of Jackson's soldiering took place later the same year when the Georgia patriots attacked the Tory base below Savannah on Tybee Island. Captain Bryan, his commanding officer, was ordered back to Savannah and the command of the light infantry fell on Jackson. The enemy was driven out and all but one of the buildings on Tybee destroyed. Jackson noted in his autobiography that for this action he "merited and received" the thanks of Governor Archibald Bulloch. Shortly afterwards he made his captaincy and was placed in charge of a voluntary corps of state militia, an organization comparable to our present National Guard. Years later Jackson's obituary was to attribute this and other rapid promotions to his courage, decision, and "ardency" of temperament.[7]

The patriots had made three "annual invasions" of East Florida,[8] all unsuccessful, and now concentrated on strengthening their own defenses to which the British were obviously turning their attention.

In marshalling forces for the attack on Savannah Britain's Sir Archibald Campbell had sailed down from New York with two thousand regulars while in East Florida the British Major General Augustin Prevost sent his brother, Lieutenant Colonel Mark Prevost, and an army of four hundred men into Georgia from the south.

For the first skirmish in this struggle the twenty-one-year-old Jackson, now elevated to the rank of major by General Robert Howe, reported to Colonel John Baker on the Altamaha River, south of Savannah. Later that month General James Screven arrived with twenty American infantrymen and assumed chief command. The patriots retreated to a wood near historic Midway Congregational Church and here each side planned to ambush the other. The troops protecting the British right flank were defeated by Colonel Baker, and their ambuscade on the left was flushed by the fieldpieces of one Captain Young, assisted by some volunteers under Jackson.

In the rout Colonel Prevost was thrown from his horse. Thinking that the Americans had won the day Jackson gave the victory shout. This emotional outburst was premature, for Prevost was unharmed and, getting his men under control, he forced the patriots to withdraw. Jackson notes in his autobiography that he took part in several skirmishes with the enemy, including the one in which General Screven was killed. Jackson himself was wounded in the ankle in one of these frays.

The Prevost contingent of the British forces, apparently discouraged, however, returned to their East Florida headquarters.[9] But the British were not discouraged elsewhere, particularly at Savannah where their force of two thousand, compared to the patriots' paltry six hundred, took an easy victory. When the dead were counted the British tallied but fifteen lost compared to the Americans' staggering total of three hundred.

Jackson's commission had expired just about the time of that retreat by water when he swam the creek and fled up the Savannah River and over into South Carolina. He tells of the "prodigious hardships" he suffered and how, the militia of Georgia being dispersed and his horses being lost, as well as "every shilling of property," he was "compelled . . . to march as a common

An Adopted Patriot

soldier in Gen'l Moultrie's army from Purisbourgh to Dorchester & was in several Skirmishes in that route. . . . ." It was during this miserable march, which he described as a "barefoot expedition," that Jackson and John Milledge, dressed in rags, were arrested as spies by some of the South Carolina militia and were tried by a court-martial. In vain they pleaded their sufferings and services as proof of their patriotism. They were condemned to be hanged and the gallows was erected. Fortunately Major Peter Devaux, who knew both men well, hastened to the scene and, in the tradition of fictional last-minute reprieves, his testimony set them free.[10] Early the next year Jackson left General Moultrie and joined the troops which were active in northern Georgia and western South Carolina.

In October of the same year Count d'Estaing of France assisted General Benjamin Lincoln, the new American commander in the South, in an unsuccessful campaign to retake Savannah.[11] Jackson was supposed to have "enrolled himself" as a private in a volunteer corps under one Colonel Marbury, which led the advance of General Huger's column. In this bloody encounter, which lasted fifteen days, Jackson "behaved with his usual gallantry." Once again the Americans had taken a terrific loss—one thousand dead to the one hundred and fifty lost by the British. Jackson casually referred to the whole incident in his autobiography with the simple statement that "In Oct 1779 I was in the storm[ing] of Savannah. . . ."

Georgia and South Carolina authorities now pleaded in vain with Count d'Estaing to make another attack. "In many cases, national honor is only a convertible term for national interest," Jackson was to say in a speech made years later, illustrating his point by telling of the pleas made to d'Estaing as the count rested five miles from Savannah while his wounds healed. A final appeal for continuing the assault was made to the count's personal honor and also that of France. D'Estaing replied, "Gentlemen, if my honor is to be lost by not taking the city, it is lost already; but I deem my honor to consist in the honor of my country, and that honor is my country's interest!"

Jackson added, "The time of operation in the West Indies was arrived and the Count re-embarked his troops."

The following spring found Jackson engaged in what was to be one of numerous "affairs of honor."[12] According to his autobiography,

In March 1780 he was reappointed to his old Station of Brigade Major and in that Month was driven by the overbearing disposition of Lt Governor Wells to a personal combat which ended in the death of the latter and his being shot through both knees.

The exact cause of this duel is not fully known. George Wells was a conservative planter of some prominence and in the early days of the Revolution had been slow to break with Britain. In 1780 the patriot cause was at a very low ebb in Georgia and the state was an easy prey to foes, external and internal.

A few of the legislators had met at Augusta in January of 1779 and turned the government over to a committee. John Wereat, Jackson's old friend, became the head of this conservative group, which was now acting as the State Council, and he was by some considered the head of the government. However, George Walton, Richard Howley, and George Wells, who had recently joined the radicals, pretended to call a legislature and elect Walton governor. Thus, in addition to Governor Wright's Tory regime at Savannah, Georgia had two patriot governments wrangling over a task neither could handle.

The two groups finally came together at Augusta in January, 1780, and formed a new legislature. Howley was elected governor but in May of that year was sent to Congress. Jackson reported that he, two other Georgia officers, and the Continentals serving with them formed a guard to protect Howley's "retreat" and that this journey and "The government expenses to Philadelphia" cost Georgia a half million dollars—"so much was the money of the U. States depreciated" at that time.

Wells, president of the Council, was then asked to act as chief executive. Jackson was of a fiery disposition, as we are beginning to discover, and Wells was domineering in the assertion of an uncertain administrative authority. It was almost inevitable that the two should lock horns. Where they met for their "affair of honor" is unknown. They brought no witnesses and appear to have had a simple agreement that they would stand a few paces apart and continue firing until one of them fell. When friends arrived Wells was dead and Jackson unable to stand, one bullet having pierced both of his knees.

Charleston fell to the British in May. A few months later Jackson, having recovered from his wounds in his usual somewhat hearty fashion, left Georgia for the Carolinas where he would serve for the next seventeen months.

An Adopted Patriot

In October he fought under Colonel Thomas Sumter in a successful engagement at Fishdam Ford, on the Broad River, twenty-eight miles from Winnsboro, South Carolina. Sumter was then joined by Elijah Clarke, Twiggs, Jackson, and the Georgia militia between the Enoree and the Tyger rivers. Britain's Lieutenant Colonel Banastre Tarleton followed across the Broad and Enoree, hoping secretly to obtain a position in Sumter's rear.

Warned too late to cross the Tyger but yet in time for battle, Sumter reached Blackstock's plantation where the river turns north, runs east for a few hundred yards, then curves back south. The two armies were marching northward when Sumter turned to fight at a small stream running in an easterly direction by a large tobacco barn and emptying into the river. The bulk of the American forces were placed along the stream, in the barn, and on a hill north of the barn.

Tarleton arrived at five o'clock in the afternoon and deliberately began to place his men in the most advantageous positions but Sumter took the initiative and forced him to immediate action. The British drove back the Americans' initial attack and their cavalry temporarily turned the American left held by the Georgians. The new reinforcements in the persons of Jackson, Twiggs, Winn, and their compatriots, helped the Georgians hold their ground, however, and a forward drive by the whole American force soon put the British to flight.[13].

Later, Jackson was to write Mathew Carey that "General Sumter was wounded early in the action, and retired. Colonel (now General) Twiggs and myself fought the enemy three hours after this, and defeated them totally bringing off upward of thirty dragoon horses." He later wrote another friend, Edward Langworthy, that after Sumter was wounded "I advanced by his order in sight of the encampment & fires. . . . Two South Carolina Colonels [Richard] Winn and [Edward] Lacy . . . deserved credit, but . . . the Georgians bore the brunt. . . ." Tarleton lost between one fifth and one third of his men and the patriots suffered but three wounded and one dead.

A participant in the battle, Colonel Samuel Hammond, wrote that "In forming for battle . . . [Sumter] was ably and actively assisted by Major James Jackson, of Georgia, acting as a volunteer aide and as brigade-major."[14] Joseph Johnson stated that two of the bravest participants in this engagement were among the youngest and that[15]

In the same battle, another lad . . . first brought himself into notice. He was in the thickest of the fight, and was repeatedly seen to seize the guns and accoutrements of the dead British soldiers, and thereby equip himself for a continued fire on the enemy. This he kept up as coolly and as actively, as if he had been engaged in a game of baseball. This boy was afterwards General James Jackson, of Georgia, ...

In the fall of 1780 the patriots received further encouragement from two events: Major Nathanael Greene was appointed Commander of the Southern Department, a post which he ably held to the end of the war; and another victory was rung up at King's Mountain when the Americans were victorious over Patrick Ferguson.

In order to threaten Fort Ninety-Six and to enlist recruits, Clarke, with a group of American militia, paused for a time on Long Cane Creek in western South Carolina. Early in December Colonel Benjamin Few assumed command and Britain's Lieutenant Colonel Isaac Allen sought to drive him out of this section. The British defeated the Americans at this point and Few ordered his forces to withdraw.[16] Jackson was probably with the Georgians in this encounter but the only details are those found in the brief statement in his autobiography that "more than once such was his influence & the love the Men bore him he saved the Camp from being totally abandoned; particularly after Clarke was wounded at Long Cane."

In January of 1781 the Georgia and Carolina militia were placed under the command of Colonel Andrew Pickens. Greene took a position on the east bank of the Pee Dee River and decided to divide his forces by sending Brigadier General Daniel Morgan to threaten Fort Ninety-Six. Pickens united his militia with Morgan near the junction of the Broad and Pacolet rivers, whereupon Morgan delivered an animated address, asking for help from the Georgians who were scattered throughout this section. He ordered Jackson to distribute copies of this plea to those scattered refugees; they responded promptly, in time to take an active part in the Battle of Cowpens on January 17, 1781.[17]

General Charles Cornwallis sent Tarleton to destroy Morgan's forces before he could reunite with Greene, hoping that the Southern commander could then be pursued into North Carolina and defeated before he could be re-inforced by Washington or escape into Virginia. Greene later wrote General Francis Marion

An Adopted Patriot

that Morgan's forces totaled approximately nine hundred and seventy while Tarleton had twelve hundred. The latter also had two three-pounder cannon, while Morgan had none. In addition the British cavalry outnumbered the American mounted forces three to one. Also, Tarleton later admitted that the ground at Cowpens was well adapted for cavalry.

Cowpens is situated near Spartanburg, about three miles south of the line between the Carolinas where the Broad River runs in an easterly direction and turns toward the south. With their backs to this river Morgan's forces faced the south. The Georgia and South Carolina militia were placed in the front line under the command of Pickens whom Jackson was serving as brigade major. The second or main line, posted on a small ridge to the north, was manned by the continentals, or regulars, and some Virginia militia under Colonel John Eager Howard. On the northern slope of a higher ridge to the rear were posted the cavalry under Colonels William Washington and James McCall.

On the night before the battle Jackson congratulated the Georgia and Carolina troops upon being placed in advance of the continentals and in "stentorian" tones "animated" their spirits by reminding them that theirs was the responsibility of proving the merits of the state militia. His men, sharing the confidence of the continentals, had learned that Tarleton was rapidly moving up from the south but that scouts had been carefully posted. Thus satisfied as to the relative safety of their position the militia slept well and arose early to a day fateful and proud in American history.

After a hearty breaking of the night's fast each man stepped briskly to his appointed position. Jackson took an elevated position where he could watch both his pickets and the first line as well as the approach of the British. Tarleton drew within view at daybreak. Although his men were weary from their long and rapid march Tarleton, nervously and in rash haste, ordered them to rush the American positions.

The battle began at seven o'clock. As the British advanced in double-quick step Jackson gave the signal. The pickets fired and, according to their orders, rushed back to the first line where they reloaded. As soon as they could "mark the epaulet men" the militia of the first line gave the advancing British a well-aimed, withering fire which momentarily caused them to hesitate. Jackson then rode toward the east and the Carolina and Georgia militia in orderly ranks left the first line and rapidly followed him around the American left, joining the cavalry to form a rear guard. As these militia disappeared over the second ridge the British regained their momentum and charged the second or main line. Here they met a stronger fire from Howard's larger force. The aim of the Americans was most effective, their resistance most determined, and the British again began to waver.

Tarleton then decided that this was the logical time to order forward his reserves, and the impact of the re-inforced British troops was so violent that they began to turn the American right. To block this move Howard ordered one of his companies on the extreme right to form at right angles to the main line. In the excitement and confusion the American subordinate officers thought this order called for a general retreat and the whole line began to move back toward the higher ridge. The British mistook an orderly withdrawal for a rout and rushed forward like a mob. After a brief conference with Washington and Howard, Morgan sent the cavalry around his left to the rear of Tarleton. He also ordered Howard's men to about-face and charge with bayonets along the entire line. The militia under Jackson, having been ordered by Pickens to swing around the American right, soon broke through and made contact with Washington's cavalry. Thus the British were caught in a vise. The hand-to-hand fighting which followed soon brought the struggle to an end.

In the contest, which lasted about an hour, the American losses totaled only seventy-two killed, wounded, and taken prisoner, while the British losses amounted to eight hundred, a large number lost being commissioned officers. Their two cannon were also forfeited and Tarleton, with part of his cavalry, barely escaped.

After Cowpens Cornwallis lingered two days to collect his troops and destroy his heavy baggage. The delay gave the Americans time to cross the Catawba River with their wounded and prisoners.

In his autobiography Jackson wrote of his part in the battle:

He has been heard to say that if he ever was pleased with himself or if ever he deserved credit in action it was on that day. He led the Militia took a great proportion of the prisoners above a dozen Officers [sic] swords and among them Major McArthurs [sic] the Commander of the British infantry & whose person he delivered to Genl Morgan.

In his report to Congress Morgan gave only a general statement of praise for Pickens and his officers. In the last paragraph he stated that "Colonel Pickens, and all the officers in his corps, behaved well; but, from their having so lately joined the detachment, it has been impossible to collect all their names and rank, so that the general is constrained not to particularize any, lest it should be doing injustice to others."

Several of Georgia's military leaders shared Jackson's sense of injustice but Jackson decided to do something about it. After all, of the seventy-two patriots lost at Cowpens, eight were Georgians. In 1795 Jackson took the matter up with Morgan and Pickens.[18] He first wrote Morgan that he was requesting a statement from him in order that it might be included in a proposed history of Georgia. He said that the officers of the three Georgia companies attributed the omission of their names in the official report to the loss of Morgan's dispatches and that Major John Cunningham and Captains Samuel Hammond, George Walton, and Joshua Inman "all behaved well."

Although Jackson mentioned himself with some "difficulty" he boasted that he commanded all the Georgia and South Carolina troops; he served as brigade major to all the militia; by his own prowess he captured Major McArthur; and at "the utmost risk" of his life he temporarily seized the colors of the 71st British regiment and was rescued from imminent death only by the personal exertions of Howard. Morgan was also reminded that on the field of battle he had expressed his gratitude for Jackson's heroism. He next mailed Pickens a copy of his letter and Pickens wrote Morgan a concise note, characteristic of him. "Dear General," he stated, "Our friend, General Jackson, has shown me this letter. His merits cannot be forgotten by you!"

Morgan, however, was occupied that year with the suppression of the "Whisky Insurrection" in western Pennsylvania against our first federal excise and failed to reply. Three weeks later Jackson wrote him again, correcting two statements in his former letter and strengthening his appeal for justice to the Georgians. He explained that the Virginia militia were not under his direction and that Morgan's thanks were expressed verbally rather than in orders but were repeated when the army reached North Carolina. General Greene, Major Edward Giles, and Colonel Charles McDowell had confirmed Pickens' high opinion of Jackson's conduct at Cowpens, but upon publication of Morgan's report Jackson was chagrined that his name was not even mentioned.

In 1797 Jackson's enemies, seeking revenge for his criticism of their fraudulent Yazoo land transactions, tried to minimize his exploits at Cowpens. In order to defend his record Jackson secured from Pickens a certificate which stated that Jackson's firm, active conduct greatly aided in animating the troops and insuring the success of the day and that he "particularly signalized" himself in this battle.

A sarcastic statement once made by Morgan may explain why he never answered Jackson's letters. He stated that at Cowpens "I would not have had a swamp in the view of my militia on any consideration; they would have made for it and nothing could have detained them. . . ."

His experience at Cowpens inspired a great urge in Jackson to arouse someone to write the history of his state, particularly Georgia's part in the Revolution.[19] Failing to enlist Judge George Walton for the task Jackson centered his efforts upon Edward Langworthy, who had signed the Articles of Confederation and who, although now living in Maryland, had previously represented Georgia in Congress and had been secretary of the Provincial Congress in Georgia.

In 1790 Jackson asked Langworthy to return to Georgia for a protracted visit in order to work up a good subscription for his history. A prospectus of this proposed two-volume "Political History of Georgia" was advertised in the press as early as the summer of 1791 but several years elapsed before the manuscript was ready. When Langworthy lost his wife in 1795 he received from Jackson a message of sympathy, followed by several valuable suggestions for the history. One of his proposals was that it include an account of the effort in 1777 by South Carolina to absorb the small colony of Georgia and the vigorous, successful endeavor of Georgia's Governor John Adams Treutlen to block the plan. Langworthy's despondency over the death of his wife never lifted, however, and the history was never published. In fact the manuscript and most of his other papers were lost.

Jackson next served in Greene's campaign in North Carolina in 1781 and he tells us in his autobiography that

He was at the crossing of the Catawba by the British . . . & the surprise of Torren's where staying too long in rallying the Men & making opposition he nearly lost his life and was reported killed to Genl Morgan at Salisbury—Here when he arrived in a Most dirty plight with a Straw hat he was introduced to that great Warrior Genl Greene who took a liking to him & declared to Genl Elbert after that there was something in his countenance which struck him at first sight.

Other sources also show that William Davidson's North Carolina militia from Rowan and Mecklenburg counties temporarily retarded Cornwallis's crossing of the Catawba. Davidson was killed in this engagement and the militia fled towards Salisbury with the understanding that as many as possible would collect on the route at Torrent's Tavern. Some three hundred of the men reached this point about noon where they rested. About two o'clock in the afternoon they learned that a troop of British cavalry under Tarleton was approaching.

Jackson promptly assumed the command. The day was wet and the men were demoralized but Jackson, aided by a few other officers, rallied them and their fire killed or wounded seven of the British and fifteen of their horses. Thomas U. P. Charlton tells us that fifty of the Americans were killed and the rest fled into the woods, but a British officer who passed by shortly after the battle reported that he saw fewer than ten patriots left upon the battlefield. After crossing the Yadkin River Jackson's Georgians continued under the immediate command of Brigadier General Andrew Pickens.

Among Jackson's numerous frays in North Carolina was an encounter at the Haw River where he assisted in dispersing a group of loyalists under one Colonel Pyle. Pyle was leading between two and three hundred of these men to the camp of Cornwallis. The patriots concealed their uniforms and pretended that they, too, were hastening to report to British headquarters. They had overtaken and almost passed Pyle when some local loyalists discovered their disguise and notified the enemy. Pyle's men attacked them but were put to rout themselves.

In the certificate Pickens gave to Jackson in 1797 he stated that "Jackson's conduct during a severe tour of duty in North Carolina . . . was such as merited not only my approbation, but that of Major General Greene, who determined from that period to give Major Jackson the command of a State Corps, which was soon after raised. . . ."[20]

Cornwallis, meanwhile, after winning a costly victory at Guilford Courthouse, North Carolina, in March of 1781 moved to Wilmington and then into Virginia, where he surrendered at

Yorktown in October of that year. However, contrary to the impression given by some historians, the actual hostilities of the Revolution did not end at Yorktown. The British continued to hold parts of South Carolina and Georgia until the summer of 1782, and New York City until peace was signed in 1783.

Shortly before the battle at Guilford Courthouse Greene had sent Pickens to South Carolina to check the ravages of the British in the area of Fort Ninety-Six. From then on Jackson's fighting was confined to his own state and South Carolina. In fact the Georgia and South Carolina militia did much of their bloodiest fighting during the last nine months of 1781 and the first six months of 1782, most of it on Georgia soil.

According to Jackson's autobiography Pickens had ordered him to Augusta, Georgia, and then into South Carolina where he assisted "Gallant" Colonel Samuel Hammond in recruiting 250 volunteers.

The patriots were attempting to retake Augusta, which was held by the British under Colonel Thomas Brown, a Georgia Tory. When Jackson again arrived on the scene he found all "in utmost confusion." In the absence of Colonel Clarke, Colonels Baker and Williamson and Major Stirk had declined the command. Instead of acting as a unit each of the officers and men was "possessed of different views," the cry being "every Man to his tent O Israel." If this state of affairs had continued for two more hours the siege would have failed but "the recollection of his former conduct made them appeal" to Jackson. At his request the besiegers remained and heard him the next morning when, in "a single speech" from horseback, he reminded them of the prospect of a continuance of tyranny, exile from their families, other "miseries," and "the object they were about to lose." The speech was dramatic and "his presence reanimated the whole" and "induced them unanimously to insist on his taking the command," as they vowed "they would go to the Worlds end with him." He accepted the leadership and promptly directed the men to bundle long wooden sticks into fascines (for raising the batteries, filling ditches, and strengthening the ramparts), to mount "a five-pounder" and to erect military works before Fort Grierson.

After "one half the struggle was over" Jackson was relieved of his position by the arrival of superior officers. Clarke first resumed the command and later was followed by Harry Lee, who in turn was succeeded by Pickens. Jackson said that Lee and Pickens had failed to name either Clarke or himself in their official reports and "assumed to themselves the whole merit of the siege." He claimed that his preliminary efforts had laid the groundwork for Lee's and Pickens' success and, while under their command, he had led one of the advances on Fort Grierson, captured two "Grasshoppers" (three-pounder cannon), and killed several officers and men.

In the Fort Grierson assault Pickens and Clarke struck the northwest side. Majors Pinkertham, Eaton, and Jackson marched down the Savannah River and attacked the northeast sector and Lee took a position to the south in order to support Eaton and attack Brown should the latter attempt to march from Fort Cornwallis to the aid of Grierson. For a time the Georgians bore the brunt of the fighting. Grierson finally left the fort and attempted to escape down the river to join Brown. He was captured and later was shot in prison by an unidentified soldier. Jackson wrote, "it is supposed Capt Alexander shot the fatal ball."

Brown surrendered on June 5, 1781, under the condition that he be taken under guard to Savannah, where he would remain a prisoner on parole. Pickens and Lee hastened with the prisoners to join Greene in the vicinity of Ninety-Six. Later Brown was exchanged and vigorously renewed his activities against the patriots.

Clarke then left Jackson in charge at Augusta and moved some of his forces north into Wilkes County, Georgia. Again, Jackson's claims to merit are verified by Pickens' 1797 certificate that "At the siege of Augusta Major Jackson's exertions, in the early period . . . laid the groundwork for the reduction of that place. He led one of the advanced parties as Capt. Rudolph did another, at the storming of Grierson's Fort, and had the command of a moving battery, at the time of the surrender of Fort George, in which he conducted with honor to himself and his country."[21]

With Augusta now in the hands of the patriots and his own forces reinforced by Pickens and Lee, Greene started in June to the relief of Ninety-Six. In order to be more evenly matched with what was presumed to be Rawdon's superior strength he endeavored to collect the rest of the available militia. Accordingly, Pickens promptly wrote Jackson that "Gen. Greene has ordered me to write you to collect all the men you possibly can, and join the army without loss of time, or if it is more convenient to you to join Colonel Leroy Hammond. . . ." He concluded with Greene's express orders that the fortifications at Augusta be leveled and that Jackson use his own judgment in disposing of the artillery. Complying with these orders Jackson marched thirty miles north into South Carolina where, learning that Greene had retired from his encampment in front of Ninety-Six, he decided that his mission was impracticable and returned to his headquarters at Augusta.

As another British attack on Augusta was evidently not imminent Jackson next marched north to the relief of Clarke, who was threatened by both a group of Rawdon's South Carolina loyalists and the British garrison from Ninety-Six. Again returning to Augusta, Jackson held that post until the Georgia legislature met there later in August.[22]

Shortly after the siege of Augusta Jackson was promoted to Lieutenant Colonel and authorized to raise and command a force of his own. He tells us himself that General Greene "in compliance with a prior promise sent the Major a Col [sic] commission for a partisan Legion which was filled and himself made Commandant of Augusta." In his *Notes On Ramsay* he also tells us that his commission was later confirmed by Congress. He maintained this post despite Lord Rawdon's march between General Greene and himself. The newly created force, known as the "Georgia State Legion," was formed by the legislature on August 21, 1781, and was composed of two companies of one hundred men each, one of cavalry and one of infantry. They were to be raised for a period of twelve months.

On January 10, 1782, a simpler organization was set up. This time the commissioned officers were: Lieutenant Colonel James Jackson; Major Thomas Washington; Captains Henry Allison, Sherwood Bugg, John Morrison, James Stallings, and John Lyons; Lieutenants Thomas Hamilton, Ezekiel Stallings, "Mad" Benjamin Hawkins, Stephen Blount, Benjamin Harvey, and Nicholas Millar; Adjutant Benjamin Hawkins; and cornets or standardbearers, Ezekiel Stallings and Benjamin Hawkins.

Jackson was authorized to purchase one hundred horses for his cavalrymen (sometimes called dragoons or mounted infantrymen) and to give in payment state certificates, payable with interest in four months, which could be used in paying state taxes or redeemed in cash secured through the sale of confiscated or "sequestered and absentee estates." Some of the camp followers were pro-

An Adopted Patriot

vided for in an act authorizing twenty-five and one half rations per day for the women and children. On one occasion the governor was ordered to furnish the Legion with twelve dozen "cartridges."

In June of 1782 the British were still in possession of Savannah but the finances of Georgia were at such a low tide that a bill to reduce the State Legion cavalry to "one Troop" was passed by the legislature. Jackson, who was a member of the legislature, voted against the measure. In July the legislature also resolved that the dragoons "be paid the bounty out of the Negroes Provided for that Purpose" and the "Infantry be allowed a Compleat Suit of Clothes and one bushel of Salt to each man," and that the former loyalists who aided Jackson in the assault on Savannah in July of 1782 be rewarded with a bounty of one Negro each. The financial affairs of the Legion were not completely wound up until 1783, when the Council ordered Jackson to make a return of the "Public Horses" which had belonged to his troops during the preceding year.[23]

Shortly after the Legion's organization some twenty of its Tory recruits in the militia company conceived a plan to have Jackson's "own quarter guard" bayonet him in his bed, recapture Augusta, and take Governor Nathan Brownson and his Council to Savannah. The leader of the plot communicated it to Alured Clarke, the British General in Savannah, who promised the traitor a generous reward if he succeeded. In the late summer General Clarke sent one Captain Brantley to the suburbs of Augusta with forty-five British soldiers who were instructed to come to the aid of the plotters about the time they planned to have Jackson killed.

David Davis, a dragoon serving as Jackson's waiter, overheard two of the plotters discussing the dark scheme. Davis began to quietly circulate among the subversive group, expressing such contempt for his superior that he was admitted to the inner circle. He then reported the detailed plan to Jackson who immediately ordered his dragoons to mount their horses and appear fully armed before his tent. The infantrymen were then ordered to appear without arms under the pretext of searching them for stolen clothing. With drawn swords the dragoons then arrested the twenty who were involved in the plot.

Seventeen of the men, when questioned individually and promised immunity for turning state's evidence, named the three whom Davis also had implicated as the leaders. The seventeen were pardoned and restored to their places but the ringleaders — John Goodgame, William Simmons, and a man identified only as Honeycut — were tried before a general court-martial and hanged. As soon as Captain Brantley learned of this unexpected turn of events he hastily retreated to Savannah. In July, 1782, the legislature rewarded Davis with "a Compleat Suit of Clothes, a good Horse Saddle and Bridle, a likely Negro and three hundred Acres of Land. . . ."

In 1781, the year the Legion was formed, the patriots were in control of the upper parts of Georgia. General John Twiggs, who headed the state troops, conceived a plan for retaking the middle and lower parts. Part of his plan was to order Jackson to move his Legion some miles down the Savannah River and from his new base to make occasional raids upon the enemy, withdrawing whenever he felt it expedient. Late in October Jackson stated in a letter to Twiggs that, upon arriving at a place called Martins, he found a Captain Grant encamped with about thirty patriot troops. An unnamed girl camp follower who had just arrived from Savannah reported to Jackson that the British had abandoned all their outposts except those at Governor Wright's plantation and at Ebenezer. As Jackson gradually moved towards Savannah he engaged in frequent bouts with the enemy. As the British retreated they burned the bridges and carried away or destroyed the supplies. Notwithstanding all these hindrances he captured Ebenezer in the fall and made it his headquarters.

Jackson's troops suffered the hardships experienced by the other Georgia militia and the private citizens. In an address some years later he stated that for the five-year period beginning in 1778 the Georgia people lost each year their total crop of corn, rice, and indigo. An idea of the scarcity of food and supplies is given in a letter Lieutenant Thomas Hamilton wrote Jackson from Augusta in 1782. Hamilton said he was sending him some brass spurs and several articles of clothing which his troops had made, and that all in his outfit were keenly distressed because there was "not one Mouthful of Bread to be had, no Salt, and nothing to Subsist on but poor Beef — I shall Think myself happy . . . to be Recall'd."

In 1795 Jackson wrote Langworthy that he was enclosing Hamilton's letter to show the "horrid condition" of his Legion in 1782 when frequently they went for periods as long as forty-eight hours without bread, beef, rice, rum, whiskey, or any drink other than the "common swamp water" with which to "quench their thirst."

As a result of this "absolute want" and without costing the "State of Georgia a farthing," his "Dragoons were clothed and armed, except pistols, by themselves — even their Caps and boots & spurs their Coats were made of Deerskins dressed & turned up with the little blue cloth I could procure. . . ." To further substantiate this gloomy picture he quoted Thomas Jefferson as having written, "It must be remembered that state had peculiarly suffered; that the British army had completely overrun it; had held possession of it for some years and that all the Inhabitants had been obliged to either abandon their Estates, and fly their Country or to remain in it under a military Government." Jackson added that a new work written in England confirmed his account of the suffering of the Georgians. He probably referred to C. Stedman's *The History of the Origin, Progress and Termination of the American War,* published in 1794.[24]

In order to continue receiving supplies of food from the loyalists and furs from the Creeks, the British in 1781 sought to keep the road open from Savannah to the lower counties. They erected strongholds at Sunbury and Great Ogeechee Ferry on the Ogeechee River, a few miles south of the city. General Twiggs feared that these fortifications would prevent him from driving the enemy back into Savannah and ordered Jackson to take the dragoons of Carr and Stallings, along with McKay's riflemen, and try to take the Great Ogeechee Ferry by surprise.

Jackson attacked in November. He quietly captured the British scouts and then made such a violent thrust at the White House, the chief defense of the ferry, that he also quickly surprised and captured a Captain Johnston, who was in charge. Johnston "pulled off his coat & presented his sword to Col. Jackson" but Captain Carr of the militia "imprudently" killed a British officer just as he was handing over his arms and the enemy concluded that no quarter would be given. Johnston rushed his men back into the building and they now fought with such abandon that Jackson had to relinquish what otherwise would have been a brilliant victory and retreat, with the loss of Captain Grant and several others.

Later in the day at the Butler house, about a mile from the ferry, he discovered fifteen loyalists under Captains Goldsmith and Howell, the latter being ill. Jackson attacked the house with such spirit that he killed the two captains and five of their men.

Meanwhile Colonel Archibald Campbell, with slightly less than ninety British dragoons, had taken a position near Butler's house. He had just been reinforced by Captain Johnston with the troops from the ferry and by Captain Wylie, recently arrived with some Tory rangers from East Florida. About four o'clock in the afternoon Campbell ordered his men to march against the retreating Americans. The American riflemen under McKay and all but eight of those under Lieutenant William Greene had deserted, the better to remove the spoils of their recent victory. This left Jackson with only thirty other militia besides the Carr and Stallings riflemen — a total of fifty-seven. The British had eighty-five dragoons. In order that the enemy might not realize how greatly they outnumbered his forces Jackson concealed the cavalry behind a small round hill and as his militia met the first shock of the attack his cavalrymen, armed only with swords, assaulted the British center.

The Americans killed a Lieutenant Hardenbrook and the total loss to the British was forty-two, "near his whole amount of men." Only six of the Americans were killed, seven wounded, and five taken prisoner. Jackson then forced the enemy to retreat a short distance where they made a stand under the shelter of a fence. As Jackson "found his column divided and engaged in the rear" he led them in regular order to the shelter of an adjacent swamp. Neither side renewed the attack and this "induced him to make it a draw battle" although he later wrote that "The British . . . confessed the crippling of their Horse by this action & they never were able to recover it." As night came on he returned to his headquarters at Ebenezer.

General Greene, upon receiving the reports of this encounter, wrote Governor Nathan Brownson of Georgia and applauded Jackson's courage and brilliance against a much superior force and promised to report it to Congress, but "no further notice was taken of it!" A slightly different account of these two engagements was published in a Savannah paper by an unnamed British reporter. This scribe claimed that in the attack on the "White House" Jackson's troops outnumbered the British two to one and that he lost Captains Grant and Lucas; that in his successful attack at Butler's house Britain's Captain Goldsmith was "butchered" by Samuel West; and that four British privates were "murdered in cold blood."[25]

Towards the close of 1781 General Greene ordered Brigadier

General Anthony Wayne to assume the supreme command in Georgia.

On January 12, 1782, Wayne crossed the Savannah River, accompanied by a detachment of artillery and four hundred dragoons under Colonels Anthony Walton White and Wade Hampton. Shortly after Wayne's arrival Jackson's Legion, now numbering one hundred and fifty, joined him at his headquarters at Ebenezer. Jackson brought Wayne a letter from Governor John Martin, which was to be delivered by "Col. Jackson of the Georgia State Legion, a friend of mine. He is a gentleman and a soldier. I beg leave to introduce him to your acquaintance as one worthy of your confidence."[26]

When Wayne was on the march Jackson was usually placed twelve or fifteen miles in the advance of the main force. In the autobiography Jackson tells us that upon joining Wayne he was

... instantly appointed notwithstanding there were older Officers & who complained to the Command of the Advance of that army and in which he baffled every art & stratagem of the enemy to surprise him which was repeatedly attempted—The Col frequently took the Horses out of Waggons & prisoners off the Commons of Savannah in presence of & within gunshot of the Enemy—burnt Sir James Wrights [sic] barns under the nose of the British Garrison & harassed them continually—

Jackson also wrote that his Legion was "almost every day or two engaged with British parties." One account stated that the British failed in two attempts to surprise him. At Cuthbert's Sawmill in February he was attacked by Colonel Hezekiah Williams but the British got the worst of this encounter. Later in the month Wayne sent Major Robert Barnwell to destroy the British supply of rice on Hutchinson's Island and Jackson was instructed to perform a similar task on the plantation of Governor Wright, half a mile southeast of Savannah. Barnwell failed but Jackson, with thirty dragoons, drove in the British pickets and the rice barns of the Tory governor were soon in flames. On his way back to Ebenezer he passed through a prison camp of two hundred wounded loyalists and refugees. So great was the hatred of the Georgians for those loyal to the Crown that Jackson had to sternly order his men to spare their lives.

It was daring raids such as these that influenced Wayne to write Greene that he was "bullying the enemy at the line of Savannah with Jackson's little legion and some *crackers*, another species of Tories who have surrendered themselves and joined our arms." Jackson's Legion, serving as the advance guard, must have experienced the conditions Wayne had in mind when he wrote that "It is now upward of five weeks since we entered this State, during which period not an Officer or Soldier with me have undressed for the purpose of changeing his Linnen."[sic]

Wayne's attitude toward Jackson varied. While at times he gave praise to an officer presumed to be Jackson, at other times his attitude was marked by angry criticism. On one occasion some of the militia of the Georgia Legion were ordered to guard a group of Indian prisoners. Wayne reported that, wearying of watching the prisoners drink rum and tea in their warm quarters, "through neglect or worse motive," the guards turned their backs and every Creek escaped. On another occasion, while angered by having to live on "poor beef, swamp seed and aligator [sic] water," Wayne learned that Jackson had imprisoned a soldier for impertinence to an officer. Wayne ordered that the man be released. When the jailor said that Jackson would be displeased Wayne exclaimed, "Jackson's a damned liar. Let him do his worst, God damn him, I don't care a damn for him."

Meanwhile Alured Clarke, seeing the British control of Georgia had been reduced to the fortified section immediately around Savannah, sent urgent requests to the Creeks and Cherokees for assistance, and it was finally arranged that a Creek and Cherokee reinforcement should appear at the Ogeechee River on the fifteenth of May. On May 19th a detachment of British cavalry under Captains Ingram and Corker was sent to greet the Indians. Wayne ordered Jackson to take a position on the Ogeechee Road, eight miles south of Savannah, near the plantation of James Habersham.

Learning through his scouts of the movements of Ingram and Corker, Jackson left his infantry at Little Ogeechee River and moved his dragoons three miles farther south where he met the enemy's advance guard and drove them back upon the main body. At Fox's he was defeated by a force of British militia and regulars. Then, retreating north a short distance to Struthers' plantation, he stationed his entire force in a swamp on each side of the road. When the British dragoons under Atwood arrived they were speeded on their way towards Savannah by a warm volley from the patriots. Jackson reported that he "almost un-

An Adopted Patriot

horsed the British & if his own Dragoons had behaved equal to his Infantry — must have captured the whole party."

He later learned that Thomas Brown had been sent to assist in bringing the Indians into the city and that his force had reached Little Ogeechee, eight miles south of Savannah. As Jackson's force was too weak to attack the reinforced British troops he sent word of these movements to Wayne, who was stationed at the plantation of Mrs. William Gibbons, six miles northwest of Savannah. Wayne hastened to the scene and, by a surprise night attack with bayonets, routed Brown and probably would have captured his entire force if some local people had not guided them along a little used trail back to the city. This battle occurred on May 21 and was mentioned in Jackson's autobiography with the brief comment that "In May he had the brunt of the action with Col Brown altho the conclusion of the business was effected by Genl Wayne. . . ."[27]

On May 23 Sir Guy Carleton issued an order from New York to Tory Governor Wright to prepare for the evacuation of Savannah and promised transportation for all British sympathizers. At four o'clock on the afternoon of July 10 Wayne issued the following order:

As the enemy may be expected daily to evacuate the town, the troops will take care, to be provided with a clean shift of linnen [sic], and to make themselves as respectable as possible for the occasion. . . . Lieut. Col. Jackson, in consideration of his severe and fatiguing service in the advance, is to receive the keys of Savannah, and is allowed to enter at the western gate, keeping a patrole [sic] in town to apprehend stragglers, who may steal in with the hopes of plunder.

The last of the British troops were out of Savannah by two o'clock on the afternoon of July 11, 1782, and that evening Jackson received the keys of the city from a group of British officers.

According to his autobiography, "he was the first Man who entered the British Gate of what might be termed his American native town." It is not known whether this honor went to him through the decision of Greene or Wayne or, as one account states, through the vote of the army.[28]

A few days later Wayne was ordered to join Greene in the assault on Charleston, and Savannah was left under the command of Jackson and John Habersham. On July 25 Jackson had a skirmish with some British forces on Skidaway Island. The details of this encounter are unknown but it is known that this was the last fighting to be done on Georgia soil during the Revolution.[29]

A month before he received the keys of the city Jackson had bought on credit a house in Savannah. On July 30th the legislature made him a present of this property. The resolution, passed with an overwhelming majority, reads:[30]

Whereas Lieutenant Colo Jackson hath rendered many great and usefull [sic] Services to his Country, for which he is entitled to the notice and Attachment of the Legislature,

Be it therefore Resolved that the House which heretofore belonged to Mr. Tattnall in Savannah be granted to Colo Jackson as a mark of the sense entertained by the Legislature of his merits.

After the Revolution he turned his attention to the practice of law and other civilian pursuits.

II

BLENDING ROMANCE WITH BUSINESS, RELIGION, AND CULTURE

◊ • ◊ • ◊ • ◊ • ◊ • ◊ • ◊ • ◊ • ◊ • ◊ • ◊ • ◊ • ◊ • ◊ • ◊ • ◊

ACCORDING to Jackson's own estimate he made "an ample fortune" in his practice of law in the Savannah repossessed by the Americans. With George Walton as his legal mentor he soon achieved distinction as an animated attorney at a time when flamboyant oratory was essential for the successful lawyer.

As early as 1783 he claimed that his legal practice "as my books will prove, afforded me from three thousand to three thousand five hundred pounds sterling per annum." This was in spite of the fact that during these years "law books indeed, were scarce, owing to the ravages of war." However, Jackson reported that the legal library of Judge Walton was "open at all times, for my young men; and that library I purchased. . . ."

A large part of Jackson's legal practice from 1786 to 1804 was concerned with settling legal estates, and the young attorney received some high fees in those early days. In 1782, as executor for the estate of Daniel Wolecon, he received slightly over three hundred and eighty pounds. In 1784 the state legislature appropriated ten guineas as his "retaining and pleading fees" for several actions in which he was called to assist the attorney general.[1]

In 1783 he began to use his influence to bolster the unsavory reputation of the legal profession, especially in some of the southern counties where an organized effort was being made to cripple the lawyers. From Richmond County Jackson wrote to a friend, concerning the propaganda of one Frice:

I have been amazed at the attempt of his Brownsboro plan—An association has actually begun in this County and is now pushing forward for the total exclusion of lawyers—and with them why not Law—Many plebeians have joined his standard but the sensible see through the disguise . . . and it is by some conjectured the high mettled hobby horse he rides will some day give him a tricky fall.

The original sources throw no light on the nature and success of the Brownsboro plan.

Jackson himself did not escape these attacks. In 1784 he explained in a letter through the press that during the previous year he had overlooked a rumor that he received a bribe from one Dr. M'Cleod as he had another rumor that "I had received 60 guineas from Mr. Thomas Young to serve his purposes. . . ." The last report left him "unhurt" because it was "unfelt" and, like the former, it would have met with contempt were it not his duty to his friends, who had denied it, to repudiate it himself. Concerning one young man who had circulated one of these reports that Jackson was "a secondary planet in Mr. Young's business" Jackson wrote

Did he know me, he would be convinced my pride, however deficient I may be, will never permit me to rate myself second to any at the Georgia Bar—and therefore, was I to be bribed, it would take as large a purse to buy me as any of my profession. . . .

There followed in the same issue of the paper a sworn statement by Benjamin Maxwell and Jacob Waldburger, clerks to Jackson, to the effect that since coming into his employ in 1783 they had had access to all his papers and knew him to have turned down many bribes offered to induce him to support certain measures before the legislature. One prominent Tory had offered two large plantations if Jackson would persuade the legislature to restore his confiscated property. Jackson resisted any temptation he might have felt to enter into these alliances.

He also on occasion criticized lawyers who charged excessive fees. Georgia allowed the governor to employ attorneys to aid those citizens who were defendants in writs of error in the federal Supreme Court. Jackson, during his governorship, ordered one hundred dollars each paid to Dallas and Ingersoll, attorneys for William Mein and one Williamson. He added the comment that "Lawyers have their peculiar kind of *reasonable* consciences and which in pecuniary matters *I mean in receiving* — are more extensive as to limits than those of other professions."

In 1790 he qualified to practice before the federal Supreme Court but no records are found to indicate if he ever appeared in this capacity.[2]

Blending Romance With Business, Religion, and Culture

Among the prominent citizens of Chatham County in 1772 was William Young who was speaker of the colonial House during the governorship of Sir James Wright. In 1774 Young had shown his Whig sympathies by acting on a committee to send food to Boston after its port had been closed by the British blockade. In 1775 he was a member of Georgia's first Provincial Congress and of its Committee of Safety. Jackson's active participation in politics had given him ample opportunity to know Young personally and he was often a guest in Young's home. When the latter died in 1777 Jackson was summoned occasionally by the widow for a conference on legal and financial matters.

Mary Charlotte, Young's daughter, was six years old when Jackson reached Savannah and only nine years old when she lost her father. Jackson no doubt knew the child during these years and must have observed with great admiration how she later blossomed into young womanhood. If, for a time after her father's death, Mary Charlotte looked on James Jackson as a family adviser and he looked upon her as a ward, the relationship developed gradually into one of personal comradeship. Although Jackson continued to make his home with the hospitable Wereat family for some time after the Revolution, he evidently continued also to dine often with the Youngs.

There also was a daughter, Nancy, in the Wereat household but Jackson's relationship with her seemed more in the brother-sister category. Nancy may have knitted the stockings which Wereat sent him during his most trying time in the Revolution and she may have been looking over her father's shoulder as he wrote the young colonel, prompting the suggestion that Jackson notify them when he needed more stockings. The letter stated that "Mrs. Wereat and Nancy send a great many good wishes." Wereat then assured his foster son that "I feel a very sensible pleasure in the esteem and confidence of this Country which you deservedly possess, as I was concerned in bringing you to it."

No doubt friends were speculating as to whether the "brother" relationships with Nancy and Mary Charlotte would persist or if one of the girls would eventually become his sweetheart. Distance lent enchantment in this case and Jackson's visits to the Young plantation became a little longer each time as they increased also in frequency. He doubtless joined the community in calling Miss Young by her nickname of "Polly" and eventually addressed her as "Maria." Although her mother had trained her for the duties and responsibilities of her future home the slaves released Polly from many dull household tasks and she found time to take horseback rides with young Jackson along the fragrant magnolia trails. On these rides the varied musical notes of the mockingbird and the more sober mating call of the small ground dove matched the young couple's tender mood.

In due time the friendship flowered into romantic love and they became engaged. On the mild Sunday afternoon of January 18, 1785, the Wereat, Farley, Walton, and other prominent families gathered with relatives at the Young home to witness the beautiful, solemn Anglican marriage service uniting the two. Jackson was twenty-eight, Polly seventeen — considered at that time an ideal age relationship. The customary brief notice appeared in the *South Carolina Weekly Gazette,* "married last Sunday Co. James Jackson to Miss Polly Young, dau. of the Hon. Wm. Young, dec'd."

The Jacksons immediately set up housekeeping at the Tattnall house in Savannah, which had a sentimental value to Jackson because it was a gift from the legislature. It was to be their home from the minute he lifted the bride across the threshhold until it was burned in the great fire of 1796.[2] Jackson's will, which referred to it as the "trust lot fronting Oglethorpe Square . . . ," bequeathed it to one of his sons with the wish that "it will be the last piece of property he parts with. . . ."

After the fire the Jacksons moved to Cedar Hill, a plantation a few miles from Savannah. There they spent the rest of their lives except for the three years of Jackson's governorship when they made their home at Louisville.[3]

When away from home Jackson was most faithful in writing to his wife and on one occasion he was both grieved and vexed that she did not write him as promptly as he thought she should. He wrote her from Philadelphia in 1794:

Is it possible that I am so far forgotten by you, as to permit Robertson & Webb's sailing for New York, and Hotchkiss for this port, without one solitary line from you—not a single expression to declare to me that you are happy in my safety? I arrived here this day, and my first inquiry was of Mr. Footman respecting arrivals from Savannah. Judge of my disappointment when I learnt the arrival of Hotchkiss, and had eagerly flown to the Post Office to be informed that there was no line for me from you. Oh Maria, to what am I to impute this silence? Shall I harrow my soul in concluding it to be indifferonce [sic] towards me, and about me? That idea is too torturing to be admitted as fact.

Blending Romance With Business, Religion, and Culture 29

Altho your strange silence flashes it sometimes on the imagination—a fear of your illness. . . . Perhaps . . . my Maria languishes on the bed of sickness, or one of our little prattlers droops its head, and she . . . dares not inform me of it. . . . I ardently and anxiously long for the hour of my return . . . we shall not sit above twenty days, and I shall fly to you.

In his will he speaks of his Maria as the "best of Mothers" and as "my dear bosom friend and most deserving Wife . . . in whose affections and consolations I have ever found relief amidst the multitude of political and personal struggles." They were bound together, not only by mutual affection but by the many griefs which they shared. Eight children were born to the couple. Three were girls, all of whom died in infancy. John, the fourth son, died at the age of six but four sons lived to maturity. William Henry was a merchant and served for over forty years as a trustee of the University of Georgia where his brother James Junior taught French and chemistry. The third boy, Jabez Young, was a member of the United States embassy at London. Joseph Webber served in Congress as did James a grandson. Apparently none of the numerous descendants of this family now bear the name of Jackson.[4]

Mrs. Jackson died in 1807 at the age of thirty-nine years, outliving her husband by about a year and a half. She is buried in Section B of the Old Colonial Cemetery in Savannah.

Jackson and his family were members of the Christ Episcopal Church of Savannah and in 1788 he served as a vestryman of that congregation. He frequently quoted the Bible in his speeches and his letters referred occasionally to a favorite minister and the baptism of one of his children. Other than that we have no record of his religious beliefs and experiences.

Jackson's military and political duties caused him to be absent from home a large part of the time but his letters reveal a tender devotion to his family. His numerous enemies accused him of many errors but at no time did any of them ever hint at any unfaithfulness to his wife. Jackson's many personal and political conflicts must have given his wife many anxious and worrisome days. One of these occurred in 1786 when a political feud of long standing culminated in a duel between Jackson and Mayor Thomas Gibbons of Savannah.

Early in the Revolution Gibbons had taken the oath to the Crown and had been attainted of high treason by the Georgia patriots. His Whig relatives, however, after the treaty of 1783, secured his restoration to citizenship and the practice of law. After this he increased his unpopularity by representing several loyalists in recovering their confiscated property and in collecting their debts, made before and during the Revolution. The loyalists, and later the Federalists, supported him politically in opposition to Jackson and other Republicans who later were to be known as Democrats. Gibbons had just returned to Savannah after having fought a duel with one Fishbourne, a member of the Jackson faction. Arriving at the home of Captain William McIntosh he found a man named Davis and two other men, representing themselves to be "a committee from Gen. Jackson and some other gentlemen then at the coffee house."

Davis accosted Gibbons "in an ungentlemanlike" manner, giving him the choice of himself or of Jackson. The latter, who was deemed to be the real instigator, was chosen. While plans were being discussed Jackson was reported to have remarked that he "would not fight God almighty until 10 o'clock the next day." Gibbons advertised rather freely to the little world of Savannah that his opponent "drank a few glasses of brandy and water and then purposed sending for pistols and determining the matter immediately."

After being quieted by his friends Jackson finally selected Major Seth John Cuthbert, state treasurer, as his second. Cuthbert conferred with Captain McIntosh, Gibbons' second, and the duel was planned for eight o'clock on the following morning "at the forks of the roads about a mile from town." Two postponements followed, however, delaying the encounter first for forty-eight hours, then for several days. Nine days after the challenge Gibbons issued a statement to the public. Jackson then named John R. Stafford as his new second and sent him to Captain McIntosh with a note announcing that "Mr. Stafford will tell when and where Mr. Gibbons may satiate his Tory appetite by shooting as much as he pleases at your obedient servant, James Jackson."

Finally, on the first day of October Gibbons and Jackson with their seconds and a surgeon, a Dr. Tetard, crossed the river to the South Carolina shore.

After the first shot Jackson exclaimed, "Damn it, Gibbons, you're a brave man and a good marksman, for I believe your ball hit my pistol."

"You are a brave man, General Jackson," replied Gibbons.

Blending Romance With Business, Religion, and Culture 31

When asked if he wished to speak further with Gibbons, Jackson uttered a sharp negative and asked that the pistols be promptly reloaded. After both duelists had fired three harmless shots, their seconds sought to conciliate them. Jackson said that Gibbons would have to apologize and the latter agreed. When Jackson added that he particularly objected to the reference to "brandy and water" Gibbons acknowledged that he had spoken in jest and had not seriously questioned the General's courage. Jackson hesitated a minute but finally offered his hand, saying, "I shake hands only in this affair, as it is a private one. In a public cause I shall always be your enemy."[5]

Some contemporary records are conflicting as to what Jackson's attitudes and personality were. Although he claimed to be a benevolent slaveowner, some of his slaves ran away. In the *Georgia State Gazette* or *Independent Register* appeared the following advertisement:

Run away from the subscriber . . . a Negro fellow named Jemmy, . . . Has his country (Ebo) marks . . . on his face. . . . Likewise run away . . . Joe . . . speaks little or no English. . . . Whoever will deliver said negroes in Sav. or to Hon Col. Fishbourn in Augusta, shall receive Reward of $8 each & sum of Five Pounds will be given on information & conviction of their or each of their being harbored. . . . James Jackson.

There are two portraits of Jackson still preserved. One, possibly made near the beginning of his political career, shows him in full military attire. The eyes seem to indicate alertness, temper, pride, and self-assurance. The second portrait, made near the close of his life, suggests strength of character, determination, and dignity. An admirer, writing in 1849, many years after Jackson's death, recalled that he was about five feet seven inches tall, erect, with thin, sandy hair, broad shoulders, full chest, large penetrating blue eyes, high forehead, and prominent features.[6]

While practicing law Jackson broadened his interests by becoming a planter, slaveholder, and landowner. His land holdings were obtained chiefly by purchase at public sales of confiscated estates and by land grants. Much of the property of certain Tories had been confiscated by legislative acts in 1778 and 1782. Jackson showed his business acumen by purchasing some of this confiscated property in 1782. Included in the sale from the estates of John McGillivray, James Dill, and John Mulrine Tattnall were twelve slaves for five hundred and sixty-five pounds, an average of forty-seven pounds per slave. He also bought from the plantation of Sir James Wright 150 acres at about fourteen pounds per acre.

Later that year Jackson invested two hundred and thirty pounds in two hundred acres on the north side of Bryer Creek. In 1783 he added to his holdings the five-hundred-acre Rocky Comfort plantation of Charles Burnett at a cost of one hundred and sixty-two pounds. Before that year was out he also had acquired a tract of several hundred acres in Jefferson County, where he later "lived a part of the time."

Some years later, in 1803, Jackson accused Daniel Sturges, Surveyor-General of Georgia, of making a new survey of this Jefferson County land in order to steal some three hundred acres of it. Sturges replied in a published article that he had surveyed some land between their plantations and that the new line might deprive Jackson of a few acres of unimproved land. For this small error, he stated, Jackson's agitation might cause the loss of his job. In another article Henry Jackson accused Sturges of taking advantage of his brother James while the latter was eight hundred miles away in the nation's capital at Washington. This article further stated that Sturges had used a "pretended plot of the original survey" in order to prejudice the public in his favor. Sturges did not lose his job on account of this controversy but neither did he gain the disputed land.

During the period of Georgia's inefficient system of land surveys in the latter part of the eighteenth century Jackson had given bonds totaling nine hundred and ninety-three pounds for lands near Monteeth. Although he had met part of these obligations the property could not be located. At his request the House cancelled the bonds and credited the amount already paid toward any other land he might purchase from the state.

In 1785 he applied this credit to a grant of 1300 acres in Glynn and Camden counties. That year he had an experience similar to what happened when he made payments on land near Monteeth. He bought two 500-acre tracts from the confiscated estate of George Kincaid in Glynn County, only to discover later that Kincaid had only 500 acres to begin with. When the matter was brought before the legislature in 1804 it was ascertained that Jackson had paid for and kept up taxes on 1,000 acres, yet had received only 500. Upon further investigation it was found that under an old Carolina grant of 1763 Kincaid had received 1,150 acres in another part of the county, 550 acres of which remained unsold. An act was passed granting this unsold portion to Jackson. In 1784 he gave bonds of 2,589 pounds for purchases of other sequestered or confiscated estates. In addition to his purchases of confiscated estates he received several state grants.

During the Revolution Georgia had sought to increase its population by a liberal use of its public domain, and later its old soldiers were rewarded by grants of land and by being allowed to purchase confiscated estates. Between 1789 and 1796 the "headright" system of selling land in the public domain was corruptly administered in Georgia, three times more being sold than existed. Jackson did not take advantage of the questionable generosity of Governors George Walton, Edward Telfair, and George Mathews and never expressed any sympathy for this speculation.

In 1784 Jackson was remunerated for his Revolutionary services in Georgia and the Carolinas with grants provided for in the Georgia land grant acts of 1781 and 1784. During the latter year two certificates were issued in his behalf by Colonels William Candler and Elijah Clarke stating that he was a "Refugee & Citizen since the fall of Augusta." Clarke also certified that Jackson was entitled to one thousand and fifty acres of public land. In 1784 and 1796 Jackson's grants from Governors John Houstoun and Jared Irwin totaled 4,594 acres, some of it located in Washington and Effingham counties. Since he sold very little real estate he could not, however, be classed with the active land speculators.

In 1798 Jackson wrote a letter to the press defending himself against a public statement by Sheriff John Bryan that he had failed to meet an obligation of ten guineas to Colonel Lemuel Lanier for the purchase of some land in Screven County. Jackson's explanation for not making the payment was that he objected to the long extension of a line along the Ogeechee River. His reasons were that the line had been run in his absence and that it would cut off much of his property from access to a navigable stream.

"I wish the sheriff had been a little more candid in his description of the nature of this obligation, . . ." he wrote; "—I believe I have been as seldom charged with a wish of evading just debts, as any of my fellow-citizens."

Jackson's residence as a planter was at Cedar Hill, a few miles south of Savannah. While living at home he wrote letters mostly from Savannah. After the summer of 1796 his correspondence came chiefly from Cedar Hill, with his letters referring to cotton and rice as the chief products of his plantations. In 1798 he bemoaned the fact that these crops had been lost at Cedar Hill and he was very much disappointed at the yield at the Hammock. In a happier mood in 1802 he wrote: "Sea Island cotton 44c. in demand; upland 17, on the rise. Rice—brisk."

In his numerous letters to John Mitchell he stated that his salary scarcely paid expenses after 1789, since his services to the public demanded most of his time and talents. During these years, however, he had some legal practice. He also gave as much time as possible to his plantations, but illness in the family and the education of his children kept a continuing drain upon his resources.

His plantation superintendent at Cedar Hill in 1794 was named Schermerhorn. No correspondence between them has been preserved but a letter from Jackson to his wife that year stated: "I think that I could have made the crop go further myself. I hope he is managing rightly this season. . . . Do give Hercules [his slave driver] a charge for me; I greatly depend on him."

It would be extremely hard to estimate accurately the amount of Jackson's wealth. His holdings consisted largely of city buildings and lots in Savannah, farm land scattered over Georgia, buildings and their furnishings, and slaves. The total number of slaves and all the land he owned, with their respective evaluations, is not known. His will referred to a tract of five acres "near the Jews burying ground," four city lots, "my Bay lot at Brunswick. . . ," and a plantation known as "Holscombe." One of his letters referred to his having settled his Rocky Comfort tract near the Ogeechee River, and to his house in Louisville.

Jackson's preoccupation with public duties probably called for overseers on his plantations at Cedar Hill, Holscombe, Rocky Comfort, and the Hammock. A letter to one McAllister in 1798 modestly declared, "All my property, a few negroes, and a little furniture, exclusive of some lands excepted lays in the City and its vicinity. . . . There are a hundred estates in the vicinity and City of Savannah of double the value of mine. . . ."

For the year 1806 one of his executors paid Chatham County ninety-two dollars and seventy-eight cents as taxes on his estate. While this statement gives no exact clue to his financial status it possibly confirms Jackson's modest admission that he was in the lower brackets of the wealthy men of his community. Nevertheless his income was sufficient to enable his family to maintain the high social standards of the planters.[7]

Shortly after reaching his majority Jackson became active in Masonic circles. In the period following the Revolution it was felt that the Masonic Lodge in Georgia had departed from its pure European form. In 1785 Jackson offered a resolution at a Masonic meeting that they reconstitute themselves from a "modern" to an "ancient" lodge and his was the first name on the roll formed under the new constitution. He served during the greater part of 1786 as Worshipful Master of Solomon's Lodge, Savannah. During his term of office the Lodge received as members "the most prominent men of the times." From 1785 to 1786 he served as Junior Grand Warden of the Grand Lodge of Georgia and Deputy Grand Master in 1787-88. In 1789 he achieved the highest state office, Grand Master of the Grand Lodge. On February 6, 1796, "William Stephens, grand master, James Jackson, a past grand master," and others secured from the legislature a charter for the Grand Lodge.

Jackson's essays, addresses, and letters indicate a wide acquaintanceship with the works of such political scientists as Vattel, Grotius, Beccaria, Locke, Rousseau, Montesquieu, and Blackstone. He was also an avid reader of the third edition of the *Encyclopaedia Britannica* and eagerly looked forward to each new volume of this work. Writing to Milledge in 1796 he asked, "I beg you to call and take my Encyclopedia from Dobson & to pay him. Perhaps there may be two volumes out—the last I have is the fourteenth—the 15th & perhaps the 16th are in print—I hope you will trust to my repaying you, ..."

In the secondary and higher schools of Jackson's era the ancient classics took priority over other classroom subjects. Among the teachers he personally knew was the Reverend Bothwell, who "has had my Boys under him since the period of their coming up [to Louisville]; he is a complete Latin, Greek, & Hebrew scholar, besides a knowledge of French. . . ."[8]

Perhaps if James Jackson had given his undivided attention to speculation in land and to his legal and agricultural pursuits he would have become one of the wealthiest men of his day. However, in order to have a springboard for political advancement he found it expedient once again to take up his military career. The nearness of the revengeful and militant Creeks demanded a considerable portion of his energies for several years after the Revolution.

III

THE MILITIA GUARDS AGAINST THE TOMAHAWK

JACKSON'S interest in military affairs was rekindled shortly after the Revolution. In 1784 the legislature commissioned him Colonel of the First or Chatham County Regiment of Georgia Militia and in 1786 he was made Brigadier General. Then in 1792 Georgia gave him its highest military honor by naming him Major General of its First Division of Militia.

Since all his military activities had been in the state militia and he was not an officer in the continental or national army, Jackson was not eligible for full membership in the Society of the Cincinnati. The Georgia chapter of the Society, however, meeting at Savannah in 1786, praised him for his "faithful" and "distinguished" services during the Revolution and unanimously elected him to honorary membership.[1]

Some of Jackson's military duties after 1782 were concerned with checking insurrections among the troops as well as threats of uprisings among the slaves. His chief task, however, was the defense of the Georgia frontiers against the Indians.

In August, 1785, Jackson, William Few, and Edward Telfair were commissioned by the Georgia Council to attend a conference with the Creeks at Galphinton in October. This commission was to "aid and assist . . . the said Commissioners of the United States . . . as far as they by the Articles of Confederation . . . are authorized to go, . . . [and] to protest against any measures . . . [contrary to] . . . the constitution and Laws of the State." Jackson and Few declined to serve and were replaced by Thomas Glascock and John King.

Discouraged by the poor attendance of the Creek chiefs the federal commission withdrew but some of the Georgia group held a conference with the representatives of two Indian villages, persuading this small group to declare that they were acting for the entire Creek Nation. In this so-called Galphinton Treaty the Creeks confirmed the cession they had made in an earlier conference at Augusta. Of greater importance to Georgia, however, was the large tract ceded to it at Galphinton. This tract, known as "The County of Tallassee," was situated south of the Altamaha River and west of a line running southwest from the junction of the Ocmulgee and Oconee to the most southern bend of the St. Mary's River. These leaders also pledged that all Creeks henceforth would consider themselves "members of" the state of Georgia.

Although no detailed record of Jackson's military activities of that particular period is available, the fact that they were of some value is indicated by the fact that the Council appropriated twelve pounds "in favor of Colonel James Jackson, Colonel of Chatham County Militia, . . . in order for the said Regiment to celebrate the anniversary of American Independence on the 4th of July next; . . ."[2]

In contrast to these satisfying events Jackson had an unhappy encounter with his old Revolutionary commander, General Nathanael Greene. The Georgia legislature had made Greene a present of Mulberry Grove, a confiscated plantation located on the Savannah River some miles above Savannah. Greene's estate had become involved and he was ill; so, after retiring for a time to his old home in Rhode Island, he moved to Georgia in 1785. Soon after his arrival Jackson was asked by his friend, Captain James Gunn, to deliver a challenge to Greene. Jackson felt obliged to abide by the honor code and accede to the wishes of Gunn, who had charged Greene with injustice in a sale of some horses at Charleston, South Carolina, near the close of the Revolution. Greene, on the advice of George Washington, refused the challenge. Jackson then advised Gunn to consider the matter settled and dropped out of the affair. When Greene refused to deal with another second Gunn threatened to make a personal assault upon him the first time they met. Fortunately their paths did not cross again.

On a hot summer day in 1786 Greene suffered a partial sunstroke on his way home from Savannah. From Richmond, his own Savannah River plantation, Anthony Wayne hurried to the bedside of his old friend and was present when Greene died on

June sixteenth. Wayne immediately sent the following message to Jackson:

Mr Dear Sir:—I have often wrote [sic] you, but never on so distressing an occasion. My dear friend General Greene is no more. He departed this morning, six o'clock A.M. He was great as a soldier, greater as a citizen,—immaculate as a friend. His corpse will be at Major Pendleton's this night; the funeral from thence in the evening. The honors—the greatest honors of war are due his remains. You, as a soldier, will take the proper order on this melancholy affair.

Jackson made the military arrangements as requested and sent the Georgia Council a bill for one hundred pounds. On the following day the body was taken to Savannah where Greene's admirers had organized a procession composed of civic and military groups. The Chatham Artillery, leading the procession, fired minute guns as they advanced to the Colonial Cemetery on South Broad Street. At the grave, located in the old section of the cemetery, a salute of thirteen guns brought the sad rites to a close.[3]

Shortly after Greene was laid to rest Georgia's troops were readied for renewed frontier warfare. In the former treaties (of 1733, 1739, 1763, 1778, and 1783) the Indians had ceded to Georgia the area north of the Altamaha and east of the Oconee rivers but each side occasionally trespassed on the territory of the other. In 1786 Alexander McGillivray, the colorful American-Creek chief, sent his braves upon the warpath and hostilities continued for several years.

In August the Committee on Indian Affairs reported to the legislature that during the previous May several parties of Creeks, painted as for war, "without provocation or aggression on the part of the white people," had killed six citizens and burned several houses. The report, typical of the unfair attitude manifested by most white men towards the Indians, affirmed that the governor and Council were "at a loss to account for the unproked [sic] attack." The committee further stated that they had shown their eagerness to prevent war by sending Daniel Murphy, Georgia's Superintendent for Indian Affairs, to investigate the causes of the trouble but he had been unable to get at the facts.

As a result of this report the legislature passed an act authorizing the governor to send among the Creeks nine commissioners empowered to raise 1,500 men in three divisions with a brigadier general over each. An expenditure of ten thousand pounds for the

The Militia Guards Against The Tomahawk

expenses of the proposed campaign was further authorized, as was one thousand pounds in presents for the Indians. The governor was also instructed to report to Congress that Georgia was merely protecting lands the Indians had voluntarily sold and was therefore acting purely on the defensive in these conflicts. Jackson supported this measure. He supported another bill, unsuccessfully, to call to the colors the young academy students who by a former law were exempted from military service. Still another bill Jackson tried to put through would set aside 50,000 acres in the bend of the Tennessee River as a reward to the men who participated in these "defensive" measures. This bill, too, failed to receive the approval of the majority.[4]

When the campaign against the Indians was started Jackson was in charge of the Eastern Division of the State Militia. Several years later one of his enemies stated in a Savannah paper that Jackson took advantage of his membership in the legislature to persuade that body to appropriate one hundred pounds to each brigadier in order that Jackson himself might be included, while the privates, serving on the very frontier, received no additional funds. This enemy further stated that in the first alarm Jackson barely crossed the Ogeechee River. Jackson replied in the next issue of the paper that this sum was all he received for his services during several years after the Revolution. He added that he had spent more than this amount of his own money and when his remuneration was audited it proved to be "worth less than six shillings and eight pence in the pound."[5]

Meanwhile Twiggs, supported by 1,500 troops, stood in readiness and by late summer the more aggressive Elijah Clarke had driven the Indians out of the Oconee section.

In April of the following year Governor George Mathews advised Jackson that a letter from Dr. James White, America's Indian Agent for the Southern Department, indicated that the Indians were preparing to attack. Jackson was ordered to "please have your Brigade put in as good order as circumstances will allow of and Send me ... the strength. ..."

Excitement over the Indians was rampant and some of the Negroes either ran away from their masters or threatened insurrection. Jackson reported this condition to Governor Mathews who in turn answered that the best way to preserve peace would be to prepare for war. The Indians had agreed to keep the peace until

August. The laws did not authorize impressing or confiscating goods but Jackson was assured that for the time being Georgia would pay for all provisions brought in by his officers.

In May James Gunn, one of Jackson's subordinate officers, reported that several slaves had fled to the swamps on the south side of Bear Creek. When rushed by the troops some of these Negroes had been captured and some escaped. One soldier had been wounded in the encounter. Jackson reported to the governor that he feared a slave insurrection in Georgia and South Carolina and that he had "broken up a nest" of some who had attempted to organize a band after escaping.

The Indian menace proved to be much more real than the vague rumors of slave insurrections. "Hostilities have already commenced," Governor Mathews' secretary, John Cobb, wrote Jackson and the other brigadiers in June. He added that the militia should be formed in proper order and scouting parties sent out.

A few days after Cobb's letter was posted the governor wrote the brigadiers that the situation had improved. Returning from a trip to the frontier, Timothy Barnard, Georgia's Special Agent among the Creeks, also reported that both the Upper and Lower Creeks desired peace. The chiefs stated that the "murthers" were committed by the Okejoys without the knowledge or consent of the other villages. Accordingly the brigadiers were instructed to accept Barnard's advice that no scouting parties be sent over the Oconee and to encourage the troops to return to their farms. By August 7th, however, the situation had taken a turn for the worse. The governor had received a discouraging report from Barnard whom he had sent again to the Creeks. He advised Barnard that "the talk from the fat King" had a military ring but that the newly proposed State of Franklin in Tennessee would send 2,000 rifles and some light horse and that Governor Richard Caswell had warned McGillivray that North Carolina would give full support to Georgia. In September Governor Mathews instructed Clarke and Jackson to send some of their militia to guard the frontiers. Later that month he wrote Jackson that he wished all the ammunition in the magazine kept in reserve and beyond the reach of the people.[6]

Jackson had personal and political enemies among his brigade officers. One of his subordinates sent him a letter of more than two pages through an Augusta paper. It was signed "Cassius" and it charged that his military orders fatigued and insulted the brigade officers, harassed the citizens, and, furthermore, were never obeyed. "Your flings are so venomous," "Cassius" stated, "that you have been known for years in the Legislature, by the name of the *Chatham Wolf*." The letter further charged that (instead of demanding that he protect the citizens against the Creeks) his friends justified his "pluming" himself in regimentals on Sundays.

In the fall of 1787 Jackson received a letter of praise from Governor Mathews for building a series of frontier forts. The letter also reminded him that a recent act had exempted from military duty citizens who furnished one hundred pounds of powder and two hundred pounds of lead. Jackson's troops were to receive part of this supply.

Despite these vigorous measures the ravages continued. In the next two years the Creeks killed 72 citizens, wounded 29, captured 140, burned 89 houses, and destroyed a considerable amount of property.[7]

A copy of the new federal Constitution reached Georgia in October of 1787 and was unanimously ratified the following January by the state Convention at Augusta. Jackson wrote in his autobiography that he "rendered many services to his Country during . . . the ratification of the Constitution in 1788." His name was not mentioned, however, in the official journal of the Convention or among the delegates listed in the *Georgia Gazette*. What services he rendered are not clearly defined but they were probably limited to holding the Creeks in check. Colonel Armstrong's regiment is the only military force mentioned by the *Gazette* as participating in the ceremonies at the close of the Convention.

In 1790 the legislature passed a resolution affirming its approval of the power the new national Constitution gave the federal government to make all treaties with the Indians.[8]

McGillivray, feeling that the proposed federal government would check Georgia's encroachments upon the Indians, encouraged his people to renew their attacks. Early in 1788 Jackson wrote Governor George Handley that the return of moonlight nights had kept his district in continual alarm. So many new Creek raids had been reported, he went on to say, that he had ordered 150 troops from the counties of Chatham, Effingham, and Liberty "to act in different directions." He expressed the hope that

Handley would be successful in his efforts to pacify the Indians and he would take the governor's helpful letter with him when he went southward.

In June Jackson reported an assortment of distressing incidents to the legislature: the Indians had attacked the plantation of John Houstoun "on Cathead," the state troops had been fired on in the night, a certain McCormick had been shot, a fourteen-year-old boy had his brains knocked out, and two young women and two children had been carried off.

The federal Superintendent of Indian Affairs had expressed a desire to hold a September conference with the Indians on the Tugaloo River on the Georgia-South Carolina border. The governor therefore instructed the three Georgia brigadiers to confine their efforts temporarily to defensive measures. But Jackson was evidently getting restless in his defensive role and he once more wrote Handley. He informed the governor that a reliable source in Liberty County had reported conditions bad and that no time should be lost if the troops in the district were expected to hold their ground. He also expressed fears that one "Bloggs," in whose boat twenty slaves had escaped from Chatham County, had been sent by the Spanish or the Indians to rob Georgia of all her slaves.

In the spring of 1789 Governor Handley and his Council ordered some Georgia troops to attend a meeting with the Creeks at Rock Landing but after a few days of futile conferences McGillivray led his chiefs away.[9]

In March Governor George Walton ordered Jackson to take his troops from Chatham to Camden County to quell a new disturbance by the Creeks. No advance arrangements had been made for supplies and Jackson replied that his men were in a deplorable condition. The people in the southern counties were unable to provide for his troops, he reported, but if funds from the state were forthcoming supplies could be purchased economically in Savannah by Major Forsythe, his purchasing agent and the conveyor of his letter. Jackson would carry out orders if the governor insisted, he wrote, but the response to his request might determine the future settlement of that frontier area.

A week later the aforementioned scarcity of supplies engendered a mutiny among Jackson's troops at Savannah and this situation was duly reported by him to the governor. The leaders of the mutiny were Captain William Ross, a Captain Williamson, and a Lieutenant McAvay. The rebel troops marched through

Savannah "to the beat of drums" and attempted to march through the country along the main highway "in contempt of their engagements, of the articles of war and of the public authority." Jackson had quieted them by ordering a certain Colonel Handley to supply them with a barrel of rice and four barrels of beef. He then divided his loyal troops into several squads, spaced some distance apart, and ordered them to march across the city, swing around the suburbs, and return through the city by the same route. By this manner of having the same men march repeatedly through the city, giving the appearance of great strength, Jackson was able to arrest the leaders of the mutiny without bloodshed.

Jackson placed the chief blame for the mutiny upon Ross. He asked that this man be severely punished so that, among other reasons, McGillivray would not think that discipline was lax among the white men and thus be encouraged to stir up more trouble. His letter was considered by the Council in April and the committee to whom the matter was referred brought further news that a spirit of discontent was prevalent among the troops stationed on the seaboard, that they had mutinied and quit their posts, and that although some had been furloughed by their officers a large number had deserted. The fact that the deserters were so numerous, coupled with the genuine quality of their complaints, induced the Council to leniency and they were placed on probation and promised complete forgiveness if their future conduct justified it.[10]

Early in 1789 Jackson entered Congress. His interest in Indian affairs, however, did not end with this change of office. In April, ten days after his arrival in New York City (then the nation's capital) he wrote Governor Walton that he had found many congressmen "not very favorable to our politics," and he requested copies of the official letters of McGillivray and others and the "Indian Reports of Committees." Shortly afterwards he sent President Washington some letters on the Indian problem, to which the President replied through his secretary that he was seeking fuller information and was encouraged by the reports on the attitude of the Creeks.

In August a federal House committee reported a bill which called for the appointment by the President of a commission not exceeding three members to make treaties with the various Indian nations. In the debate on the bill Jackson argued that, in spite of the Constitution's requirement that the national government protect the states from invasion, Georgia was being invaded. He informed the House that under the Articles of Confederation Georgia and two other states had named commissioners and they had united with the federal commission in asking the Creeks to name the place and date for a conference. But McGillivray had refused to meet them and had written a member of the federal commission that if the chiefs could treat with Georgia alone an agreement would soon be reached. To this Jackson had to say that "this half-breed chief, has dared to treat even the United States with indignity! . . . he has . . . torn up settlements by the roots." He had plundered, burned property, and destroyed "the offspring before the mother's face." Georgia had done nothing which it could not justify. Three thousand Indians were armed and ready to attack and so far had been held back only through fear of the federal authorities. Sensing a timidity in these authorities, they would surely attack.

After the bill, calling for no more than three commissioners, was passed, Jackson offered a resolution that, should the Creeks refuse to make a treaty, the President would be authorized to protect the Georgia frontier by the establishment of certain military posts and the calling out of the Georgia and South Carolina militia. After some revisions his bill was passed.

The question then arose as to the amount to be appropriated for holding the conference. A motion was made setting the sum at $41,000. Jackson defended this figure vigorously against those who thought it far too high. He asked if the members should listen to the claim that there were signs of approaching peace, when in letters to certain citizens McGillivray had expressed the desire to "leave the Georgians to their fate, and he will teach them reason." "Can it be supposed that a half-breed savage has more humanity than the civilized citizens of Georgia?" he asked. With considerable emotion he proceeded to describe how a Mrs. McCormick of his state had helplessly watched her daughter "compelled to submit to the lustful embrace of an Indian." Thomas Sumter then accused him of appealing to the passions of the House and asserted that the Indians seldom violated the chastity of white women. Jackson retorted that any member in his situation would be moved with passion. Reading some letters from Georgia showing that McGillivray was threatening to go to war he declared that, if the President would use them, he believed

Georgia could raise 15,000 men to meet the 6,000 Creeks McGillivray was believed to have.

Another member of the House expressed the wish to keep down expenses, especially since the Creeks were showing an inclination to keep the peace. Jackson replied that he was as careful with public money as any member but refuted once more the claim that the Creeks were seeking peace. Instead they were exposing Georgia to the horrors of a savage and brutal war. His statements were based on an official communication from the Secretary of War. McGillivray knew that the cause of an invaded state was the cause of the Union, Jackson said, but had still shown the temerity to attack defenseless citizens and had lately committed depredations beyond anything hitherto known.

Georgia had wished to send her forces to the front but "with patience she waited for justice from those with whom she had fought and conquered in the cause of liberty and safety; but that patience had been nearly exhausted." He then exclaimed:

... let them present to ... [McGillivray] for his choice, the sword, or the olive branch; if he declines to receive the latter, let him be assured he will feel the keen edge of the former, and perhaps his prudence may induce him to treat on better terms.

... The Union is to protect each State from invasion; Georgia is invaded, and requires that protection. ... I declare this publicly: my arm shall be lifted on the occasion; we must, if too weak ourselves to accomplish the object, league with the arms of Spain or Britain.

As a compromise Madison offered an amendment that the appropriation be for the sum of $40,000. Jackson voted for this motion and it was passed but when it went before the Senate Washington persuaded that body to reduce the amount to $20,000, enough for but one treaty.

In August Washington carried out the mandate of Congress by naming an Indian commission composed of Benjamin Lincoln, David Humphreys, and Cyrus Griffin. Two futile efforts were made by the three men to hold a conference at Rock Landing during the year. On their way back to New York in the fall the commissioners conferred with Georgia's governor and were convinced that Georgia had legal title to the Oconee lands and to Tallassee County by virtue of the treaties previously made with the Creeks at Augusta, Galphinton, and Shoulderbone. The commission later recommended to Washington that an effort be made to have both of these cessions confirmed and that, should the Indians continue their attacks upon Georgia, they be punished as enemies of the United States. The President rejected this advice, however, and the three were replaced by Secretary of War Henry Knox as sole commissioner.[11]

In March, 1790, William Few, Jackson, and others of the Georgia Congressional delegation delivered to the President an address from the Georgia legislature requesting federal aid in quieting Indian titles to its frontier lands. Washington replied that he was aware of the danger Georgia felt but that obviously state politics had "blended" with the address and that he would let Few know when he could give it official consideration. The following June found Jackson becoming very impatient with the manner in which the Indian question was being handled. Nevertheless, he voted for a motion to supply Washington with presents to be used in dealing with the Indians.[12]

In August of 1790 Secretary Knox concluded the Treaty of New York. The President's great desire for peace was shown by the fact that the Creeks received more than they demanded. Their titles to the large tracts of Tallassee County and the disputed territory in the Ocmulgee section were confirmed. They in turn agreed to abide by the Treaty of Augusta which had ceded to Georgia the land east of the Oconee. In return for this cession they were to receive $1,500 annually. The United States also agreed to protect the Indians by licensing each of the white traders who went among them.

In a secret paragraph McGillivray was named federal agent to the Creeks with the title of brigadier general at an annual salary of $1,200. Each of his five most important chiefs was to receive $100 per year. The Creeks also were promised that should their trade with Spain be interrupted within a period of two years they might annually receive through American ports $60,000 worth of imports without duty.

In his message to the Senate asking for ratification Washington said: " . . . it is to be hoped that it will afford solid grounds of satisfaction to the State of Georgia, . . . [because it provides for the] relinquishment . . . of . . . the . . . [land east of the Oconee River] in the utmost extent in which it has been claimed by that State, . . . the Creeks in this city absolutely refuse to yield [the Tallassee section]. This land is reported to be generally barren, sunken and unfit for cultivation, . . . it is stated by the Creeks . . . to be of the highest importance to them as . . . some of their most valuable winter hunting ground."

The Georgians, who had been ignored in the New York Conference, instead of finding "solid grounds of satisfaction" were first stunned, then angered. They were particularly offended by the provision that "the United States solemnly guarantees to the Creek Nation all their lands within the limits of the United States, to the westward and the southward of the boundary described by the preceding article."

Jackson attacked the New York Treaty the following December. He reminded the House that in the fall of 1789 the United States had sent three men from states other than Georgia to secure the facts. These men had reported to the President that they approved Georgia's claims to three million acres in the Tallassee country. Their report was ignored in the treaty with "a savage of the Creeks," and this land, guaranteed to Georgia by the Constitution, was "ceded away without compensation." Georgia's rights were further sacrificed by the clause in the treaty stating that should a citizen pursue his property into Indian lands the tomahawk would be allowed to settle it. Jackson remarked that even English laws require that citizens be tried by their own courts. This savage, McGillivray, had been brought to the very seat of government and "there loaded with favors, and caressed in the most extraordinary manner."

Jackson's anxiety was increased by persistent reports of secret agreements. Declaring that "Treaties by the Constitution are to be considered the supreme law of the land; but will Congress permit the laws of the United States, like those of Caligula, to be placed where they cannot be read, and then punish the people for not obeying them?" He gave notice that he was going to offer a motion that the House ask the President for the secret agreements. Some months later Washington did send them to Congress.

Jackson returned to this subject in a Senate address in 1803 in which he asserted that although Georgia was greatly injured by the New York Treaty "not a single small State came forward to support her protest against a great wrong when a treaty was sanctioned that violated her rights and parcelled out her . . . county of Tallassee to a parcel of tomahawking Indians . . . it was only two years ago that half justice was done; for half what was taken away by usurpation, has not been restored by justice."

In 1791 the Georgia legislature sent to Congress a formal protest against the treaty,[13] and many wondered if Georgia would ever forgive Washington for his partiality to the Creeks. The President himself, as he approached the Savannah River on his Southern tour in 1791, must have wondered what effect the New York Treaty would have on his reception by the Georgians for he wrote in his diary on June 4th:

In Georgia the dissatisfied part of them at the late treaty with the Ck. Indians were evidently Land Jobbers, who, maugre every principle of justice to the Indians and policy to their Country would, for their own immediate emolument, strip the Indns. of all their territory if they could obtain the least countenance to the measure. but it is to be hoped the good sense of the State will set its face against such diabolical attempts.

To what extent Washington's attitude toward Georgia's Indian problem was influenced by this tour is not known. However, later in the year a joint resolution of Congress appointed a commission of Blackbourn, Twiggs, Armstrong, McNiel, and Fort to hold a conference with the state leaders in Georgia. On December 3rd it was announced at the Georgia Executive Office in Augusta that Jackson, Taliaferro, Tattnall, Irwin, Milledge, Ellis, and Abercrombie had been named by the legislature as state commissioners to confer with those sent by Congress. The result of this conference was probably negligible, as no record of it is found, and the New York treaty was a failure from the beginning. Since neither the Georgians nor the Indians cared to know where the line was it was not surveyed for years. Much to the anxiety of the President each side renewed hostilities.[14]

As he remained in Georgia during these years Jackson was able to give considerable time to Indian affairs in 1791, 1792, and 1793. In the spring of 1793 he announced in the Savannah press that the lantern at the Tybee Lighthouse had been burned and that the Creeks were supposed to be the guilty parties. He claimed the frontier citizens in Liberty County were becoming jittery with constant alarm and were begging for an effective plan by which the ungrateful Creeks "shall be taught to respect the Union." Jackson had just returned from some frontier points in this county and at the fort of Beard's Bluff he had assisted the federal troops of Lieutenant Clay in setting up temporary defenses.

In May Jackson began to fear complications in East Florida for he wrote Governor Edward Telfair that James Seagrove, federal Indian Agent, had informed him that the Spaniards had built some posts on the St. Mary's River ten miles above Coleraine, in Georgia territory. The Spaniards explained to Seagrove that these fortifications were erected for protection against such raids as that by Galphin and a party of Indians who, while over on the Florida side, had stolen eight Negroes and some livestock, burned a house, and fired on a citizen.

Throughout this year Jackson's correspondence reflected a struggle between optimism and pessimism as rumors of peace and war alternated. Early in June he again wrote Governor Telfair that, in view of reports of a growing peace sentiment among the Creeks, he had thought of reducing his forces but more recently he had learned of the scalping of four Indians who were reported to have come on a peace mission. He expressed his intention of ordering Major Hammond to erect a stockade on Doctor's Creek in the vicinity of Beard's Bluff for garrisoning troops of an officer named Way. President Washington had promised to send one hundred cavalry, which Jackson felt would be inadequate. He recommended that the governor keep on active duty the Camden troops and those of Way and Williams.

In August Telfair's patience became exhausted and he called to a council of war at Augusta Major Generals Twiggs, Jackson, and Clarke and Brigadier Generals Glascock, Morrison, Clarke, Irwin, and Gunn. The conference decided upon an expedition in October against the Creeks for which they would need "At least two thousand horse, and three thousand foot" to serve sixty days. These plans were then sent on to Washington for his approval.

The President replied through his Secretary of War that a general and open Creek war would be a complicated evil of great magnitude and urged Georgia to desist from its military preparations. However, as a concession to Georgia and a warning to the Indians he had, earlier in the year, ordered an increase of two hundred in the regular troops stationed in the state. Telfair only partially complied with the President's advice. In September he sent two hundred cavalry into the Indian country and notified the War Department that in the next conference with the Creeks he thought Georgia should send its own commissioners to share in the deliberations.[15]

For some unexplained reason Jackson showed less enthusiasm at this time than formerly about going to the front. He requested Indian Agent James Seagrove to recommend to the Secretary of

War that he order the United States, North Carolina, and Georgia troops to move simultaneously against the Cherokees and Creeks. He hoped the War Department would not know that the suggestion originated with him lest it be thought he wished to serve. He explained that Twiggs, Clarke, and Sevier were more experienced Indian fighters than he.

This same month a mutiny occurred among Jackson's troops in Camden County. Brigadier General Gunn and Captain Carr were at odds in the dispute. Jackson wrote Carr that he would give him all possible support but he could not send men from another regiment to quell the mutineers. Before the final disposition of the matter Jackson was elected to the Senate and his absence from Georgia for several months during the next two years placed a severe limit on his military activities. However, he supported a bill which passed the Senate, authorizing the President to call out the militia from adjacent states when a state was threatened by the Indians.[16]

In 1793 the French minister, Edmond Genêt, landed at Charleston and began to call upon American sympathizers to render military assistance against French enemies in America. In response to this appeal Elijah Clarke enlisted several hundred Georgians with the aim of marching against the Spanish in the Floridas. In 1794 the French called off this proposed invasion. Clarke then led his pioneers across the Oconee and made a settlement on the soil of the Creeks.

Jackson watched this movement with interest and concern and in July wrote one of his subordinates that "From Official accounts given to me by James Seagrove esquire, it appears that the Creek Nation is much divided, and that the one half is bent for War—, the ostensible reason for their resentment is General Clarkes settling over the Oconee." Clarke evidently decided to discontinue his opposition to the Creeks, Georgia, and the Union, for in October he returned to the east bank of the Oconee.

Seagrove also expressed uneasiness over the governor's order to establish a post on Creek lands at Doctor's Town in Glynn County. He feared this action might cause the Creeks to think that Clarke was advancing on them and that Georgia was extending its laws over their territory. Until further advisement from the governor Jackson ordered one Armstrong to check the advance of the Georgians in Liberty County. He feared the Indians would come out to the frontier and he was grateful for the swollen streams which thus far had held them back.[17] In September he wrote Mathews, governor of Georgia at that time, that he planned to sail for Philadelphia on October 20 to resume his seat in the Senate. He might be unable to carry out all of the latter's orders but what could not be accomplished by this time he would pass on to the commanding officers of the two brigades in his division. The letter concluded with an appreciation of the governor's praise for his "zeal in promoting the interest of my Country."

In February of 1795 Jackson informed the Senate that he and his colleagues were again required by Georgia to ask the United States to secure a treaty for extinguishing the claims of the Indians to its frontier lands. The Senate then passed a resolution in which it agreed to consider any treaty the President would make, provided Georgia would bear the expense. In March its members debated "An Act making provision for the purpose of treaty and trade with the Indians." Jackson moved an amendment that the act apply specifically to the Tallassee tract but it was defeated and the original motion prevailed. The Senate preferred to give the President a general rather than a restricted directive.[18]

Returning to Savannah in October Jackson renewed his militia activities. His first step was to request of Governor Mathews supplies and back pay for the troops. The governor complied, complimenting Jackson on his eagerness to defend the frontiers, also reminding him that the Constitution and laws of the United States allowed any governor to call out the militia in cases of invasion or insurrection.

President Washington, acting in compliance with the legislation passed by Congress the previous spring, named Benjamin Hawkins, George Clymer, and Andrew Pickens to a commission to confer with the Creeks at Coleraine. In April, 1796, Georgia sent as its commissioners to this conference James Jackson, James Hendrix, and James Simms. The state looked to these appointees to secure from the Indians title to the Oconee River section and the Tallassee country farther to the south.

Jackson wrote Governor Irwin that he had been elected to the commission against his will and, as he knew himself "not to be versed in Indian matters," he had requested the legislature to name another in his place. Evidently he feared the Georgians would accomplish little and that his Yazoo enemies would use their lack of success as another weapon against him. However, the appointments had been made late in the session and George

Watkins and Judge Taliaferro, president of the state Senate, persuaded the legislators not to hold a second election.

Jackson was in charge of the district nearest the site of the conference and was instructed to furnish as many troops as the Georgia commissioners required. Military guards were also being sent from the federal government. On May 30 Jackson wrote Colonel Gaither, in charge of the federal troops, that the Georgia militia were "cooped up" in their ship, the *Fair Play,* on the St. Mary's River, and asked permission for them to be quartered on land.

Meanwhile Hendrix had asked the federal commission how the state militia were to be supplied. The latter replied that, inasmuch as the Secretary of War had notified Governor Irwin that the national troops were adequate, the Georgia guard could be sent home. Hendrix then informed the federal commission that Georgia had only about twenty in its guard and, as the governor had ordered their presence, they could not be sent home. Also, Georgia was bearing one half of the expense of the conference and "should have a say" about its citizens attending.

The requests of Jackson and Hendrix were denied. Over the protest of the Georgians Seagrove persuaded the federal authorities to move the conference from Coleraine to his home at Muscogee on the Ogeechee River, a short distance. As the chiefs and three hundred and forty Creek warriors marched under the United States flag to the new site they occasionally performed the Eagle-tail dance and smoked the peace pipes with the six commissioners. It was June 16, 1796, before the conference, which was to last fourteen days, began.

On the first day speeches were made by the three federal commissioners. On the second day Jackson spoke at great length. He vigorously recounted numerous instances of "faithless observance" by the Creeks of their treaties with Georgia, presenting as evidence two long sheets of paper filled with items of property the Creeks had stolen. He bluntly demanded that they be restored. The chiefs listened respectfully and abruptly departed for the day. McGillivray had died and Big Warrior was now the most prominent chief. He answered Jackson at the next session with this laconic assertion, "I can fill up more paper than Jackson has done, with a list of similar outrages of the Georgians upon my people."

The results of the conference were that the chiefs refused to cede any territory but did allow the United States to erect trading posts on their soil. Each post was to have a plot five miles square. They also agreed to abide by the New York Treaty of 1790 and to refrain from attacks upon the whites. The federal commission, in return, gave the Indians six thousand dollars worth of goods and promised to send them "two blacksmiths with strikers, . . . with the necessary tools."[19]

Before the treaty was signed the Georgia commission sent the federal commission a written protest. Copies of the protest and the replies made by each side were sent to the press. The complaints revolved around the questions of slights to the dignity of Georgia's commission and violation of certain rights of the state. The state commission's first complaint was voiced in slightly different phraseology by Jackson's statement in the press that the Georgians took some of their militia but they were turned back, although Coleraine was several miles within the county of Camden, Georgia. A federal guard was placed before the Indians' quarters and the Georgians were not allowed to talk with the Creeks except in the presence of the federal commission although the federal agents visited them at will. This procedure had caused the Indians to boast that "one Creek could beat ten Georgians." Furthermore the Indians were permitted to have their weapons but the Georgians were ordered to disarm. Jackson asserted that Pickens was the most friendly and Hawkins the most unfriendly to his state and expressed the opinion that if the Georgia commission had been given free access to the Creeks the latter would have made a cession.

Another grievance was that the federal authorities prejudiced the Indians against Georgia by encouraging them to speak and act with deliberation, assuring them that whatever they decided the federal government would protect them. They also complained that the federal commission offered the Indians but six thousand dollars in presents while Georgia's larger offering, valued at $20,000, was ignored. Other complaints dealt with the time and place of holding the conference and the requirement that Georgia bear a part of the expense while her representatives were pushed into the background. Also, without obtaining the state's consent a cession had been obtained from the Creeks of trading posts on Georgia soil.

The United States government had also assumed the power to annul the treaties of Galphinton and Shoulderbone. Georgia had made these treaties with the Creeks when it was a sovereign state under the Articles of Confederation, before the Constitution had given the federal government the sole right of securing cessions from the Indians. The repudiation of these treaties offered "a melancholy prospect, and more melancholy tie to the union, . . ." The federal commission answered that the conditions they laid down were in their instructions; the Georgians alone were dilatory; and in making the treaties of Galphinton and Shoulderbone Georgia had assumed powers which under the Articles belonged to Congress. Also, the Indians preferred to make their decisions apart from the whites. The Georgians insisted, however, that the Articles divided the authority to treat with the Indians between the national and state governments.

If the estimates of *Chronicle* editor James McNeil and one of his reporters (unnamed) are accepted, Jackson was a total failure as a conciliator. "It is my opinion that Jackson and Simms have damned the treaty . . . it seems to me the former is deranged, his arrogance overleaps anything I have ever seen," the reporter wrote. "From his want of temper he disgusted the Indians as well as the Federal Commissioners," he continued. "Declamatory invective made up all his oratory, and pervaded his whole deportment . . . . Jackson's mean endeavors to shift the blame off his own shoulders will, I fear be too successful with the misguided people: . . . ."

Another unnamed correspondent, writing from Coleraine, was quoted in the same paper as reporting that the federal commission had told the Creek chiefs that the Union had no interest in Georgia's efforts to secure more land. He added that Hendrix, the most deliberate and unbiased of Georgia's representatives, hesitated for a time. At last, concluding that the federal group was working against the interests of the state he, too, signed the protest.

In ratifying the treaty the federal Senate modified it to provide that the Union must obtain the consent of Georgia before establishing trading posts among the Indians. However, Georgia's sovereignty over the Oconee, Tallassee, and other frontier lands was left an open question.

Shortly after this ratification the federal House received a new protest from the Georgia legislature, which was referred to a committee composed of Thomas Pinckney, Robert Goodloe Harper, Nathaniel Macon, Albert Gallatin, and other prominent congressmen. This committee reported that it saw no adequate reason for the repudiation of the Treaty of Galphinton other than the general national policy of keeping the peace and recommended that Georgia be remunerated for the loss of the Oconee and Tallassee lands. The nearest the House ever came to acting on this recommendation was a resolution passed in 1799 which authorized President John Adams to negotiate a treaty for the cession of Tallassee.[20]

Georgia's bitterness, dating back as far as the New York Treaty, was deepened by the Coleraine decision. With emotion Jackson wrote Milledge in 1797 that the Coleraine matter had caused the legislature's representatives from the Oconee section to offer a bill for opening a land office west of the Oconee River. A joint committee from both houses had unanimously approved the attitude of the state's commissioners and Jackson added that a proposed spirited remonstrance to the President and Congress remained "the only mode to preserve peace between the Union & Georgia, & that, without redress, will not answer the purpose . . . in Hancock, Washington & Greene, the people are swarming . . . they must, & will, rush like a torrent over the Oconee in search of subsistence. . . . The election of Mr. Adams will add to the fuel, ..." It was not only the rabble but the most influential citizens as well as those most friendly to good government who favored the extension of white settlements into the section Congress had reserved to the Creeks.

When Jackson later became governor his official actions reflected the reluctant decision of Georgia's leaders to abandon force and seek relief through local and national legislation. Congress concluded treaties with the Indians at Fort Wilkinson in 1802 and at Washington in 1804, securing the Ocmulgee-Oconee section for Georgia.[21]

Jackson's military duties were not entirely concerned with the Indians. In 1791 the troops of the Eastern District were asked to help celebrate a pleasant civic event. In May of that year President Washington reached Purrysburg, South Carolina, on his southern tour, and was rowed down the Savannah River to Savannah. He landed at a pier in the upper part of the harbor, and was saluted by the guns from the wharves and "by the shipping in the port." At "the foot of the stairs" leading up to the bluff he was met by Brigadier General Jackson and Colonel Gunn, who in turn introduced him to the mayor and the aldermen. In the account of this visit in Washington's diary Jackson is not mentioned but as he had been one of the most active members of Congress and had been a guest at the Executive's mansion he presumably was remembered by the President.

Washington was honored with several banquets, a reception, and a dance. He attended the Sunday morning service at Christ Episcopal Church and then began his journey toward Augusta. Just outside the city, at Spring Hill (the scene of some bloody fighting during the Revolution) he was met by Jackson, in charge of the artillery and the light infantry, and was greeted by "39 charges from field pieces & thirteen vollies of platoons." The President then proceeded to Mulberry Grove where he dined with the widow of his friend General Nathanael Greene.

The following day Jackson delivered through the press his congratulations and gratitude to Captain Else and his artillerymen, Captain Montfort and his "Volunteer Infantry," and "the Commissioned and non-commissioned Officers and Privates of each corps" for their "soldierly conduct" during the recent ceremonies. He said that Washington had commended the artillerymen in particular "in the warmest terms." This statement would seem to indicate that Jackson and his officers participated in all the public ceremonies connected with the President's visit to the city.[22]

Once these festivities were over, personal matters engaged Jackson's attention. On July 24, 1782, he had sent to the Georgia House a letter which was referred to the committee on petitions. The records of this legislature throw no light on his object or the decision which was made. That this probably was a request for remuneration for a part of his services in the Revolution is indicated by the fact that in 1793 he petitioned the legislature for fifteen hundred dollars for his services as lieutenant and captain of some of the state militia from 1776 to 1780 and as brigade major of all these forces from February 11, 1780, to June 7th the following year. A legislative committee recommended that he be given a certificate for eight hundred dollars but it was decided that "the House do disagree to this report." One of his enemies, in a public letter of 1796, stated that Jackson made his petition "eleven years after the evacuation of Savannah" and while he was a member of the legislature, that the sum requested was fifteen hundred dollars, and that it opened the door for all of the state's militia officers to claim the same pay as the continentals.

Jackson replied, also through the medium of a public letter, that he never received the fifteen hundred dollars although it was justly due him and since the Georgia Senate had voted to grant it he felt that it had been properly considered later by the House, of which he was a member. He also claimed that he had served as brigade major from early in 1779 to the middle of 1781, "during which period, the most trying service in America was experienced, ..." His letter continued: "General Clarke, and the western officers, had their accounts audited for like services, ... Continental officers . . . have received commutation, of twice the sum, ... Why should it be more criminal in me, to make application, than in other officers?"

In 1793 he was preparing to enter the United States Senate, and it was necessary that he work through his friends. In a letter to Milledge, who was a member of the Georgia legislature, he wrote:

> I shall hold you to the conversation we had together respecting my little petition. I really, my Friend, worked hard for it, and my increasing Family compels me to make the claim. Indeed Debts of that nature, are Debts which no Nation, or State on earth, can get rid of, but by discharge. . . .

For several years following we find no further mention of the petition. Then in 1803 Jackson was encouraged by indications that Congress would appropriate a substantial sum for Georgia's past and future defense against the Indians; this grant would enable his state to complete payment for his services during the Revolution. He forthwith renewed his petition and wrote Governor Milledge that

> I have again almost totally lost my crop, and cannot afford to do publick business for nothing. I am getting old and . . . , the prime of my years have been spent in the service of the State to the detriment of my private interests, and it is too late now to reburse [sic] it. The State must do me justice as well for the Commissioner's duty as my demand against her during the war, which you can assist me in. In right they owe me 2,000 dollars for house rent whilst Governor, and I spent more over my salary than that sum comes to.

This legislature, also, was as unresponsive to his petition as had been those approached in the past.

Later that year Daniel Sturges, Georgia's surveyor-general, published a private letter from Jackson dealing with this subject.

The letter asserted that "at this moment . . . [Georgia] owes me nineteen hundred dollars, for military services. . . . I had possession of this state one twelve month before Wayne shewed his nose in it." Although seemingly willing to give Jackson every honor within its power Georgia never paid him all he demanded for his services during the Revolution.[23]

For a generation Georgians remembered 1796 as "the year of the great fire" in Savannah. A series of fires, which George White thought began in a "bakehouse" in Market Square, destroyed two thirds of the city's buildings, including two hundred and twenty-nine dwellings. The total property loss was estimated at one million dollars. Governor Irwin ordered Jackson to hold one half the militia of Liberty, Bryan, and Effingham counties in readiness to "check the repeated nefarious attempts to lay in ashes that City." The Maryland legislature, acting out of compassion for the sufferers, sent two thousand dollars. Jackson voted with the Georgia legislature the following year to provide additional relief.

In 1802 a wave of excitement swept through Georgia and South Carolina over reports of an organized attempt to land some Negro brigands from the French island of Guadaloupe in southern ports. In September Governor John Milledge ordered Jackson to resist such an effort in the state's ports and to charge the expense to the governor's contingent fund. No serious attempts to land the brigands were made however.[24]

We find no reference to Jackson's connection with the military during the last three years of his life. During the nineteen years he served in this field his activities were largely defensive but, since the frontiersmen were continually encroaching on the Creeks, Georgia needed an organization to stand guard in order to prevent its population from being destroyed. Jackson made good in a defensive role but in offensive Indian warfare he admitted that Clarke and Twiggs merited greater recognition.

If one is to discover Jackson's greatest contribution to society he must turn from Indian affairs to the field of politics.

IV

THE "CHATHAM WOLF" IN THE GEORGIA LEGISLATURE

◊ • ◊ • ◊ • ◊ • ◊ • ◊ • ◊ • ◊ • ◊ • ◊ • ◊ • ◊ • ◊ • ◊ • ◊ • ◊ • ◊ • ◊

IN HIS autobiography Jackson writes that after leading his victorious troops into Savannah in 1782 he entered into civilian life, resigned his commission, and was elected to the assembly, "having been appointed or having served in every legislature for the State from the evacuation . . ." until 1789. He failed to mention the fact that his name also appeared on the rolls of that body at its session held at Augusta in August of 1781, eleven months before the British evacuated Savannah. At this session he was named a justice of the peace for Chatham County, a position of considerable social and political importance in that era, and the appointment was renewed annually for several years.

His services in the legislature were confined to the lower house during the eleven years of 1781 through 1787, 1789, 1791, 1796, and 1797. The first eight of these years were during the era of the Articles of the Confederation (1781–1789) and the last three were during the Federalist regime of Washington and John Adams (1789-1801).

In 1782 the legislature met at Ebenezer first but moved down the river to Savannah after July 11 when the British retired from Georgia. During Jackson's political career the state capital was changed five times, being located in turn at Augusta, Savannah, Augusta again, Louisville, and finally at Milledgeville.

In 1782 Chatham County again named Jackson as one of its representatives but the Committee on Elections and Privileges reported that at the time of his election he held a post (undesignated) which excluded him from the House and he was denied his seat. For some reason the legislature adjourned to the fourth of January, 1783, and then reorganized. In the meantime Jackson either had resigned from the objectionable office or had met some other requisite and the committee, reversing its position, gave him his seat.[1]

He had the distinction of being elected to the legislature by the two counties of Camden and Chatham in 1788. The Georgia Constitution of 1777, which was still in effect, allowed the frontier counties of Glynn and Camden to be represented by citizens from any of the more populous counties. The House forgot this when it ruled, regarding one of the county returns, "That James Jackson returned from Camden County is not eligible because of non-residence." As he had refused a similar election by his own county of Chatham Jackson evidently was not in a mood to accept any public office at that time. In the following year Glynn County, in which he owned some land but had never resided, sent him to the House. The members then apparently recalled the Constitution's provision for this county and he was seated.

Among the numerous committees upon which he served in various sessions were Finance, Indian Affairs, Education, Judicial Affairs, and Ways and Means. The latter enabled him to assist in the guidance of much of the over-all legislative program.[2]

Jackson's leniency towards the Revolutionary Tories was a prime example of his conservative leanings in economic affairs. Much of the property of these men had been confiscated by the state. In 1782 the radical element, hoping to buy these properties at bargain prices, sought to induce the legislature to take over what remained; but Jackson and his conservative friends were lukewarm in their support of such measures and from 1782 to 1789 sought to soften the punishment of disloyal "loyalists." In 1783 he served on a committee which reported an act authorizing the governor to limit the confiscation of loyalist property to a maximum of six hundred pounds per person.

But Jackson's mercy was often tempered with stern justice, as in the case of Tory Thomas Gibbons of Savannah. Although he stood with the majority in voting to restore Gibbons' confiscated estate, Jackson later helped pass a resolution that "Thomas Gibbons be not allowed to plead and practice in the Courts of Law of this State for fourteen years. . . ." In 1796 the "Chatham Wolf" also introduced and helped pass a bill which restored to citizenship loyalist John M. Tattnall. Jackson must have regretted some of his forgiving, charitable gestures, for in his autobiography he bitterly asserted that "his patriotism and humanity prevented many unworthy Characters from suffering who ungratefully repaid him for it. . . ."

In financial affairs Jackson occupied a position to the right of center. In 1782 the House requested him to form "a depreciation Table of the difference . . . between Georgia and Continental Money issued, and Specie, to commence from . . . January," 1776. His conservatism is seen again in his opposition to a futile effort to pass a bill "for the relief of debtors" and in his support of a successful bill to "settle and liquidate all demands against this or the United States, ..."

In 1786 the majority of the state's planters and yeomen promoted an act which authorized the printing of fifty thousand pounds in paper currency for rewarding Georgia's Revolutionary soldiers but only thirty thousand pounds of this legal tender was actually issued. Opposing its issue were a group of sixty-six mechanics of Savannah who publicly announced that they would not accept this "cheap" money as wages. A majority of Chatham's planters and merchants must have agreed, because the county's entire delegation, including Jackson, opposed the inflationary measure. This issue of currency was based on the state's public lands and it was later redeemed. Sympathy for the veterans, rather than radical principles, influenced those planters who supported the bill.

Jackson also fought successfully in 1789 to have Georgia's outstanding bonds redeemed although he failed to secure several amendments which would have strengthened this conservative measure.[3]

During the 1783 session Jackson worked with House committees which handled such matters as greeting General Nathanael Greene as the military commander of the Southern Department and conferring with him on the defense of Georgia.

In an adjourned session of this body held in Augusta Jackson's name was first mentioned in connection with the subject of public education. He and a man named Davis were instructed to draw up a bill for "erecting a University or Seminary of Learning" and for "laying out" the reserved land in Augusta for the support of an academy. But for some reason no law on education was passed at this session. The legislature of 1784 appointed a self-perpetuating Board of Trustees and set aside twenty thousand acres of public land in each of the newly created counties of Franklin and Washington for the establishment and support of a state university. Then in January of the following year this body passed "AN ACT. For the more full and complete Establishment of a public School of Learning in this State." It also issued a charter and named a Board of Visitors and a new Board of Trustees. The two groups formed "The Senatus Academicus" of the university, a body which was instructed to "consult and advise" upon university problems and the literature of the state.

Thus the University of Georgia was the first state university to be chartered, although not the first to function. Jackson was one of its principal founders. The records are silent as to his part in enacting the laws of 1784 and 1785 but an act of 1786 named him a trustee of the proposed institution. He also served on a committee to plan the establishment of a public school or academy in each county as directed by the state Constitution.

Jackson as governor signed "The University Act" on December 5, 1800. This act decreed that the university should be established in either Jackson, Franklin, Hancock, Greene, Oglethorpe, Wilkes, or Warren county. It also named Jackson to a new Board of Visitors. The trustees were asked to order "all persons . . . in possession . . . of any funds papers or books belonging to the said University . . . , to deliver over said property" to them. The legislature seemed determined that the university should begin its operation as soon as possible, for the act of 1800 instructed the officials to "carry this institution completely into effect"; and its doors opened in 1801.

In 1791 Jackson served as trustee of two Chatham County educational units. One was a proposed Chatham Academy; the second was the private Bethesda Orphanage, a controversial institution in the management of which Jackson had found himself not a little involved. Before he was through he was to be accused of trying to divert the assets of one to the other.

Bethesda Orphanage, with its surrounding plantation, was founded in 1739 by the Reverend George Whitefield of England and was by him enlarged into a preparatory school, Bethesda College. Whitefield died in Massachusetts in 1770, leaving the school in trust to Madame Selina Hastings, "Countess Dowager" of Huntington and widow of the ninth Earl, Theophilus Hastings. The countess had been the founder of the Calvinistic Methodist sect known as "The Countess of Huntington's Connection," which supported Whitefield against John Wesley. The countess was so far removed from Georgia that the institution languished from the very year she was entrusted with it, and when she died in 1791 the legal status of the school became highly involved. No orphan received any aid from its administration after the Revolution began. On the contrary, according to Jackson, it had been maintained for "several lazy dronish Parsons, most of whom have been too supine to perform the common duties of Clergymen, and some of them have actually spent their time in Racing and Hunting with the Overseers of the Estate."

Shortly before her death the countess had vainly sought to sell the property "to the highest bidder" and her executors named the Reverend John Johnson, a dissenting Anglican clergyman, the "President" of the school. They also appointed him to serve with Savannah's Mayor Thomas Gibbons as legal representative for the institution.

According to Whitefield's will the trust did not devolve upon the countess's heirs or her attorneys but upon James Habersham of Georgia. However, the legislature in 1791 ruled that the property was without heirs. Since it was originally intended for the benefit of orphans the state would act as guardian and see that the purposes of Whitefield and his supporters were carried out. Sir George Houstoun was named president of a new board of thirteen trustees.

Johnson resisted several efforts to dispossess him, even arming himself against those who arrived with eviction papers. He was later forcibly removed and placed in prison and was released only on the understanding that he and his wife would leave for England. Before he left he published his version of the controversy, claiming that Jackson had planned to introduce into the legislature a resolution "for taking away the Orphan House Estate & applying it to the purpose of an Academy for the County of Chatham—."

Jackson previously had warned the legislators that certain Northern papers had been urging a plan "for exposing the Orphan House Estate for sale as private property—," but evidently he later found it politically expedient to leave the property intact. Johnson claimed that he found "the clamor against Jackson & Clay because the people are aware of their intentions against the Orphan House; but in consequence of their declaration against any such intentions, Gen'l Jackson was elected" to the House.

Georgia's economic plight in early days is reflected in many of Jackson's legislative experiences. In 1782 he helped a committee prepare a letter to Congress which expressed the state's regret that poverty compelled it to meet only a part of the requisitions by the federal government (under the Articles of Confederation). The legislators were also ordered to help in the grave financial emergency by serving without pay, and the officers of the state militia had to be content with a bare subsistence. Another economy move was the state's decision to pay its contingent expenses with certificates for confiscated and public lands. Jackson supported this bill but revealed his fear of a political dictatorship by successfully opposing a bill which would name a manager with broad powers to husband Georgia's economic resources.[4]

During his House terms Jackson naturally had some relations with the national government. He worked on several committees which prepared instructions to Georgia's Congressmen. He also helped in the writing of letters to federal Presidents John Hanson and Elias Boudinot. In 1783 the Georgia legislature named six Congressmen but provided salaries for only two of them. As chairman of an investigating committee Jackson reported that Governor Lyman Hall had even refused to give credentials to one Congressman who had agreed to serve at his own expense. Jackson helped pass a bill which rebuked the governor and his Council for their negligence.

In 1787 he supported a motion to approve a proposed amendment to the Articles. This amendment would authorize Congress to levy a tariff of five per cent, but the House defeated it by a vote of 25 to 39. Thus because of the negative attitude of Georgia and other states our first federal Constitution never received the unanimous ratification of the state legislatures necessary to secure an amendment.

Little is known of Jackson's representation of Chatham County in the legislatures of 1791 and 1792 inasmuch as the only extant official records for these years are the journals of the Senate. However, the Senate journal of 1791 shows that he led a House committee in convicting one of the state's officials in the disputed Congressional election of that year.

In 1792 Georgia appealed to state sovereignty when two non-Georgians won suits in federal courts against the state. In one of these, "Brailsford v. Georgia," the court awarded a British merchant property which Georgia claimed by virtue of one of its confiscation acts. In the second case, "Chisholm v. Georgia," the state was ordered to pay a certain sum to one Chisholm of South

Carolina. By refusing to appear before the court Georgia lost the decision by default. As an outcome of these suits Jackson secured enactment of a House resolution advocating that the federal Constitution be amended so as to prevent a person from suing a state of which he was not a citizen. The eleventh amendment in 1798 incorporated this principle, by the approval of each of the state legislatures.

Jackson's appeal to the lower middle class is reflected in his views on the state militia. In 1784 he helped enact a law which exempted from state militia service the larger part of Georgia's politicians and professional men. This law, which held except in cases of alarm, exempted members of the Council, legislators, chief justices and associate justices in each county, state treasurers, secretaries of state, attorneys general, county clerks, sheriffs, collectors of ports, pilots, mariners, ferrymen, teachers, clergymen, physicians, justices of the peace, "Sworn" attorneys, "Idiots, and Madmen."

Georgia was slower than some of the states in completely freeing its government from certain obligations to the churches. The Anglicans had been disestablished by the state Constitution of 1777 but many of the legislators felt that religion was still a vital concern. In 1784 Jackson worked on a committee which prepared a legislative act "for the regular establishment and support of the public duties of religion." By this law the churches were encouraged to reorganize and erect suitable houses of worship and the legislature came to the relief of the poverty-stricken congregations with appropriations based on membership. In passing this bill by a vote of forty-three to five the House reflected the widespread dread that private and public morals would collapse in the distressed conditions following the Revolution. It became evident, however, that this policy conflicted with the growing American conception of the separation of church and state and it was soon abandoned.[6]

In the spring of 1786 Jackson joined a group of Chatham politicians in a controversy with Governor Edward Telfair. Since the state government had been moved to Augusta the legislature directed the governor to have the state's records moved from Savannah to the new office of Secretary of State John Milton. James Pearre, Jr., was directed by Telfair to take his wagon to Savannah and make the transfer. Upon learning of this decision Chatham's justices of the peace—William Stephens, Richard Wylly, Peter

Deveaux, Samuel Stirk, and James Jackson—determined to retain these documents in Savannah. Following one unsuccessful attempt they finally gained entrance to the old executive quarters and moved a large part of the records of both the colonial trustees and the lower counties to the office of the county clerk of Chatham. Their explanation to the protesting state officials was that, while meaning no disrespect, they believed the executive department had exceeded its authority in demanding the removal of all the books from Savannah. The Council branded this action as anarchy, suspended each of the justices, and employed private counsel to assist them in forcing the transfer.

In retaliation the newly elected assistant justices—General Nathanael Greene, Joseph Habersham, and William Gibbons, Jr.— refused to serve. The Savannah press severely criticized the executive department for interfering with the judiciary and the legislature. Considerable personal and factional bickering followed and the timid legislature dodged its duty by postponing further action. The justices must have felt uneasy in their stand, however, because in November Milton reported that the disputed documents had been received in Augusta.[7]

Although he had declined to serve in the legislature of 1788 that body elected Jackson to the governorship. On the seventh of January the speaker of the house wrote him that a large majority of the legislators had been influenced enough by his "approved patriotism" and "repeated exertions" in the service of his country (Georgia) to elevate him to the "Chief Magistracy." Following the announcement of this honor in the press an editor broke the news that "General Jackson has *refused the government, the only instance in Georgia.*"

All knew that he was one of the most ambitious young men in the state, and his refusal must have caused considerable speculation. The only explanation of his motive in the original sources is this statement in his autobiography:

in 1788 . . . he was elected Governor . . . which he had fortitude & prudence . . . to refuse—it being certain that however uprightly a Man in the Cols [sic] conspicuous situation might walk the eye of malevolence would reach him so he was about this period harassed by factions who wished & tried to destroy his reputation in vain however they disturbed the peace of a beloved Family. . . .

During this same year he was also elected one of Georgia's four presidential electors by an overwhelming vote.

In both 1796 and 1797 the Georgia legislatures were known as "Yazoo" legislatures, and the sale of the state's western lands consumed much of the time. In the latter year Jackson was selected to serve during 1798 in the legislature and in the state constituent Convention. He was elected governor in 1798, however, and thus his activities in the state legislative branch ended in 1797.[8]

Years later, while commenting on the puzzle of Georgia's politics from 1819 to 1833, Hezekiah Niles wrote in his *Register* that "We know not what they differ about—but they do violently differ." His remarks would be applicable equally as well to the period in which Jackson served in the Georgia House; this was approximately from 1781 to 1797.

Although political divisions did exist in Georgia's early history they were slightly milder on most issues than those of other states. The cleavage between the conservatives and the radicals began with the Revolution. In opposition to radicals Button Gwinnett, John Houstoun, George Walton, and George Wells such conservatives as John Wereat, Joseph Habersham, Lachlan McIntosh, and William Few succeeded in postponing the break with Britain until 1775. Each of these groups insisted on dominating the government and conducting the war. When he first arrived in America Jackson supported the radical patriot side but in 1775 he affiliated with the conservative Wereat political faction.

When the middle and upper counties complained of having to travel long distances to Savannah to transact governmental business the governor and his Council decided to reside three months annually in Augusta. And, while Jackson's opposition in 1786 to the permanent removal of the capital from Savannah revealed his predominant sympathy for the aristocratic coastal region, his blusterous temper and his devotion to the common man also made a strong appeal to the frontiersmen.

While the five counties of the lower district were all on the coast, only Chatham and Effingham were controlled by the planters. Camden, Liberty and Glynn were on the frontier. The reports of the first congressional race under our present United States Constitution failed to show the section in which Jackson had the greater strength. And in the second congressional campaign Chatham was carried by Jackson, a conservative Republican. Effingham was credited to a more conservative Federalist, Anthony Wayne. Jackson carried the frontier counties of Glynn, Liberty, and Camden, the most thinly settled of the five. Again the evidence was too inconclusive to show positively which class or section gave him the greater support.

The legislature again elected Jackson to the governorship in 1798 and 1799, and it sent him to the United States Senate in 1793 and 1800. While the sectional alignments are not given his majority increased with each election. In his first campaign for the federal Senate he spoke of having strong support from the frontier, and in 1796, as a result of the Yazoo fight, his support in this section was still stronger. His most serious opposition came from personal enemies and the Yazoo purchasers. In retiring from the governorship in 1801 he boasted to Baldwin that he had the support of all the citizens of the state, "a few aristocrats excepted." Since he won all of his political campaigns he must have had considerable support among the small farmers. But taking his career as a whole it appears that he probably received a slightly larger proportion of the planter vote.[9]

The first eight years of Jackson's experience in the legislature proved to be a valuable stepping-stone to the term he was soon to serve in the federal House during Washington's first two years in the presidency.

V

A PIONEER IN THE FIRST CONGRESS

A FEW months after he refused the governorship James Jackson became a candidate for the lower House of the First Congress. The election was to be held on February 9, 1789. In January he had spiked a rumor that he was not in the race, pledging through the press that if elected he would "attend my duty in that House."

The federal Constitution determined that until such time as the first census should be taken Georgia should have three members in the House. The Georgia election act of 1789 accordingly divided the state into three congressional districts. This act further specified that in the congressional election there should be a general ticket, each voter throughout the state voting for one candidate residing in each of the three districts. The candidates for the three positions were: Abraham Baldwin, George Mathews, James Jackson, William Houstoun, Henry Osborne, Job Sumner, Henry Allison, Isaac Briggs, J. M. Schiver, Baptist Hillegar, Joseph Clay, John Graves, William Few, William Pierce, Thomas Gibbons, and Edward Telfair.

Upon opening the returns on February 26 the Council announced the successful candidates and their total vote. George Mathews, for the western or upper district, polled 1,054 votes; Abraham Baldwin for the central or middle district, 1,000; James Jackson for the lower district, 583.

Only the returns from the seven counties of Richmond, Wilkes, Effingham, Chatham, Liberty, Burke, and Washington were received in time to be counted. The returns from Greene, Glynn, and Camden came too late to be counted but the Council had them published. Had the votes from these three counties been counted in the official tabulation Jackson still would have won.[1] Ten days before Washington's inauguration Jackson was officially seated. This was April 20, 1789, two weeks after the organization of the two houses and the count of the electoral votes.

Travel to and from the capital at New York City was none too easy. In 1790 Jackson and Mathews were caught in a storm at sea, landing with great difficulty at Cape May, New Jersey, and afterward travelling one hundred and sixty miles in a wagon to Philadelphia.

Jackson wrote Milledge that

I . . . should have been present on the Constitutional day, had I not as usual met a severe Gale between Lookout and the Frying Pan. . . . I never made up my mind to die before, but I tasted of death at that time and feel a satisfaction when I reflect, that I was perfectly resigned. . . . I have ever since been thinking of an expression of old Qua's in Savannah, a few days before I sailed—The rascal had the insolence to tell me to stay at home, & not fret myself about Publick [sic]—"What Publick care for you, Massa? God! Ye get drowned bye & bye. Qua tell you so, & what going come of he Family den?"

Jackson served in Congress during the administrations of Washington and Jefferson and so can truly be called one of the "founding fathers" of these United States. The republic was young and debate at the capital helped to determine the present and the future character of the national government.

In these early years the Constitution was interpreted, important precedents were set, and our system of federal courts was set up. In addition our nation sought solutions for such varied questions as the tariff, federal and state finances, Indian relations, the public land policy, naturalization, and foreign relations. Upon these questions it was natural that there should be two viewpoints, namely the aristocratic or Federalist (now Republican) and the Republican (now Democratic).

Republican Thomas Jefferson believed that government should be by the talented few but of and for all, including the masses, but Federalist Alexander Hamilton believed that government should be of, by and chiefly for the wealthy. To his way of thinking the common people should have but a very modest share in the wealth and happiness of a great nation. William Maclay in the Senate and James Jackson in the House opposed Hamilton's aristocratic policies before antagonism to them fully developed in the thinking of others. As a modern historian phrased it, "The astonishing thing is that the comparatively crude Maclay from the wilds of Pennsylvania and the leather-lunged James Jackson from sparsely settled Georgia should have caught the full significance of it all before it dawned on Jefferson and Madison."

With impetuous and untiring presentation of their thought, Maclay and Jackson undoubtedly paved the way for a democratic viewpoint, thus earning the right to be considered two of the forerunners of the Republican (now Democratic) party. In forming the opposition to the aristocratic viewpoint, a little later Madison took the lead in the House and Jefferson began to clash with Hamilton in the cabinet. Near the close of 1793 Jefferson resigned his post as Secretary of State and concentrated on the task of laying the foundations of the Republican party. In national politics Jackson was an independent Jeffersonian Republican.[2]

Naturally one of the first questions faced by Congress was a suitable method of addressing the President. Jackson led the House in ridiculing certain Senators for proposing such titles as "Most Honorable," "His Grace," "Mightiness," and "His Most Serene Highness." He said that such terms trifled with government and "exalted one man to a station as high as Haman's gibbet. These titles have been echoed even in the Boston papers, a town which, fifteen years ago, would have acknowledged no Lord but the Lord of hosts." While the matter was under debate the House began introducing Washington as "The President of the United States." The Senate soon followed suit.

Jackson was only thirty-two when elected to the House and in a speech before that body once declared that he was "as young a politician as any on the floor." He also boasted in his autobiography that in Congress he "was at least not of the lowest order of Speakers." Fisher Ames of Massachusetts, a Federalist member of the lower House, wrote Thomas Dwight in 1790 that "Mr. Jackson then made a speech, which I will not say was loud enough for you to hear. It disturbed the Senate, however; and to keep out the din, they put down their windows. Mr. Smith (S.C.) followed him, ... Jackson rebellowed." On another occasion Ames wrote that Jackson sounded like a "furnace bellows." Jackson may have been reminded by his friends that his manner was unnecessarily vehement; at any rate in the midst of a warm debate he felt called upon to offer this apology: "Gentlemen will excuse me, if my language should not be adapted to that delicacy to which so respectable a body is entitled. I have accustomed myself to a blunt integrity of speech, which I hope the goodness of my intentions will excuse."[3]

In his recorded speeches and writings Jackson only occasionally referred to Washington. While they differed on many political measures Jackson's attitude was one of respect and admiration for the character and abilities of the President. In January and March of 1790 he was a dinner guest at Washington's New York home.

Jackson was not very active in committee work during his term in the House except for occasional service on committees of conference when the two houses were endeavoring to agree on important legislation. He wished to prevent the development of too strong an executive department, voting with the opposition when a bill to create a Department of Foreign Affairs was passed by the House.

Early in this First Congress Madison moved that the President be authorized to remove the heads of the three departments of State, Treasury, and War. Jackson objected, claiming that the Constitution suggested the Senate should appoint and remove, and that he thought the President should be allowed only to suspend an official until he could be tried for treason. Madison agreed that judges should be removable by impeachment but argued that to impeach all unworthy appointees would tax the time of the Senate.

Jackson replied, "I am, sir, a friend to the full exercise of all the powers of Government, and deeply impressed with the necessity there exists of having an energetic Executive. But, . . . I value the liberties of my fellow-citizens beyond every other consideration, ..." He pointed out that since a majority of the Senate must approve the President's appointments, the powers of government are blended and that there is no government in history where the legislative and executive powers are fully separated. The President has a part of the legislative power and the Senate has a part of the executive power. He was opposed to "this thirst of power."

Some had argued that the President should have the power of removal because the Secretary of Foreign Affairs, for instance, might have a fit of lunacy. Jackson answered that this was possible but not probable and that the President, the Senate, and the House members might all "suffer from lunacy." If the President should be allowed to remove the Secretary of the Treasury he could obtain another who would back him with money and, as he also names the officers of the army, he could become a tyrant. There would be no danger of this during the presidency of Washington, Jackson said, "but alas! he can not be with us, forever...."

He claimed that the power of removal is not granted. In seeking ratification of the national Constitution, the Federalists in supporting that document had assured the country that what was not specifically given to the nation was reserved to the states and a proposed amendment would incorporate this view in the Constitution. Jackson further declared that if Congress should ignore this principle of reserved powers it would take an arbitrary stride towards a despotic government. While America was giving vigor to the executive arm it ought to be careful not to lay the foundation of future tyranny, for a wise people will not trust their freedom to one official and then give him the sword and the strong box.

Madison's bill, however, passed by a small majority.[4]

Throughout much of his public life Jackson was a strong advocate of state rights and democracy. In 1788 he favored the adoption of the Constitution because Georgia wished the protection of a strong federal government against the Indians and the Spanish. When in 1790 Washington showed a strong sympathy for the Creeks Jackson began to favor building up the state and limiting the national powers to those definitely delegated to it in the Constitution. He wanted the federal government to be stronger than the Confederation but not too strong. In social life he was an aristocratic planter but in political theory he supported democracy. During a House debate he said,

My heart, sir, is federal; and I would do as much as any member on this floor, . . . to promote the interests and welfare of the Union. But, . . . I conceive the liberties of my fellow-citizens too deeply involved to suffer me to risk such a precious stake, though to secure the efficiency of a National Government.

In still another debate he spoke of the states as the sixteen pillars of "our empire" and urged that nothing be done by Congress to shake them. Taxes which touched the poor should be replaced by those which would tap great estates made through speculation whose "holders are now like drone bees, sucking honey out of the hive, and affording no aid in its procurement. This is my opinion and I care not who knows it."[5]

The "democratical" Jackson probably surprised his friends by becoming the chief opponent of the first efforts to amend the Constitution. He sought the protection of Georgia against its enemies through a reasonably strong central government and he felt that the Constitution would be weakened by hasty amendments. When certain members of Congress spoke of holding another Convention and rewording the whole Constitution Jackson opposed it: in due time it could be amended but hasty revisions would undo the work of the people.

Madison moved that the members form a committee of the whole to consider the question of amendments. Jackson objected because "the ship of State" had just been launched; its course was untried and it was too early to consider amendments. Georgia had unanimously adopted the Constitution and its citizens were not eager for immediate change. If some amendments were voted now, then when North Carolina and Rhode Island entered the Union others would be demanded. Jackson wished Congress first to complete the matter of "collections," lest they have no revenue with which to run the government. If they wished to prevent other nations from despising America the first task was to organize the government.

"I am against inserting a declaration of rights in the Constitution, ... If . . . not . . . improper, it is at least unnecessary; . . . ," Jackson said. Do not congressmen belong to the people? Why fear the congressmen? The people's rights were not more safe under state government than under a limited federal government. He asserted that in 1789 there were no bills of rights in the constitutions of Virginia, New York, New Jersey, South Carolina, or Georgia and he asked if the people were less safe in those five states than in the other eight. He inferred that if certain reserved rights should be specified for the states then all other rights would be considered granted to the United States. He did not wish to have the Constitution patched up from time to time like "Joseph's coat of many colors." Congress had power to regulate commerce, war, and peace but he failed to see that it had any power to control the press. And why secure what was not in danger?

Nevertheless the question was taken up by the committee of the whole and in the debate Jackson opposed most of the proposed amendments. Many advocated that the federal Constitution should guarantee trial by jury but he saw no reason to fear that the people would be denied this privilege. The motion prevailed and the state legislatures ratified it as the seventh amendment. In August another proposed amendment would have prevented Congress from voting direct taxes so long as the tariff and requisitions upon the states sufficed to meet the needs of the national budget. Jackson stated that requisitions had failed under the Confederation and that taking such a backward step might lead to civil war, or handicap the country in time of invasion. The resolution was defeated.[6]

One of the first problems facing Congress was that of financing the government. The Confederation had bequeathed to the new government the burdensome heritage of both an empty treasury and a large debt. Also, inasmuch as direct taxes must await a federal census, Congress turned to a tax on imports. When the tariff committee reported a bill imposing a duty of fifteen cents per gallon on spirits of highest proof, Elias Boudinot offered an amendment that it be reduced to twelve cents. Jackson seconded this motion. He thought the rate was so high that it would be impossible to collect it without erecting customhouses at intervals of ten or twelve miles along the entire Atlantic coast. The amendment was rejected.

In order to encourage our merchant marine as well as raise revenue, the tariff committee wished to punish the unfriendly and at the same time reward the friendly nations. Thus its first tariff bill proposed to make the rate per ton on imports from lands like Britain, which refused to make a commercial treaty with us, higher than those from France and others which had made such a treaty. Jackson objected and moved an amendment charging the nations out of commercial relations with us only twenty cents tonnage instead of the suggested thirty cents rate.

He admitted that the high duty on rice would greatly aid the planters were it not for the fact that in two or three years Britain had reduced the price of that staple from fourteen to nine shillings per hundredweight. All of Georgia's staples were selling abroad at a lower figure than before the Revolution and he feared that a high tariff would further lower them. The returns received in Europe on rice, indigo, and tobacco were so low that instead of exporting them Southern planters were exporting specie, forty thousand dollars recently having been shipped on one boat. This was a daily practice and soon Georgia would have no specie with which to meet its obligations abroad or to pay its duties in America.

In addition, high discriminatory duties would prevent Britain from coming for Georgia's goods, and until such time as America could build her own ships the planters would suffer. There were piled up in Southern warehouses five thousand hogsheads of tobacco and large quantities of rice and lumber awaiting shipment. Should the planters in order to help the building of American shipping be compelled to suffer their stuff to rot? "I hope the government will not insist on our walking before we are able to creep, or compel us to make bricks without straw," he said. High duties would weaken the loyalty of the people to the new national government and "rivet them in their distrust." He wished Congress to "draw in, by tender means, the States that are now out of the Union, ..."

At this point Ames suggested that if Georgia needed more shipping high duties would offer the means of procuring it. Jackson answered that he preferred to see the shipping first and that as soon as Americans could do the hauling he would not object to fifty cents per ton, or even total prohibition of foreign shipping.

"Are we of the Southern States to lose our agricultural advantages?" he asked. "If we cannot carry our product to market we are cut off from the means of paying our debts or improving our country; and in the South this would 'unpeople our lands.'"

Jackson's amendment to reduce the rates charged nations having no commercial treaty with the United States to twenty cents tonnage was defeated and the proposal of the committee for thirty cents was approved. The committee's bill also proposed an extra import duty of fifty cents per ton on goods from any nation if they were hauled in ships belonging in whole or in part to nations refusing to enter into commercial treaties with us.

Madison spoke in favor of a motion to lower this discriminatory duty. Jackson also thought this rate was too high for his section. Even New England would be willing to accept a forty cents duty. Maryland and Pennsylvania, in demanding the higher sum, reminded him of the Biblical king Rehoboam who, when his people begged that he begin his reign with a lowering of taxes, replied, "My father did lade you with a heavy yoke, but I will add to your burdens." In spite of attempts by Jackson and others to lower the rate the original bill remained unchanged.

Many Senators and some Congressmen from the Middle States

A Pioneer in The First Congress

wanted the tariff rates made permanent but Jackson successfully supported the effort by Madison to limit their duration to seven years. Some parts of the bill were "exceptionable" to the South, he argued, and the House was less permanent and closer to the people than the Senate. The Revolutionary veterans would prefer to leave the public finances in the hands of the popular branch and it would be unwise for the House to give in too often to the Senate. The expiration date was finally set for June 1, 1796.

In May of 1790 Jackson said that the "carrying trade" brought no benefit to America other than the training of seamen, and that if invaded we would not look to a navy but to our yeomen of the West. Ships were already being built in New England, and Congress should not burden the South to speed up the process. The Southern States were a good "milch cow" to the Union, Jackson continued, but if the Union milked the cow they should not ride it at the same time—the additional tonnage appeared to him to amount to a double advantage. The true interest of America lies in its agriculture, he averred; the country ought therefore not to depend upon the carrying trade alone but also upon its yeomanry.[7]

In 1791 Hamilton had a bill introduced to bolster the national revenue through an excise. The excise bill proposed a duty of from eleven to thirty cents per gallon on spirits distilled from molasses, sugar, and other foreign materials, and a duty of from nine to twenty-five cents on those distilled from domestic articles (such as grains). Concerning the debate on this bill Ames wrote Thomas Dwight that

Mr. Jackson flamed forth yesterday, before the first paragraph was read. He was stopped to hear it out, and then he moved to strike it out, after a violent speechicle [sic] which was not answered.

After reviewing the whole financial policy of the government Jackson spoke at length on the subject under debate. He thought the excise was odious, unequal, unjust, unnecessary, and clearly another blow at the South.

Defeated on his motion to strike out part of the bill, he said that the members were silent because they were unable to answer him. He felt it was absurd to plead that the bill would encourage industry and agriculture, raise revenue, and promote morality. Ames was successfully challenged to deny that on a former occasion he had ridiculed the idea of reforming the people by an excise on spirits and had said that the members were not to consider themselves as at school or church and compelled to listen to the harangues of speculative piety. Jackson quoted Necker as saying that it was unfair to compare the tax burdens in different lands, while ignoring the "gnawing vulture [of perpetual taxation] whose appetite increases daily with what it feeds upon. I hope, Sir, we shall not feed him too daintily in America."

He thought an excise would encourage the smuggling of spirits from abroad and added, "I will here remark my surprise at the memorial of the college of physicians [of Philadelphia] against the use of spirits and their poisonous effects. Sir, a dozen colleges would not persuade the common people of the southern states, that . . . grog, is unnecessary." He believed that overeating was as injurious as overdrinking and that the sin of overdrinking should be punished only in the next life. He had no doubt but that a copy of the Reverend Jedidiah Morse's *Geography* was "in this house," in which Morse held that drink was necessary in the South. The South did not have access to beer, ale, or cider, and these would remain cheap because the bill placed no excise upon them. Hence taxes should not deprive the Southern people of the only luxury they possessed. The law would be hard to enforce, Jackson insisted. In the light of past experience with excises he held that if this bill became a law there would have to be in each American village from one to twelve federal appointees charged with the law's execution. Nevertheless, the original bill was passed.[8]

In 1789 Congress also faced the problem of organizing a federal court system. A bill was introduced to have a Supreme Court, three Circuit Courts, and thirteen District Courts. Jackson sided with Hamilton in opposing Circuit and District Courts, holding that "the State courts would answer every judiciary purpose," and "the people, their liberties and properties, would be more secure under the legal paths of their ancestors; under their . . . known methods of decision. They have hitherto been accustomed to receive justice at their own doors in a simple form." A round of appellate courts would favor the rich over the poor, he felt, and appeals from a state court to one higher court was sufficient.

With inferior federal courts, citizens would be tried by strangers two hundred to three hundred miles away. It was extreme in the Articles of Confederation not to provide for any federal court, but the present government should not go to the opposite extreme of having one in each of the states. If Congress should create only a Supreme Court the judicial system would be sufficiently centralized. This body could then hold a check over the state courts. The state courts should be given a fair trial and if they failed then "a more energetic mode" might be tried. But the bill setting up the three classes of federal courts passed the House in September of 1789 and later received the approval of the Senate and the President.[9]

One of the most bitter debates of 1790 was upon Hamilton's recommendation that the federal government assume and fund or redeem its financial obligations at par by converting all its bonds and paper bills into a more or less permanent debt with new bonds bearing regular interest. The motion to assume and fund, or redeem, the foreign debt was passed without opposition.

It was then proposed to take over and redeem at par the entire domestic debt of the Union. Then the fight really began. This measure would enable the holders of depreciated bonds of the bankrupt, defunct Confederation to exchange them for the new federal government's paper, which was worth its face value.

Madison moved an amendment which would enable the secondary purchasers or "holders by transfer" to receive only the highest prices which the old federal securities had ever brought. Jackson supported Madison and laid down the general principle that any largess to the speculator must eventually be paid by the producer and that Hamilton's plan would lay a first lien on future labor. An account sent to the Georgia press stated that Jackson "pathetically described the situation of the officers and soldiers of the late army, who had been obliged through necessity to part with their certificates for a trifling" sum.

Hamilton had anticipated these objections by stating that he wished to avoid discriminations among public creditors as "original holders and transferees." Jackson said that he formerly adhered to something like this, but recent circumstances had converted him to Madison's view. His anger had been aroused when within two weeks three ships sailed from New York loaded with funds for purchasing public securities in the hands of uninformed though honest citizens of the Carolinas and Georgia. His "soul became indignant" at the avaricious and immoral turpitude which so vile a conduct displayed and such speculation in England would have made a Hastings blush.

He hoped the states could find some way to check the speculators and make them burn their fingers. He realized that all public debts encourage speculation; but the citizens at the center of government, having prior knowledge of Hamilton's plans, were taking advantage of those living at a distance. He wished Congress had been on the Susquehanna, the Potomac, or at any place in the woods. If so, warning could have been sent of the "rapacious wolves" seeking whom they might devour. In a later address he stated that America must re-establish its public credit by meeting its obligations to its own creditors, its foreign supporters, and especially its "brave soldiers." He saw no immediate necessity for funding, however. Florence, Genoa, Venice, France, Britain, and Spain had been seriously crippled by funding their national debts. Hamilton's plan would only temporarily increase our credit and enlarge our circulating medium. In the end it would demand taxes which would transfer money from the producing masses, where it circulated freely, to the idle purses of wealthy speculators. Thus the workers would part with their necessities to provide luxuries for the bondholders or creditors and to the extent that this plan would boost New York and Philadelphia it would depress the frontier.

The pittance which was the reward for distinguished service should not be torn from the Revolutionary soldiers by the "arts of insidious speculators!" The foreign debt must be paid before even considering the domestic debt. And in both foreign and domestic securities Jackson desired a distinction in favor of the original purchaser. If this distinction were not made he feared that the soldiers and other citizens who had sold their securities eventually would pay ten times as much as the speculators. Why should Congress imitate the British by saddling the bulk of the people with a large debt? Jackson asked. Hamilton's supporters had claimed that a permanent debt would be a blessing, but the best authorities on finance taught that it would be easier for each generation to meet its own obligations.

Jackson realized that in the debate the weight of experience was against him on account of his youth but he could not be silent upon so important a national subject. Some of those who had spoken against Madison's plan mentioned the injustice of interfering with private contracts, but Jackson felt the House had the right to guard against fraud.

"Public justice, . . . had not been done," he cried; "the war-

A Pioneer in The First Congress

worn soldiers were pining in retirement, in the most cruel situations, and condemning the injustice of that country, whose Congress . . . is legislating here this day." Do justice and credit will follow, and we should avoid injustice more than impairing of contracts. Some had said that if the soldier had kept his securities he would now get the full twenty shillings to the pound. To this Jackson exclaimed:

Unfortunate, foolish soldier indeed! . . . why didst thou not steel thy feelings against the wife of thy bosom, and behold thy beloved, without a murmur or an exertion, starving on a dung hill? Then thou mightest have kept thy . . . twenty shillings until it became a real pound. But, . . . is this the language of mercy, or of justice? What will a man not give in exchange for his life? And if he has feelings, for that of his wife and children?

One House member had said that if the original purchasers were rewarded the money would be thinly distributed. To this Jackson answered, "the tears of the afflicted would be dried up, and widowed hearts be made to sing for joy."

Madison's motion was defeated by a vote of thirteen to thirty-six.[10]

The next proposition called for assuming and funding at par the debts of the thirteen states, again making no distinction between the original creditors and "transferees." This proposition greatly intensified the bitterness of the debate. On March 1 Jackson reminded the House that North Carolina had tardily ratified the Constitution but had recommended that Congress refrain from interfering with the state debts. Georgia and some other states had already extinguished a great part of their debts. He asked why generosity was voluntarily offered the creditors and he wondered if these wealthy men had even thought of asking the aid of Congress. He agreed that Hamilton was a man of genius whose "talent in report was admired," but he was not infallible. He was trying to bind remote sections to the federal government by taking over the load of the states, but the certificates were then in the northern cities or abroad, and his object would be defeated.

Hamilton was also setting a precedent for making federal taxes exceed those of the states. This would reverse the assurance of the Federalists in 1787 and 1788 that in the American pyramid the people would form the broad base, the states would be in the middle section and the national government would form the smaller top. Jackson asked if the Confederation, the Constitution, or the states had demanded assumption of state debts. The idea originated with Hamilton, not with the creditors.

He ridiculed the debts of two states, Massachusetts and South Carolina. The former would have the nation pay for its Penobscot expedition while the latter would have it pay for the building of its ship, the *South Carolina*. Neither of these state projects had been authorized by Congress. "If States choose to run into those balloon exploits on their own account their neighbors ought not to pay for it. . . ." The provident states disliked to be doubly taxed to assume the obligations of two improvident states and "to mortgage themselves and posterity for a funded debt."

During the Revolution Georgia placed most of its troops in the state militia and their only remuneration was state certificates, five hundred thousand dollars of which had been liquidated and burned. Hamilton's plan ignored this situation; hence assumption of state debts was inexpedient, impolitic, and unjust. Smith of South Carolina smarted under this attack by Jackson and replied that although Georgia had supported its own troops it had received outside aid against the Indians. Jackson denied this and asserted that during the Confederation era South Carolina's Congressmen had sided with McGillivray and blocked federal aid to Georgia.

As some private creditors seek to control their debtors by loading them with larger burdens, so Hamilton would have the United States bring its citizens under the power of the Union, Jackson said. If the national and state debts should be paid by tariffs, New York and Philadelphia would import more than southern ports. Because the North manufactured a considerable part of its goods, however, most of the imports would be reshipped to southern ports; so in reality the tax load would be carried by the southern consumers.

The other taxes Hamilton had suggested might prove inadequate, the tobacco manufacturers already having reported that he had overestimated what could be obtained from that source. If federal taxes should prove "disagreeable," he thought the army might have to back up the collectors in some states. He also warned that Hamilton's plan had deliberately failed to provide any final liquidation of the national debt.

Later Jackson offered a motion that Congress decline to assume the state debts; after a short debate this motion was defeated by the close vote of twenty-nine to thirty-two. Immediately thereafter a motion was made to allow the original holders of the state certificates the exclusive right of subscribing during the first six months after the offices were opened and that the whole of their claims should be funded. Jackson said in support of this motion, "I do not believe that there are twenty original holders in Georgia." The motion lost by a vote of fifteen to forty-five.

A compromise arrangement between Hamilton and Jefferson enabled the South to get the national capital and Hamilton to get assumption and funding of the state debts. The Senate then passed a new assumption and funding bill and sent it to the House where it was carried by a vote of thirty-four to twenty-eight. It was then approved by the President.[11]

The debate on the location of the national capital began while there were only eleven states in the Union. Most of the speakers in the early part of the discussion were northern men and Jackson sarcastically declared that the members from New York and New England had already made the decision. "This is not proper language to go out to freemen," he said. "Jealousies have already gone abroad. This language will blow the coals of sedition and endanger the Union. I would ask, if the other members of the Union are not also to be consulted? . . . Why not . . . [let New York and New England] fix the principles of Government? This looks like aristocracy! . . ."

He objected to two proposed places as not being in the center of the country. From New York to the nearest point in Maine is two hundred and fifty miles, and from New York to the nearest point in Georgia is nine hundred miles. From a point on the Susquehanna to the nearest point in Maine is four hundred miles, and from a point on that river to the nearest point in Georgia is nine hundred miles, or more than two to one. He prophesied that Georgia would soon become the largest state in the Union and he preferred to select a place on the Potomac or else to postpone the decision until North Carolina came in. It had been suggested that he was helping to make a deal between Jefferson and Hamilton as early as September of 1789 but he denied involvement "in any bargaining whatever."

The Senate finally passed a bill which would temporarily locate the capital at Philadelphia in December of 1790. In December, 1800, it was to be moved to a place on the Potomac which would be selected by a group named by President Washington. This bill later was enacted into law, Jackson voting with the majority.[12]

He also entered heartily into the debate on the naturalization bill. In 1790 Congress took under consideration a bill requiring of foreigners seeking American citizenship only one year of residence and an oath of allegiance to the Constitution. Jackson believed that a foreigner should be required to reside here some time before applying for citizenship. He favored progressive naturalization as a protection against a "common class of vagrants, paupers, and other outcasts of Europe." He opposed a leniency which would make "the rank of an American citizen the maygame of the world."

As an example of poor citizenship he quoted an article in an unnamed Pennsylvania publication concerning a contested local election in Philadelphia. Most of the sailors from the ships anchored there paid the half crown required for registration and cast their votes. On the return voyage the sailors of one of the ships were discussing a shoal of porpoises off Cape Henlopen, Delaware. A sailor asked, "What merry company have we got here! I wonder where they are going so cheerfully?" Another answered, "Going, why, going to Philadelphia, to be sure, to pay taxes, and vote for Assembly men!"

The naturalization bill was defeated, and a law was enacted requiring two years of residence, proof of good character, and an oath of allegiance.

Shortly after Congress moved to Philadelphia a bill chartering a national bank passed the Senate with very little opposition but was vigorously opposed in the House. Jackson and William Branch Giles attacked the whole banking system as a plot for enriching the few at the expense of the many. Jackson quoted the Philadelphia newspapers as stating that the bank bill was unconstitutional. He asserted that if Congress should make the "necessary clause" of the Constitution a rubber or "sweeping clause," as the friends of the bill requested, Congress would soon be in possession of all possible powers and the charter under which it worked would be nothing but a name.

Some had based the right to form a national bank on the same authority as the right to raise armies but he presumed that no one would claim that this was a bill for the national defense. Others had argued from the right of Congress to borrow money but he affirmed that it had already borrowed money without a bank. Some wished an advantageous place in which to deposit the surplus of the national revenue but he thought there never would be a surplus. We had what he believed was a perpetual debt but he hoped we should never have a perpetual corporation.

Some had said that a bank did not necessarily need a charter but that the proposed corporation was necessary in order that it might have a hold on the government. This frankness astonished him as there was "no saying" where this precedent would stop. He feared that a new federal bank would infringe on the charter of "The Bank of North America," also located in Philadelphia. He praised this bank because its stockholders were not speculators.

The proposed bank appeared to him as unconstitutional and monopolistic, planned solely for the benefit of the corporations and large merchants. State banks were to be preferred, he said, as they could more easily detect the efforts of counterfeiters. The checks of state banks would circulate widely but those of the proposed bank would circulate only in Philadelphia and Connogocheque. He had not seen a bank bill in Georgia and he was certain that the yeomen of that state and New Hampshire would receive no aid from the proposed bank. The "general welfare" provision of the Constitution was intended for Georgia and New Hampshire as well as for Philadelphia, New York, or Boston and if all the East was for the bank certainly all the South was opposed to it.

The Bank of Vienna and the Bank of Amsterdam were successfully conducted without any connection with their governments but he reminded the House that when the Bank of France became a royal institution it began to issue paper and soon came to ruin. He thought it unwise for the United States to hold shares in a bank. Borrowing leads to anticipation, he said, anticipation means debts, and debts prophesy bankruptcy. A week later the Senate bill passed the House by a vote of thirty-nine to twenty.

In 1790 Jackson declined an appointment to the militia committee but at his suggestion Mathews of Georgia received the honor. However, his views on military affairs were expressed at some length in several speeches. If Quakers and other pacifists wished to be excused from military service each should pay for a substitute. To excuse them without substitutes would establish those faiths more effectually than any positive law could do and would tend to make the whole community Quakers. He held that protection and service are reciprocal and any other plan unfortunately would force the nation to resort to a standing force for the general defense. He supported a bill for a uniform militia. However, he was not eager for the young nation to rush into war.[13]

In planning for the national budget Eastern Congressmen favored small salaries for federal officials. Like most of the other members from the South, Jackson wanted federal officials to be well remunerated. In a spirited debate he supported the act which placed the President's salary at $25,000.

Jackson spoke with much greater warmth in the debate about the salaries of Congressmen. The Senate sent down to the House a bill to pay Senators six dollars per day and House members five dollars. This amount was in addition to an allowance of one day's salary for each twenty miles of travel to and from Congress. Jackson opposed this discrimination and declared that rather than accept the proposed rate he would prefer to work without salary. "Is it expected that a Senator shall eat more, or drink more costly liquors than a member of the House of Representatives? . . . The duties of both Houses are equal, and the pay ought to be alike." He distrusted the request for larger pay to Senators because "All Governments incline to despotism, as naturally as rivers run into the sea."

The bill was rejected and another motion placing the salary at six dollars for each was enacted into law.[14]

One of the warm debates of the First Congress was upon the subject of slavery. In February, 1790, the yearly meeting of the Friends, or Quakers, of Pennsylvania and Delaware petitioned the House to end the African slave trade. The petition was violently opposed by Jackson, Baldwin, Smith, and Tucker (all from Georgia and South Carolina). Jackson's first speech in this debate was reported at some length in the Georgia press. That slavery was an "evil habit" he did not deny, but that habit was already established, he said, and peculiar conditions in Georgia and South Carolina justified it.

Rice was grown in soil where white people could not live, he claimed. "Are Congress willing to deprive themselves of the revenue arising from that trade . . . and to throw this great advantage into the hands of other countries?" He quoted one Millar to the effect that in Africa the Negro wife walks behind her husband, and she eats what he leaves. In Georgia the master was as liable to punishment for killing a slave as for killing a white person.

A Pioneer in The First Congress

He quoted Jefferson's "Notes on Virginia" as stating that it would be unwise to free the Negroes and leave them among the whites lest one race destroy the other. Jackson also asserted that it would be unwise to have the races intermarry. Evil results had followed when the Spaniards absorbed their former slaves, the Moors, and "however fond the Quakers may be of this mixture and of giving their daughters to negroes' sons and receiving the negro daughters for their sons, there will be those who will not approve of the breed (and a motley breed it will be)."

The *Virginia Gazette* stated that when Britain transported some of its slaves (who were voluntarily emancipated) to Sierro Leone in West Africa, some of them took with them British girls as wives. Some of these white wives soon died and a Negro, King Tom, of a neighboring island, enslaved the others. Jackson believed that if the Southern Negroes were colonized in America the Indians would re-enslave them, and this was proved by the fact that the Creeks already had numerous slaves.

Should the North and Maryland and Virginia, with no use for slaves, work against the economic interests of Georgia and South Carolina?

National unity demanded compromises in the making of the Constitution; the South had to give in to the North on commerce, and slavery was left to the decision of each state. Congress had no more legal right to abolish slavery than to destroy the Eastern fisheries, he felt. The North should first free its few remaining slaves and thus remove the large beam from its own eye before trying to remove the mote from its neighbor's eye. No European nation had freed its slaves, and Britain with its numerous colonies "dared not." Why then could not the South be allowed to handle its own problems in its own way?

Roman law allowed a father to sell his son into slavery three times before he was certain of his freedom, and Moses permitted Jewish fathers to sell their sons as slaves and their daughters as concubines. Christ and His apostles also condoned slavery. In the tenth and eleventh verses of the Book of Philemon Paul ordered Onesimus, a fugitive slave whom he had converted to Christianity, to return to his Christian master, Philemon. Slavery was also justified by such Biblical passages as: Romans 13:1; I Corinthians 7:21, 22; Ephesians 6:5; Colossians 3:22; I Timothy 6:1,2; Titus 2:9,10; and I Peter 2:18. These passages required that in all things slaves were to obey their masters, both the good and the perverse.

Let the Quakers go to Africa to mix their blood and convert the natives to their view rather than cause confusion here, Jackson exclaimed. "I hold one thousand acres of tide rice on the Altamaha. On the expectation of importations these . . . are worth three guineas per acre; take away this expectation . . . , and you take away that value altogether; restrict that importation, and you diminish that value one-half. . . . How, Sir, are [the slaveholders] to be compensated? Can or will Congress and the Quakers reimburse them?"

The petition of the Quakers was referred to a partisan committee of one each from New Hampshire, Massachusetts, Connecticut, New York, New Jersey, Pennsylvania, and Virginia. In its report the committee expressed the belief that Congress would exert all its powers towards the accomplishment of each of the humane objectives of the Quaker memorial. Scott supported the report on the ground that one man cannot have property in other men. Jackson's position was that "the slaves are better off than if freed. What are they to do if discharged? Work for a living? Experience has shown us that they will not."

In Maryland the freedmen became pickpockets and practiced other forms of crime, he said. The slaves in America were not in a worse condition than the Negroes were on the coast of Africa, for between wars African parents sold their children as slaves, and during a war the victors sold their captives wholesale. Those who came to America merely exchanged one form of slavery for another, and they were better off in America where interest and law provided comfort and support in old age. He was opposed to such high respect for the Quakers and insisted that the planters were equally useful citizens and "equally susceptible to the refined sensations of humanity."

. . . But suppose all this to have been wrong, let me ask the gentleman if it is good policy to bring forward a business at this moment likely to light up the flame of civil discord; for the people of the Southern States will resist one tyranny as soon as another. . . . The gentleman says, if he was a Federal Judge, he does not know to what length he would go in emancipating these people; but I believe his judgment would . . . be of short duration in Georgia, perhaps even the existence of such a Judge might be in danger.

In the debate which occurred on March 8 the reporter stated that Jackson "animadverted with great severity on the memorialists, and introduced an account of the mischiefs which had resulted from the interference of a sect called Anabaptists in the State of Georgia."

Although he was not a member of the Society of Friends, Benjamin Franklin supported their views on slavery and the last article he wrote was a sarcastic parody on Jackson's speech in defense of slavery. Writing under the name of "Historicus," he sent the article to the *Federal Gazette*. Franklin died a few weeks later and Jackson never publicly referred to the criticism by this venerable statesman.

Jackson never altered his views on slavery but during his governorship of Georgia the importation of slaves into the state from abroad was forbidden by the new state Constitution of 1798 and by an act of the legislature in the same year. Jackson was active in the Georgia Convention of 1798 and signed the bill abolishing the foreign slave trade.[15]

Jackson's term in Congress expired on March 3, 1791, and, having been notified of his defeat by Anthony Wayne for a second term, he retired to his military, legal, and agricultural pursuits in Georgia.

In the two years he spent in the federal House, Jackson, the aristocratic planter, advocated "democratical" simplicity in addressing the President. His opposition to aristocracy in government, a high tariff, the excise, the establishment of inferior federal courts, the United States Bank, and the assumption of state debts shows that he was a state rights man and a pioneer in opposing the Hamiltonian program as well as a leader in the formation of the "Republican" Party. His defense of slavery may be explained on the grounds of his economic, sectional, and political interests.

VI

JACKSON IN THE SENATE

JAMES JACKSON'S retirement from public life lasted only a few months. He gained more notoriety during his "retirement," through challenging Anthony Wayne's right to a seat in Congress, than he had received as a member of that body.

In 1787 Wayne, desiring to enter politics, had requested his friends in the Pennsylvania legislature to send him to the United States Senate. He had also sought the aid of Jackson to obtain a seat in the Georgia legislature. Failing in both ventures he established citizenship in Georgia in 1788. In 1789 he supported Jackson for Congress. The following year Jackson announced his desire to be returned to the lower House by the Eastern district. Wayne entered the race as an opponent to Jackson. Both he and Jackson left the electioneering largely to their friends and Jackson remained in Congress during the entire campaign.

Several events in this period favored Wayne's candidacy. Shortly before the election Congress presented him with a medal for bravery at Stony Point during the Revolution. The *Georgia Gazette* (Savannah) published his correspondence with President Washington concerning this honor, and also republished an account of the battle as reported in the London *Gentleman's Gazette* in 1782. In addition Wayne recently had been elected president of the Georgia division of the Society of the Cincinnati and at a banquet had been toasted as a vice-president of the Pennsylvania branch of that organization. The faultless attire and engaging manner of "Dandy Tony" opened wide to him the best homes in Chatham County. In 1790 he was appointed chairman of the committee to entertain President Washington on his visit to Savannah. All these things were on the credit side and helped boost "Mad Anthony" in the regard of the people.

The election was held January 3, 1791, and again a general ticket was used. Wayne was declared the winner by a majority of twenty-one votes. In April of that year financial stress caused Wayne to sell his property in Georgia and when he left for Congress in October he never returned to the state.[1]

For a time Jackson accepted his defeat with outward calm. Through the medium of a letter in the press he thanked his supporters, assuring them that "he retires from public life with the pleasing satisfaction of having done his duty."

In May he received this eulogy through a Savannah paper:

Sir, We the Mayor and Aldermen, of the City of Savannah, . . . congratulate you on your return to . . . your domestic enjoyments. . . . We regret that you have been deprived the opportunity of continuing your services to the State, . . . as we are assured that your conduct would have been uniform in the support of our rights. . . .

Jackson publicly acknowledged this statement as "among the most valued testimonials of my life."[2]

Reports of corrupt election practices in some of the lower counties soon began to reach Savannah. Jackson had fought with the Georgia troops during seven years of the Revolution and they were closer to him than to Wayne whom they had known but seven months. Many of these veterans, taking it for granted that Jackson's election was a certainty, had not voted; but when they learned of the frauds their anger was so aroused that they quickly secured the affidavits needed in exposing Jackson's enemies.

Since President Washington was expected to arrive in a few weeks Jackson bided his time in taking action against the exposed irregularities. Late in July, however, his anger found outward expression in a public letter denouncing the election.[2] He then decided to carry the fight to the state legislature, and as a first move obtained a seat in the lower House of that body.

The records of the Georgia Senate show that in November, 1791, the House impeached Henry Osborne, judge of the Eastern district, for corrupt practices in securing Wayne's victory. Jackson served on a committee with Jacob Waldburger, John M. Tattnall, and one Walker in conducting the trial before the Senate. The articles of impeachment contained six charges.

First, on the night of the election in Camden County, Osborne reopened the polls after the legal hours of closing, and acted as one of the managers in a second or illegal election.

Second, Osborne and his associates reported that Camden gave seventy-nine votes to Wayne whereas at the legal election the officials reported but fifteen for him. The votes for Jackson—ten—had remained the same.

The third article stated that Osborne permitted absent Camden citizens to vote by proxy.

Fourth, he suppressed or detained the returns from Glynn County with the result that they reached the governor too late to be counted.

Fifth, by descending from the office of judge of the Superior Court to hold a second or illegal poll Osborne brought to pass a "perversion of Justice . . . in direct violation of his oath of office, and . . . Committed the dignity of the State, and . . . disgraced the sacred character of a Judge."

Sixth, his actions resulted in "setting a precedent for the subversion of the government and the tearing of the same up by the roots; . . . and has been also highly instrumental in sending on to Congress a member who has not the free voice of the Citizens of the State."

H. E. Wildes accused Jackson's friends of counting twenty-one more votes than were legally cast in Chatham County but the chief criticism was against Osborne and other friends of Wayne.

Osborne selected as his attorneys Seaborn Jones and three others named Sullivan, Stirk, and Porter. Early in the proceedings the defense advanced four arguments. First, only Congress could investigate a congressional election. If a trial were held in Georgia the defendant would be placed in double jeopardy. Second, a crime could be tried only in the county where it was committed. Third, if Osborne was being questioned about his conduct as a judge the only charge which could be introduced was of an official nature. Fourth, an affidavit signed by Osborne was introduced which stated that "deponent . . . saith he verily" believed that he could not get justice because a "publication in the Savannah and Augusta prints, signed James Jackson accompanied with a number of Ex parte Affidavits relative to the matter [had purposely been published] with ye intent of . . . prejudicing the public mind. . . ."[3]

Before the trial began Jackson had not failed to present his case in the press. The affidavits and other statements offered in the trial covered the entire front page of the *Georgia Gazette* (Savannah) of July 28th. The first official report in 1791 had given

Wayne 266 and Jackson 245. Jackson wrote that a just tabulation would have given him a total of two hundred and seventy-three votes to two hundred and fourteen for Wayne. This estimate would have given Jackson a majority of fifty-nine, and more if nine other questionable votes were thrown out.

Chatham and Liberty were the only counties where the conduct of the election was not challenged by the House. Certain citizens in four of the counties sent written criticism of their election officials to the legislature. A majority of the registered voters in Camden protested Wayne's receiving five times the number of votes cast for him. Protests of like nature were signed by seventy in Liberty, one hundred and twenty in Chatham, and one hundred and forty in Effingham. Grand juries in each of the five counties recommended the impeachment of Osborne.

According to these protests the election in Camden County was held at Saint Patrick's, a small outpost of civilization on the Satilla River. When the polls opened a Wayne supporter suggested that as there were so few Jackson men in the county the votes should all go to Wayne without spending the whole day conducting an election. Sheriff Samuel Smith and the managers objected, saying that they would hold a legal election. The sheriff testified that when the election ended at sundown only twenty-five had voted, that he had seen the polls closed, and then had ridden to his home two miles away. Not only were Osborne and his cohorts charged with illegally reopening the polls but the report turned in by Osborne (in his handwriting, and with some erasures) showed more votes than there were voters in the county.

Thomas Gibbons was the leading figure in the Effingham County election, held at Elberton on the Ogeechee River. Gibbons secured as managers Nathaniel Hudson, John London, and Jeff Bell. Hudson and Bell later admitted that they were not qualified. Several local citizens swore that there were nine more votes than registered voters and that some minors were allowed to vote. John Moore testified that he saw a minor vote and one man cast two ballots.

John Eigle swore that Wayne gave him a drink and "10 or 12 cut dollars to treat the men of the German Company & said that General *Jackson* was not minded in Congress," adding that "Jackson had been there two years without doing anything" but if Wayne should be elected "he would drive off the Indians."

The trial ended December 21, 1791. Osborne was unanimously

convicted on five of the counts. The Senate decided, however, that the prosecution had failed to make good the charge that he suppressed or delayed the returns from Glynn. Osborne was indefinitely disbarred from the practice of law in Georgia. He was also forbidden to hold office in that state for the next thirty years. In addition to all this he was fined six hundred dollars.

Immediately after the verdict was rendered the House returned to its quarters and passed a resolution in appreciation of Jackson's leadership in the prosecution. Two days later the Senate concurred in this laudatory statement.[4]

Naturally the bitter enemies of Jackson were displeased with the verdict.[5] About the time of the Osborne impeachment John Burrows published a card asserting that Jackson was intoxicated with appointments and felt "the rankling murmur of small passions . . . embarrassing a small mind." He urged Jackson not to feel that his "affidavit warfare" was on the people's account. He stated that Jackson was hackneyed in his expressions and that he engaged in

a continual campaign of paper wars, . . . it is a morsel . . . to keep alive your vanity if the boys of the city would say, Little Jackson talked loud to-day. I was pleased to see the passion little Cayenne put himself in. Thus you furnished entertainment for the lobby, but always disgusted the members, on whose votes the interest of your constituents depended. . . .

Come forth, thou brawling pigmy, and say whether you have any cause to doubt my character as a soldier, a man of honor, integrity, and truth. . . .

Jackson was not content with securing vindication in his home state alone. He had meanwhile been making plans to appear before the federal House and contest Wayne's right to a seat in that body. A month before the Osborne decision Abraham Baldwin presented to the federal House "a Petition from General *James Jackson*, . . . complaining of the *undue Election* and *Return* of General *Anthony Wayne*. . . ."

The petition set forth several charges. In the election in Effingham nine more votes than there were voters were counted and two of the managers were not qualified. In Glynn County votes were suppressed, the original results having favored Jackson. In Camden County Wayne was credited with fifty-four votes whereas only twenty-five voted. After Camden's legal poll was closed the certified statement of the results was suppressed or destroyed, an illegal election was held, and the illegal poll was sent to the governor.

After three motions on separate days had failed Baldwin finally had the petition referred to a committee, which was instructed to report on the proper mode for conducting such contests. With a slight change in the recommendations of the committee the House decided to set the trial for February 7, 1792. It was agreed that the evidence must be confined to the points made in the petition and the depositions must be confined to those obtained at least twenty-five days before the trial should begin. Jackson informed the House that he had not received notice in time to procure the needed evidence and requested that the trial be postponed until February 27th.

On November 24th Wayne reminded the House that eleven months had elapsed since the election and asked why his seat was contested at such a late day. He asserted that Jackson had been busy securing evidence and lining up the Georgia legislature in his behalf, and that he delayed presenting his petition because he lacked evidence which would carry weight outside of Georgia. Wayne further asserted that Jackson had aroused Georgia's grand juries to act, caused its press to teem with affidavits of perjured witnesses, and had published *"ex parte"* evidence on a subject which was to come before the House.

Jackson's request for a delay of twenty days met no objection and was granted. At Wayne's request the House instructed the speaker to turn over to each side such depositions as might be presented. When, on February 27th, Jackson was allowed to plead his own case he took a seat near Wayne.

Wayne stated that he had not received all his papers from Georgia and requested a further delay of twenty or thirty days. Since the plaintiff was at considerable expense and the defendant was receiving his salary Jackson made a lengthy plea for promptly proceeding with the case. He stated that he had delayed his petition eleven months because he preferred to keep silent but had finally concluded that the stories of corruption would have made silence an act of treason.

"It is not the seat," he exclaimed, "but the restoration of the people's rights which I contend for; let us both go home—let their choice be made by a fair election; and if it falls on the sitting member, I shall be content."

The Georgia people believed that they had no representative from one of their districts, and they would consider delay an evasion of justice, he claimed. Some Georgians had prophesied that no decision would be made and he wished to disprove this charge. Although the Georgia papers had spoken in his behalf, their published pleas would reveal the method of the prosecution and hence aid the defense.

"The present instance of corruption is unexampled in America, and is scarcely equalled in ancient or modern annals," he shouted.

Wayne broke in to remark that he did not suppose that Jackson would dare to suggest that he was involved in the alleged corruption.

"Whether the gentleman is or is not guilty of the corruption at the election, is best known to his own conscience," Jackson countered; "but I *dare to do my duty*, and as long as I am a public man, I will continue to do it, notwithstanding I may meet with *stern looks and menacing expressions.*"

Wayne was given a delay of two weeks and March 12 was set as the time to resume proceedings. By this time the interest was intense. According to a reporter, "the galleries were unusually crowded with spectators." During the next five days the House gave its undivided attention to the trial. Attorney Lewis, representing Wayne, asked that the delay granted his client be extended, claiming that new evidence was being brought from Georgia by Captain Burrows and Collings.

Jackson answered that two ships from Savannah had recently docked in Philadelphia and delay would further deprive Georgia of representation. The Revolution was fought over representation and less than ten years had elapsed since its close, he said. As a public man he was bound by duty to prevent injury to the community. It was not the favor of the House but justice which he requested and the

merits of the sitting member or himself should not be known on the occasion; . . . for his own part, whatever might be the opinion of the hon. gentleman of his merits or ability, he had not the vanity to suppose that his being in or out of Congress would affect the interest of America in the smallest degree. But that the question . . . was of the greatest magnitude, in which the lives, the liberties, the fortunes, and the happiness of the American people, were materially involved—for it could not be denied that they all depended in a greater or less degree on the representatives in that House.

The members had decided two other election contests but inasmuch as it was the first based on the charge of corrupt election practices, this one would set a precedent. The House debated the question for two hours and, on March 13, decided against further delay.

The trial lasted four more days. The interest of the members was so great that on the opening day the session was continued beyond the usual closing hour in order to give Jackson time to read and comment upon a part of his evidence. Baldwin stated that the House should have all the facts in the case and moved that the testimony in Osborne's impeachment trial in Georgia be admitted as evidence. This request was denied.

Jackson began the presentation of his case by showing that Georgia law required the sheriff of each county to select three justices of the peace as election managers. These men were to open the polls at nine in the morning and close them at sundown on the first Monday in January. The conduct of the election and the making of the returns must be in their hands. He then took up the affidavits dealing with the Effingham County election. According to a deposition by Jeff Bell, Sheriff Lane asked him to sit as one of the justices. Bell had at first declared himself not qualified to serve as a justice of the peace but, when pressed, later agreed that "he might as well sit there as anywhere else." When the polls were closed he was requested to sign as a justice of the peace but he declined and simply signed as an individual.

Hudson's affidavit showed that, although not a justice, he sat as a manager. He claimed that as early as eleven o'clock in the morning many of the voters were drunk. He also told how three Savannah men were allowed to vote although they had not been in the county the required six months. A man named Neidlinger testified that the Effingham grand jury had declared the election illegal and that he personally observed some minors vote. Jackson next offered proof that the returns from Glynn County had been suppressed, but he spent very little time on this part of the evidence.

Most of the affidavits were by citizens of Camden County. Daniel Miller, who served as clerk during the legal election, testified that only twenty-five votes were cast, fifteen for Wayne and ten for Jackson. He added that the polls were closed at sundown but

Judge Osborne borrowed the returns and, instead of returning them, substituted others the following morning. Sheriff Smith testified that not more than thirty voted at the legal poll, but the next day he learned that an illegal poll taken after sundown reported a total of eighty-nine votes. It was his belief that there were not over seventy qualified voters in the county.

Surgeon John M. Scott of the First United States Regiment testified that while visiting the Camden community at the time of the illegal election he noticed absentees were being voted. He asked Judge Osborne if "this was the common mode of doing business at elections in Georgia," to which Osborne answered "never to mind." A man named Gray also testified that absentees were voted. Jackson departed from his evidence to quote the opinions of Baron Gilbert and John Locke that judges should supplement the testimony of their five senses with that of all available witnesses. He then appealed to the House to reverse its position and receive the testimony produced at the trial of Osborne. This was again refused.

Lewis then spoke briefly for the defense. The Georgia legislators had been too lenient, he said. After impeaching Osborne they "should have hanged" him and then thrown out the returns from Camden. He claimed that if the Georgians were very eager to have Jackson represent them a larger number would have voted. He would not imitate Jackson's dissertation on Roman law, Eastern tyranny, and British corruption nor would he ape Jackson's style by referring to his client's wounds for he felt the former was too intemperate in presenting his testimony. He explained that the nine votes in excess of the qualified list in Effingham were due to the fact that the clerks were irregular in attendance and did not keep up with the count. The only fault one witness found with the election was the haste with which it was conducted.

Lewis introduced evidence to the effect that Gibbons arrived from his home in Chatham after the Effingham polls were closed and, hearing of irregularities, had suggested that nine votes be thrown out (six favoring Wayne and three favoring Jackson). He further claimed that since Effingham and Chatham were in the same congressional district Gibbons was entitled to vote in Effingham. He asserted that Hudson's warm friendship for Jackson made his testimony useless. As Wayne was two hundred miles from the scene of this Effingham election he was innocent of any corruption. Admittedly two of the managers were not justices of the peace but, if the sheriff had not persuaded them to serve, the people of this county would not have been represented in Congress. He was more concerned about Wayne's honor being upheld than his retaining his seat. If one candidate was out the other should be out. And, the defense attorney went on to say, Osborne was influenced not so much by love for Wayne as by hatred for Jackson. In a few days, he said, papers would arrive which would show that in other counties Jackson got votes to which he was not entitled.

By way of rebuttal Jackson said that he had been accused of intemperance. "I admire the lovely garb of modesty . . . ," he said, "and whilst I flatter myself that I am possessed of as temperate a disposition as the learned gentleman opposed to me, modesty must not be carried to an extreme fatal to society. . . . I have not yet learned to look on villainy with composure, nor on corruption with a lenient eye." He had said nothing about his own wounds, he claimed, and the merits of the two principals were of no concern.

He then presented other affidavits asserting that during the election Gibbons was present in Effingham and was working in the interest of Wayne. Lewis had said Gibbons was the mayor of Savannah but Jackson asked if "this fact did not aggravate the crime? He has but barely proved that bad men make bad mayors. This person, Gibbons, whose soul is faction, and whose life has been a scene of political corruption, who never could be easy under government. . . ." At this point he was called to order by the speaker. Jackson apologized to the House but insisted that he was "commenting on facts," that "the proofs were strong against Gibbons for corruption and that this corruption was in great measure of his charges."

For proof that Gibbons, Moore, and Putnam cast illegal votes in Effingham he would "only refer to the first section, fourth article, of the Constitution of Georgia, that said it required six months residence in a county to be qualified to vote." He felt certain that the nine excess votes in Effingham were given to Wayne, bearing out the statement of the Bible that "unto him who hath shall be given; but unto him that hath not, shall be taken away even that which he hath." Wayne had been given ninety votes in Effingham and "to take nine from my total would leave me barely eight." There were ninety-eight members in the federal House and if each of them could vote an absentee there would be ninety-eight different returns. Lewis had said that he favored dropping the sixty-four fraudulent votes from Camden. If this were done *"my right to a seat cannot be contradicted."*

He concluded that the "general welfare" clause of the national Constitution was so broad that

there is . . . no subject of police [power] . . . but might be comprehended within its extensive meaning . . . therefore, the only safety to the People, is in their free election of members to represent them. If the elections are pure and free, the People are free; but if the elections are corrupt—I beg pardon of the House—but this honorable House must be corrupt likewise.

. . . I beg leave to repeat, that A FREE REPRESENTATION was what we FOUGHT for, A FREE REPRESENTATION was what we OBTAINED, a Free Representation is what our *children* should be taught to lisp, and our YOUTHS to relinquish only with their LIVES!

When he thus dramatically closed his argument "there was a loud clap of applause by the citizens in the gallery." Once again Baldwin moved that the documents which had been sent by the governor of Georgia be received in evidence. This request was again refused.

Then by a unanimous vote—Wayne not voting—the House resolved that "Anthony Wayne was not duly elected a member of this House." Giles then moved that Jackson be seated. In support of this Madison said there were only two candidates from the Eastern district and unless Jackson were seated the people would lose their representation. In the most lengthy speech in this connection Findley affirmed that the facts which proved Wayne out proved Jackson in—namely that Jackson had a majority of the votes.

The vote of the House was a tie and Speaker Jonathan Trumbull, an ardent Federalist, cast the deciding vote in the negative. Another effort to seat Jackson was blocked by a ruling of the speaker which none challenged. It was that "unless a majority of votes in favor of General Jackson had been returned to the Governor and from him transmitted officially to the Speaker he could not be supposed entitled to the seat." If, after the conviction of Osborne, Governor Telfair had issued a warrant of election to Jackson he probably would have been seated. But the House unanimously declared the seat vacant and ordered that a notice be sent to Telfair in order that he might call a new election.[6]

In May Jackson published this card in the press: "The subscriber thinks it is his duty thus early to inform his friends, that he declines standing a poll at the ensuing election." So, when Governor Telfair called a special election in 1792 neither Wayne nor Jackson was a candidate. John Milledge served during the few remaining months of the Second Congress.[7]

During this trial and for several years afterwards Jackson ignored Wayne's conduct in the election. In a gloomy mood one day in 1803, however, he asserted in a personal letter that Wayne was equally guilty with Osborne in breaking down the rights of free elections "and he is now amply rewarded for his treachery." Whether Jackson's anger against Osborne ever fully cooled is not known but the Georgia Constitution in 1798, in the making of which Jackson took a leading part, restored Osborne to full citizenship.[8]

Jackson's merciless attack on Thomas Gibbons resulted in their fighting a second duel but the only known detail of this encounter is the assertion that three harmless shots were fired by each. In later years they were said to have become friends.[9]

In depriving Jackson of his congressional seat his enemies inspired his friends to elevate him to a higher position in the national scene. In 1793 William Few's term as United States Senator expired and he decided to run for re-election. Opposing him were James Jackson, John Houstoun, and George Mathews. In a letter to John Milledge, Jackson explained that several men who had been in the race dropped out in order that his (Jackson's) friends might persuade him to run. "I still resisted, and Barnett and the whole back Country then resolved to run me whether I would or not," he stated. In the election, on November 30, Jackson received twenty-four out of twenty-eight votes.

The Third Congress met in Philadelphia on December 2, 1793, and he was seated on December 16, the fourth year of Washington's administration. James Gunn was Georgia's other Senator, having been elected in 1789 for the full term of six years.[10]

Although the Senate record of yeas and nays has been preserved, the deliberations of this Congress and several which followed aroused so little public interest that no report of its debates was kept (except on a few special occasions); so we have only a limited knowledge of Jackson's activities during his first term in this body.

One of the problems facing this Congress was our relations with

Algiers, Britain, France, and Spain. "Mother Britain" intensified our conflicts with Algiers as a means of injuring our trade in the Mediterranean, Jackson asserted in one of his letters to Milledge; Gouverneur Morris, our aristocratic minister to France, was "obnoxious" to the French, he said, and in a message to Congress Washington sarcastically referred to Edmond Genêt as "the *person* representing the French nation." Spain renewed its "old claim to one-half of our State," and Britain complained against our partiality to France. Jefferson, though, "made Boys of them all. I am sorry to say that our Agent has added to the complaints against us. . . . The words *these Georgians* frequently occur."

Jackson sympathized with the original aims of the French Revolution but he regretted its excesses and sided with the Federalists in demanding the recall of Genêt. The Federalists sympathized with Britain but that country's interference with our commerce caused them to work with the Republicans in checking British aggression. Thus a resolution favoring the boycotting of British goods was passed by the House, to be in effect until the British abandoned the Western posts and remunerated Americans for losses sustained through aggression upon our neutral commerce. For some undisclosed reason Jackson withdrew from the floor and declined to vote when this bill first came before the Senate. On May 30 the excitement caused by Britain's impressment of our seamen and interference with our trade caused a joint resolution to be passed by Congress which would authorize the President to place an embargo on American and foreign ships. Jackson supported this measure and the Senate passed it by a vote of fourteen to five. Washington, however, thought it unwise to exercise this power.

The President decided in 1794 that rather than risk war he would send John Jay to London to secure a commercial treaty with Britain. Early in June of 1795 the Senate was called into special session to consider this unpopular Jay Treaty. Jackson voted for open discussions but the advocates of secrecy won by a vote of twenty to nine. He also supported Brown's motion to postpone action and request the President to secure better terms but this was defeated by three votes. Jackson then supported a resolution by Gunn that the President be requested to secure from Britain remuneration for the slaves taken from America during the Revolution. This was carried, only one vote being cast against it.

The bitter opposition of the Senate to the treaty was slightly softened by an amendment protecting our trade in the West Indies and by Washington's assurance that Jay had obtained the best possible terms. The treaty was finally approved.[11]

In a letter which revealed his partisan loyalty to the secretary of state Jackson wrote Milledge in 1793 that "Jefferson is about to resign, and his resignation will be almost universally regretted; we are at a loss to know who will succeed him"; Jefferson left the cabinet late that year.

When it came to military affairs Jackson favored a liberal policy. As chairman of the military committee he introduced a bill which authorized the President to buy or build "a number of vessels, to be equipped as galleys in the service of the United States, ..." Although the bill became a law the galleys were not procured and the intended funds were used in the construction of some frigates.[12] When the second session of the Third Congress began in November of 1794 military affairs were again taken up. Jackson supported a bill for the relief of the daughters of the late Count de Grasse of France in appreciation of the count's military service in the Revolution, a measure enacted by an overwhelming majority.

The collection of the excise resulted in a small rebellion among the distillers of western Pennsylvania. Washington's vigorous military measures quickly brought this uprising to an end. His message to Congress that year condemned the revolutionists and the "democratic societies" which encouraged them. The Senate committee which had been appointed to prepare an answer brought in a resolution couched in language even more severe than the President's. Evidently Jackson's expressed opposition to the excise during the First Congress had not abated, for he seconded a motion that the language be softened. Nevertheless, the original resolution was passed.

One worthy reform accomplished at this session was the opening of most of the Senate debates to the public. Jackson voted with the majority for the adoption of a rule which provided that the rare judicial sessions would remain secret but ordinary legislative sessions would be open to visitors. The first occasion when visitors were permitted in the Senate chamber was during the debate in 1794 upon the question of seating Albert Gallatin, a former Swiss, who had been elected to that body in the previous year by the Pennsylvania legislature. The Federalists disliked his opposition to the ratification of the federal Constitution, his sympathy with the revolt of some of his neighbors against the excise, and his friendship to France. They protested that he had acquired American citizenship one year too late to be eligible for membership in Congress. Jackson voted to seat him, but by a strictly partisan vote of fourteen to twelve he was denied his seat.[13]

During the first five years of Washington's administration few Georgians had been named to federal civil offices. Early in 1795 Jackson was requested by Georgia's congressional delegation to take up the matter with the administration. Pickering had retired from the office of postmaster general and Jackson wrote the President recommending the following Georgians for the vacancy: "Joseph Habersham, a merchant who performed signal service in the war; Richard Wylly, present loan officer of Georgia and formerly deputy quartermaster of the Southern Department under General Lincoln; Joseph Clay, Jr., a lawyer of superior talents; George Walker, the present attorney-general of Georgia. Any one of the above the delegation conceives to be capable." Habersham received the appointment.

In 1795 when Georgia was stirred by the controversy over the sale of its western lands, called the Yazoo Sale, Jackson, believing that his services were needed in his own state, sent Governor Mathews his resignation from the Senate.[14] When he reached Georgia Jackson hastened to write Senator Madison regarding certain state and national problems. He was pessimistic about anything being accomplished in the Senate until all its sessions were opened to the public, "until a change of Members" took place, and until the national authorities began to accept "the Letter" of the Constitution. The assumption and funding systems, the national bank, and the Jay Treaty "have all been consequences of construction—and construction too, opposed to the principles of our government." The people would welcome a constituent Convention to deal with such questions, he felt, and they "look to you for some amendments, which will clip the wings of Executive power."[15]

During the next six years he placed national affairs in the background and concentrated upon the political problems facing Georgia.

VII

THE YAZOO LAND FRAUD

◊ ◊

THE GREATEST recognition given by the nation to James Jackson was in connection with the sale of Georgia's western public lands. Involved in this sale were such varied questions as the sacredness of contracts, state rights, Indian affairs, the public domain, and the relations of the United States with the Spanish and French subjects on the exposed Georgia frontiers. The solution of these problems called upon the services of Governors Walton, Mathews, Irwin, Jackson, Milledge, and Troup; also Presidents Washington, John Adams, Jefferson, Madison, Monroe, J. Q. Adams, and Jackson.

Georgia's eagerness to speed up the tide of immigration from the Carolinas and Virginia caused the state to extend its liberal land grant policy of the Revolution into the periods of the Confederation and the Constitution. The realization that it would be difficult for Georgia to govern the extensive territory claimed beyond the Chattahoochee tempted the state's leaders to lend an attentive ear to the seductive offers of certain land speculators. Much of this speculation was honest but the fraudulent Yazoo sale attained national and international notoriety. A British traveler to America in the 1790's wrote "Were I to characterize the *United States*, it should be by the appellation of the *land of speculation*. . . . The last great purchase of land . . . on the confines of Georgia, was at the rate of a cent per acre; . . . ."[1] This land derived its name from the fact that its earliest settlements were near the junction of the Yazoo and Mississippi rivers, a short distance from the present city of Vicksburg.

According to the state's early head-right system each man was limited to a thousand acres in the section east of the Oconee. In the "land rush" of the 1780s and 1790s, however, speculators secured much larger amounts. During half of those two decades Jackson was in the Georgia legislature but its journals reveal no criticism by him of this policy. The fact that the grants were handled by the executive department may have given him an excuse for silence. At any rate the frauds ceased when he became governor and he stated in a letter that he had always opposed them. In 1806 he wrote that the Georgia people never sanctioned the Pine Barren speculation palmed off on "foreigners and northerners."

Georgia's growing desire to dispose of its public lands in the northern parts of what are now Alabama and Mississippi led the legislature in 1784 to pass a resolution looking towards the organization of Houstoun County on the Tennessee River near Muscle Shoals. Jackson supported this resolution but in 1786 he helped persuade the legislature to leave the organization uncompleted. He also helped to enact a law which provided that each of the commissioners who had actually performed their duties on the Tennessee business should receive 5,000 acres of the public domain in that section but no further surveys were to be made. In 1785 Georgia also attempted to set up Bourbon County on the Yazoo and Mississippi rivers but the act was repealed in 1788. Over the protest of Georgia Congress organized the Territory South of the Ohio in 1790 and the Mississippi Territory in 1798, each territory including Georgia's western lands.[2]

Concerning the fraudulent sale of Georgia's public domain Jackson wrote that the Yazoo speculation was in "embrio" shortly after the Revolution and that some viewed the Yazoo territory as "the land of Promise" but for a few only and not for "all the children of Israel." A certain Captain Sullivan, Moultrie Suchens, and Major Thomas Walsh, "the famous swindler" (who assumed the name of Washington), in 1789 enlisted certain speculators in Philadelphia and Georgia in the formation of the "Combined Society." Before the adoption of the federal Constitution this Captain Sullivan had led a Philadelphia mob to the "State house which insulted the Old Congress and . . . had to fly to the Mississippi . . . to save his life." Jackson regarded Walsh, who had served under him in the Revolution, as "a good soldier," but in 1792 he was hanged in Charleston for forgery, "having forged the South Carolina and Georgia State Papers to an immense amount. . . ."

All members of this society were required to take an oath of

The Yazoo Land Fraud 107

secrecy and they began to line up some of Georgia's leaders for the purpose of influencing the legislature to sell them much of this large western section for a very small sum. Fortunately timely publicity soon dissolved the Combined Society. Later in 1789 some of the former members of this group skillfully secured a legislature in sympathy with their self-seeking purpose. They again worked through Major Walsh and organized themselves into the South Carolina Yazoo Company, the Tennessee Yazoo Company, and the Virginia Yazoo Company. Their hand-picked lawmakers then sold them twenty million acres for $207,000 but a later legislature declined to grant the deeds inasmuch as depreciated currency had been the chief money offered in payment. Jackson was out of the state at this time.

In 1794 four new companies sought to buy about thirty-five million acres of these public lands. The Virginia Company was the only one which retained the word "Yazoo" and its title was later changed to the Upper Mississippi Company. Although the others now called themselves the Georgia Company, the Georgia Mississippi Company, and the Tennessee Company, the term "Yazoo" still was usually applied to each of them.

According to Jackson Justice James Wilson, Nathanael Pendleton of the Federal District Court of Georgia, and Judge Stith and Senator James Gunn of Georgia were foremost in influencing the legislature to pass the "pretended" Yazoo law "for a mere song." In the lobby of the Georgia Capitol there appeared the "disgraceful scene of a Wilson, Judge of the U. States Supreme Court with 25000 dollars in his hands as a ready cash payment." Gunn and Stith also were pictured as alternately using a "loaded whip" to bully and pleasant words to cajole "understrappers in Speculation."

Wereat organized a fifth group, the Georgia Union Company, the other leaders being John Twiggs, William Few, Edward Telfair, and William Gibbons. These men offered $800,000 for the same land but the legislature was persuaded by the leaders of the other four companies to reject this higher offer.

In 1794 the legislature passed the bill with the terms requested by the four Yazoo companies but Governor Mathews vetoed it. After a few minor changes had been made to give the appearance of acceding to his objections, however, he signed it on January 7, 1795. This sale disposed of about two thirds of Georgia's public lands west of the Chattahoochee for a half million dollars or about one and one-half cents per acre. Thus was completed one of the great real estate transactions of history.[3]

Washington was alarmed by the sale and in February he sent an unofficial copy of the Georgia act to each house of Congress for immediate attention. Ten days later Jackson laid an official copy of the act before the federal Senate. He expressed no opinion of the sale at this time but since it called for nullifying the Indian titles to the Ocmulgee-Oconee section and Tallassee County he introduced a resolution authorizing Washington to negotiate a treaty. His resolution was passed and a treaty was signed at Coleraine in 1796, but it gave Georgia none of the land the state sought.

In March Congress requested Attorney General Charles Lee to examine the title of the Yazoo lands. His report gave an objective history of the legal claims of Georgia, Spain, and the United States to this vast territory. In 1796 his report was published as a book. Jackson appeared to value it highly and gave a copy to President Washington. Needless to say, the book sought to justify Georgia's claim to these disputed lands.[4]

As early as 1794 Jackson was offered a half million acres if he would lend his influence to the land companies. To the unnamed citizen "high in judicial rank" who suggested that, he replied "that he had fought for her—for the people—the land was theirs, and the property of future generations; and that if the conspirators did succeed, he for one would hold the sale void."

In the fall of that same year Jackson was warned by one of his slaves that he had better remain in Georgia with his family. In a gloomy mood he wrote Milledge that

> I have really a good mind to follow his advice—leave Congress and Congress things, turn speculator and go snacks at home with the best of them. There is a damn sight more to be got by it, depend on it, & I have not got one sixpence ahead. . . . Such business . . . does not answer half the calls of a Wife and five Children.

In 1795 he wrote Tattnall that

> We are told the Sale is passed—& if so, I consider Georgia as having passed a confiscation Act . . . of your Children & mine, & unborn Generations, to supply the rapacious graspings of a few sharks—300,000 Dollars have gone from this City since October, & two-thirds of Georgia will be held & owned by Residents in Philadelphia, in Six Months. . . .
> Morris—Nicholson—Kettere—Wilson the Judge . . . are those

principally concerned . . .—they have all agents in Georgia & the others will sell to those persons in 6 Months from this day.

He later wrote—also in 1795—that he had told Governor Caleb Strong of Massachusetts "the iniquity of the whole transaction," and of his intention to resign and "at the risk of life and fortune go home, and break down the speculation, which the governor did not think his talents and influences could accomplish. . . ."

Jackson gave as one reason for resigning his seat in the Senate to run for the state legislature the fact that "he was solicited from all quarters more especially from the Mechanics and planters of Chatham County. . . ." He was also urged by letters from several parts of Georgia to hasten home in order to attend the state Constituent Convention which was to meet in May. There he was to attempt to persuade that body to undo the Yazoo sale. He sought to comply by taking passage on the ship *John* which sailed from New York but the southwest winds were so violent that more than a month had passed before he reached Charleston late in April.

Perceiving that he would reach Georgia too late to be of much help in the Convention and wishing to be back in Philadelphia when the Senate was scheduled to consider the Jay Treaty in June, he boarded the *Commerce* and reached New York in less than three days. He wrote Langworthy that "the wicked triumph—Mrs. Jackson had given me over as lost to her, and our little ones, and I have the satisfaction of learning that my supposed loss was much regretted by all ranks but those interested in unjust Speculations and some avowed enemies."

When Georgia's senators returned home in 1795 Jackson was hailed with "public approbation by all but Yazoo partisans," but "One evening in July the people at Savannah met before the State-House, put an effigy of Jay and one of their senators, Gunn, in a wagon, drew them through the streets and along the bay, and at last burned them on the gallows that stood upon the Old South Common." After this, Gunn "in many parts of the Country did not dare appear in public."[5]

On the last day of October a group of Chatham County citizens held a meeting and named Balthaser Shaffer, John Car. Smith, William Lowden, John Glass, and Thomas Palmer as a committee to urge Jackson to run for the legislature in order to fight the Yazoo Act. They assured him in a public letter that they were convinced he had always been activated by proper motives in his public conduct. Jackson agreed to run and expressed through the press his highest gratitude for the confidence imposed in him by the citizens of Chatham County and stated that he had "ever considered myself in a public capacity as a servant of the people who know where I can best serve them."

Much of the land in question had already been resold by the speculators to "innocent" purchasers and Jackson feared that Congress would be persuaded to purchase these certificates. He wrote Madison asking him to try to block any such efforts and assured him that the Georgia people would annul the sale "even should they be driven to the necessity of arming to effect it."[6]

Earlier that year Jackson had published eleven essays under the name of "Sicilius in several issues of the *Georgia Gazette* (Savannah) and the *Augusta Chronicle*. In August they were republished in a pamphlet of sixty-five pages entitled *The Letters of Sicilius to the Citizens of the State of Georgia*, which was circulated throughout the state in the campaign for seats in the 1796 legislature. This pamphlet and another written in 1805, twenty-six pages long, entitled *Facts in Reply to the Agents of the New England Land Company, by a Georgian* were the most scholarly of Jackson's works. Each presented a dignified, philosophical presentation of certain fundamental principles of political science. In the introductory number of the *Letters of Sicilius* he announced that he would discuss "the Policy, the Legality, and the Constitutionality of this grant. . . . It ought not to displease those interested in the speculation, because if their grant be founded on these principles, its value will be enhanced by the inquiry, and . . . if it shall appear, that your rights have been invaded by the sale, you may . . . take those steps which the preservation of your liberties . . . may dictate to you. . . ."

In the letters which followed he traced man's hunting and pastoral stages in which land was held in common. Later, in the agricultural stage, the land was divided and each head of a family kept a part for his own use. While later institutions violated this natural law of a fair division in this regard, republics have been fairer than aristocracies. Greece divided its land equally among its citizens. Ancient Rome gave each aristocratic family five acres but in the degenerate days of that republic when "fifty times the value of five acres of ground, was barely sufficient to furnish a freedman's supper—nations were disposed of to conquerors and favorites, and . . . Rome . . . soon sunk into effeminacy. . . ."

The feudal lords spilled the blood of millions, he wrote, de-

The Yazoo Land Fraud

stroyed the arts and sciences, and added to their former holdings what they conquered and took by fraud. What the lords spared the lazy priests took for monasteries. The United States was the first nation to abolish the principles of entail and proprietary rights. Should this old order now be restored in Georgia? Was it fair that the few should own millions of acres to the hurt of the many?

He sought to prove by the writings of Vattel, Montesquieu, and Burlamaqui that the people are supreme and the Constitution must prohibit the legislature from depriving them of their rights. Vattel held that the sovereign may use the public domain but that it belongs to the people. The kings of France gave the public lands to their favorites and the "Duc de Sully" advised Henry IV to recall those grants but France had to endure the bloody Revolution before that property was restored to the people. The Constitution may authorize the government to dispose of the public domain but only upon the condition that the laws of nature are observed and the many are not injured in the interest of the few.

Jackson held that in a democracy it is especially important that the legislature should abide by the Constitution. There was no authority in the Georgia Constitution for granting unheard-of monopolies of land to a few individuals. It had, however, authorized the legislature to make any constitutional laws which were for the good of the state. The recent sale would help to pay the debts of the few concerned but would add to the burden of the many and cause violence and "all the horrors of civil and savage warfare . . . ; and if . . . it be calculated to . . . give us some lordling among the speculating tribe," it would be a menace. The members of the legislature did not deem it for the good of the state but for their own private interests, and therefore it was unconstitutional. In private grants the Constitution should favor the grantee but in public grants it should favor the grantor who represents the people.

The *Letters of Sicilius* show that Jackson wished Congress to keep out of the Yazoo question until the legislature could annul the sale of 1795. If the sale to the land companies should be annulled he thought they would be unable to resell to the United States. This suggested the additional argument that the Yazoo sale violated the federal Constitution. In the Hopewell treaties, during the Confederation, the United States had guaranteed to the Choctaws and the Chickasaws title to the lands the four companies had pretended to purchase. The Constitution ratified all treaties made under the Articles of Confederation; therefore the treaties of Hopewell became "the supreme law of the land" and Georgia could not legally sell those lands without first quieting the Indian titles.

Jackson quoted Blackstone, who had held that if "the king is mistaken or deceived. . . . or if his own title to the thing granted be different to what he supposes . . . ; in any of those cases the grant is absolutely void; . . ." Georgia erred in thinking that it had full title to the Yazoo lands, he said; hence the act which granted to four land companies absolute title to property which belonged to the Indians was unconstitutional. That Georgia was deceived as to the value of the property was shown by the fact that the Yazoo lands contained about forty million acres or sixty-two thousand, five hundred square miles. This was an area larger than England and Wales and nearly half as large as France. Its soil was as rich as that of the Northwest Territory and its access to markets was superior. Congress sold land at one dollar per acre yet Georgia had asked but a cent and a half per acre, the same as the British colonial quitrents.

Making further comparison, Jackson wrote that the triangle of Pennsylvania on Lake Erie sold for eighteen cents per acre and the remote Genessee Purchase in Pennsylvania was retailing at ten shillings. The "Pine Barrens" of South Carolina and Georgia were valued at fifty cents per acre. Even before the law of 1795 was signed the Yazoo lands were hawked about the streets of Philadelphia at a profit of ninety-eight cents per acre, he said. Furthermore, the Georgia legislature had turned down an offer of eight hundred thousand by Wereat's Georgia Union Company, a clear loss of three hundred thousand dollars. Assuming that Georgia could have sold its land at the rate secured in the Genessee purchase it lost over fifty-one million dollars.

"The extravagances of a Marie Antoinette, are . . . eclipsed by this abominable act," he declared. "Settlement under the Western act must take place first on the Mississippi," a distance of seven hundred miles from the seat of Georgia's government. In taxing these lands it would take six months to inform the citizens and another year to make the collections. Taxes would accumulate and instead of meeting their obligations the new citizens would expect pay for serving in the militia for their own protection.

The Yazoo Act stated that "the lands to be granted in pursuance of this act, shall be free from taxation, until the inhabitants thereof are represented in the legislature"; and they might avoid taxation for generations by not asking for representation. The East alone would be governed by the legislature. Many Georgia people would emigrate to the West and no one would replace them. Taxes in the East would rise but its land values would fall. The act also reserved too little, he felt, for the private citizens. Georgia's head-right system had allowed a citizen one thousand acres and why should he be stinted in this case? Since 1777 great care had been taken to prevent speculation but in 1795 a few individuals "had whole kingdoms poured into their laps."

He also considered vicious the provision in the sale which permitted individual foreigners to purchase lands in any amount. Two thirds of "Yazoo" would go to aliens and Georgia's children would have to buy from them at enhanced rates. Many of the foreigners would be hostile to our form of government whereas if they settled along the immediate frontier they would absorb our customs and new and old settlers would both gradually spread into the West. The order planned by the speculators was: speculators first, foreigners second, citizens third. Settlers in Kentucky were ready to float down the Mississippi to lands the United States had guaranteed to the Indians. They would probably lean towards Spain, and Georgia might become involved in a war with the United States.

Most of the replies to these letters of Jackson's were bitter, personal, and emotional. One "Mentor," however, answered in a counter series of public articles, pitched on an intellectual plane. He asserted that Jackson used Vattel's statements at random and out of context to prove his point. He claimed that Jackson wrote his letters before resigning from the Senate for the purpose of feeling out the pulse of the state and hoping for a bid to take the lead in opposing the sale. The national Constitution forbids *ex post facto* laws and laws impairing the obligation of contracts, and the Yazoo sales, whether honest or fraudulent, were contracts. "Mentor" also expressed the hope that should a rescinding act be passed the governor would veto it.[7]

The Convention of May, 1795, took no action upon the criticisms of the sale other than to refer them to the next legislature and was content to order the removal of the capital to Louisville. The annual meeting of the legislature was changed from the first Monday in November to the second Tuesday in January. The term of Governor Mathews expired on November 7 and as the Georgia Constitution had gone into effect on the first of October the state had no officers for a period of two months. The old officers held on until their successors took office in January. The election for members of the legislature was held on the first Monday in November, 1795. Jackson was elected "by a large majority" to represent his county in the lower House. After the election most of the counties held mass meetings and instructed their delegates to annul the Yazoo sale.

The legislature convened in Louisville on January 11, 1796, and elected Jared Irwin governor. No one connected with the sale of 1795 was punished. The Yazoo question had been the only issue in the campaign and as the anti-Yazoo men had an overwhelming majority they promptly settled down to work on the main task, the rescinding of the "infamous" Yazoo Act. Early in the session a committee was instructed to report on the manner in which the act of sale had been passed, and its constitutionality. Those named were James Jackson as chairman, William Few, James Jones, John Moore, David B. Mitchell, James H. Rutherford, David Emanuel, George Franklin, and a man named Frazer.

While the committee was making its investigation Jackson secured the passage of a resolution which stated that the giving of a bribe to a member of the House was one of the highest crimes and that the acceptance of a bribe was "so flagrant an abuse of the sacred trust reposed in him that it ought to, and does disqualify the member. . . ."

The committee members were threatened with violence but they followed the vigorous, fearless policy of Jackson (their chairman) and reported that

the fraud, corruption, and collusion, . . . and the unconstitutionality of the same, evinces the utmost depravity in the majority of the late legislature . . . the public good was placed entirely out of view, and private interest alone consulted; that the rights of the present generation were violated, and the rights of posterity bartered, . . . the bounds of equal rights were broken down, and the principles of aristocracy established in their stead. The Committee . . . [believes that this legislature will condemn that] . . . avaricious spirit of speculation . . . , which, if it were to continue, would totally annihilate morality and good faith from among the citizens of the State.

The Yazoo Land Fraud

The rest of the report consisted of affidavits relative to frauds practiced in the enactment of the Yazoo law. One citizen had heard a legislator say that he "sold his vote for six hundred dollars, and that others had got a thousand." Another testified that a certain legislator recommended him to be in favor of selling the Western lands, because he himself was to have eight or ten likely Negroes for his part.

Still another stated that William Longstreet and other members recommended that he vote for the sale because "if he would, he should come in for shares to the amount of" 100,000 acres; but when he said that he did not think it right to sell the land Longstreet told him "if he would, he might make a fortune for himself and family forever." According to one affidavit Gunn told a certain citizen that he was afraid the bill would be defeated and if he would prevail on Senator Mann to vote for it he would give him 50,000 acres of land. Another member asserted that he was offered 50,000 acres or a thousand dollars but he demanded and got 75,000 acres, the same as the others were receiving. Others testified that 75,000 acres, 100,000 acres, and two thousand dollars were given as bribes to individual legislators. One who could not be bribed to vote for the bill was paid seventy pounds to return to his home and this was "done at the request of General Gunn." Of those who voted for the Yazoo Act of 1795 George Watkins was the only one in either house who did not profit personally from the transaction.

In completing its report the committee offered this resolution, which was adopted:

Resolved: That all such proofs relating to the fraud and corruptions practiced to obtain the act for the disposal of the Western territory of this State, be entered by the Clerk on the Journals of the House, in order that the testimony so given may be perpetuated, as well for the satisfaction of the Legislature and to show the grounds on which they proceeded, as to hand down to future Legislatures the base means by which the rights of the people were attempted to be bartered.[8]

The committee then introduced a bill commonly called the "Rescinding Act," which underwent a few minor changes and on February 13 was passed by a vote of forty-four to three in the House and fourteen to four in the Senate.

The preamble contained slightly over a thousand words and was about three times as long as the body of the act. It stated that the Yazoo Act of 1795 violated the federal and state constitutions, provided for monopoly, threatened the dismemberment of the state, and violated the rights of man. It violated Article IV, Section 4, of the federal Constitution, which states that "the United States shall guarantee to every State in this Union a republican government." The act of sale also violated Article I, Section 1 of the Georgia Constitution, which stated that the legislature may pass only such acts as are "for the good of the State."

The Rescinding Act asserted that it was not for the good of the state that foreigners should receive absolute title for lands at the rate of the British colonial quitrents or that the state should accept a sum one third smaller than an offer it rejected. The reasons Governor Mathews had given for vetoing the law of 1794 should have caused him to veto that of 1795, namely that the time was not proper for disposing of the Yazoo lands, the sum was too low, advertising would have assured larger bids, too little was reserved for the citizens, the land companies had greater advantage than the citizens, a monopoly would check settlement and expansion of agriculture, one fourth of the land should have been reserved for future disposal by the state, and to sign would be a violation of his oath of office.

The Act further claimed that the speculators sought to camouflage their crookedness by grafting the Yazoo Act upon a popular act which remunerated Georgia's Revolutionary soldiers. Thus the Yazoo Act seemed merely a further fulfillment of the act to reward the veterans. In order to remunerate the soldiers the Yazoo Act proposed to quiet the claims of the Indians to the Oconee-Ocmulgee section but it provided only $30,000 for this purpose, whereas "a larger amount than that was already in the State Treasury unappropriated." It made representation in the legislature voluntary and thereby placed the West beyond the control of the state. Nor could the legislature dispose of the state's lands without being authorized to do so by a state convention. No convention had authorized it to do so but the Convention of 1795 had referred the Yazoo Act to the legislature of 1796. A decided majority of those who voted for the fraudulent sale were personally interested. The act of sale had carried the Senate by only one vote and numerous resolutions by the citizens urged the legislature of 1796 to rescind it. It was, therefore, declared null and void.

The Rescinding Act also provided that within the next three days the two houses should expunge from all the public books and indexes all the papers and the law relative to the Yazoo sale. These papers and the "Usurped Act shall be publicly burnt in order that no trace of so unconstitutional, vile and fraudulent a transaction, other than the ignominy attached to it by this law, shall remain in the public offices thereof." In addition each superior court at its next session was ordered to destroy all similar records in the county files and any clerk who should refuse to do so "shall be declared incapable of holding office of trust or confidence in this State, and the Superior Court shall suspend him." Furthermore, any county officer who entered any record connected with the Yazoo sale on his books should be fined one thousand dollars (one half of this going to the informer) and the offending officer be barred from further holding office in the state.

No grant of the Yazoo lands should "be received as evidence in any court of law or equity in this State . . . ," except that after sixty days from the passage of the Rescinding Act the governor should order the state treasurer to pay all legitimate warrants turned over to him by the purchasers, "provided the funds are in the treasury." The state was not to be held responsible for any sums lost or destroyed and the expense of keeping guards must be borne by the grantees. Any funds not claimed within eight months would be "escheated to and for the use of this State." If the Indian titles were to be extinguished this must be done by Congress in co-operation with Georgia.

It further asserted that no federal court was capable of trying a case between a citizen and his state and if there were such a court Georgia would not acknowledge jurisdiction in cases where its sovereignty was involved. The governor was instructed to promulgate the Rescinding Act in each of the states "as soon as may be, in order to prevent further frauds on individuals." It was signed by Governor Irwin on the same day it passed the two houses and the time given the grantees for receiving their refunds was extended by a legislative act of 1799. The new state Constitution, two years later, incorporated the Rescinding Act. It also contained another section written by Jackson which declared that "all the territory without the present temporary line, . . . is now of right, the property of the free citizens of this state, and held by them in sovereignty, inalienable but by their consent."

It also ordered the members of each house of the legislature to take an oath that "I have not obtained my election by bribery, treats, canvassing, or other undue or unlawful means, used by myself, or others by my desire or approbation, for that purpose." Any legislator who should be convicted on a bribery charge would be disqualified from serving his term and from holding any "office of honor or profit" for one year.

Another requirement in the new Constitution, attributed by tradition to Jackson, was that no "law or ordinance shall pass, containing any matters different from what is expressed in the title thereof; . . . ." He is also thought to have written the clause which authorized the legislature to cede the public lands west of the Chattahoochee to the United States on "terms as may be beneficial to both parties," provided the national government agreed to extinguish all Indian titles to the land east of that river.[9]

On February 15 the legislature adopted the report of a joint committee which ordered that where the Yazoo documents had been recorded in books containing other records the offending pages be cut out with a knife and a memorandum signed by the president and secretary of the Senate and the speaker of the House should be inserted in their places. Where the Yazoo documents covered a whole volume, however, each complete document should be "deposited with the expunged pages for the purpose of being burned." The following procedure for this was then outlined:

A fire shall be made in front of the State House door, and a line to be formed by the members of both branches around the same. The Secretary of State (or his deputy), with the committee, shall then produce the . . . usurped act . . . , and deliver the same to the President of the Senate, who shall examine the same, and shall then deliver the same to the Speaker of the House of Representatives for like examination; and the Speaker shall then deliver them to the Clerk of the House of Representatives, who shall read aloud the title of the same, and shall then deliver them to the Messenger of the House, who shall then pronounce—"GOD SAVE THE STATE! AND LONG PRESERVE HER RIGHTS!! AND MAY EVERY ATTEMPT TO INJURE THEM PERISH AS THESE CORRUPT ACTS NOW DO!!!"

Accordingly, on the afternoon of February 15 the legislators and a group of citizens marched to the appointed place and stood in a circle about the fire until all the condemned documents were burned to ashes.[10] A tradition asserts that a sunglass was used in starting the fire. While most of the Georgia historians refer to it none of them quotes any contemporary or original source. Wil-

The Yazoo Land Fraud   119

liam B. Stevens' statement that "no authoritative document of the day" substantiates the tradition of fire appearing from heaven is incorrect, for in a speech in the federal Senate of 1803 Jackson described the use of a sunglass. Inasmuch as during this period the Senate did not report debates at any great length the speech does not appear in its official journal. A lengthy news article dealing with the sunglass incident did appear, however, in Philadelphia's Jeffersonian *Aurora*. The date of the *Aurora* is not given but the article was reprinted in the *National Intelligencer and Washington Advertiser* of May 6, 1803, the *Georgia Republican and State Intelligencer* of May 9, 1803, and the *Columbian Museum* of May 13, 1803.

In an editorial in the *Aurora* William Duane was quoted as explaining that he was printing "Gen. Jackson's speech to guard the public against further speculations and [to] record the facts which . . . will one day form a curious part of our history."

The federal Senate at that time was debating a bill relative to the settlement of the claims of the secondary Yazoo purchasers and, according to the article in the *Museum*, Jackson said in part,

I have as a leader in restoring to unborn generations their bartered rights, been abused, through this union, and not only here, but in the prints beyond the atlantic [sic] for *burning the records and traces of this famous transaction*—abuse, sir, of the blackest and vilest nature. . . . Sir, as if Heaven itself thought proper to shew its resentment of the base speculation—*the fire which consumed the records of it came from Heaven—it was no earthly fire—An old man never seen before, and I do not believe has ever been since, at the seat of Georgia government, drew it from Heaven and as soon as they were consumed, disappeared.*

The *Aurora* also carried in a footnote an article which narrated this incident substantially as Jackson had given it. As no reference was made to a tradition, this article and footnote apparently were printed as "news" rather than tradition. According to its account,

a venerable grey headed man, a stranger to all present, rode up to the throng, and alighting made his way to the officers of the government. His reverend grey hairs and aspect altogether excited attention—he addressed them, and declared that the act of justice which they were about to perform had led him thither to witness it, but that he did not think earthly fire should be employed to manifest the indignation which the occasion required, but that the fire should come from heaven—he took from his bosom a burning lens, and applying it to a heap of papers, the conflagration was completed; and meanwhile the old man retired unperceived; and upon enquiry for him he was not to be found, nor was he known to any of the oldest inhabitants of Louisville.

In commenting upon Jackson's speech and the *Aurora's* news article the editor of the *Museum* praised Jackson for his leadership in the fight against the Yazoo fraud but ridiculed what he called the superstition of both Jackson and the *Aurora*. The *Museum's* editor asked if "in sober seriousness" the reader was to conclude that the old man "was sent from Heaven"?

Or is he, in the spirit of the Monk, of Lewis, to conclude that this self same man, . . . was no other than the "Wandering Jew" of that fashionable literary necromancer . . . ? . . . He [the editor of the *Aurora*] must have some such belief, if he has any respect at all for the authority of our Senator—and the note is evidently to enforce it . . . while he [Jackson] is content in taking the praise of it to himself, we are willing with the rest of his subjects to cry, "well done"—but when he thus ascribes a part of it to supernatural agency, we feel ourselves at liberty to interpose our doubts.

The editorial was noncommittal as to the use of a sunglass but doubted that there was any visible manifestation of divine displeasure.

The statements by Jackson and the *Aurora* and the failure to deny them on the part of the editor of the *Museum,* all occurring within seven years of the event and further backed by the unanimous voice of tradition, pretty well establish the fact that a sunglass was used. The assertion of divine intervention is to be attributed chiefly to the informality and vehemence of Jackson's oratory.

A man named Tom Bigby sarcastically reported to the *Chronicle* of February 27, 1796, that on the fifteenth of that month the Yazoo papers were destroyed "by fire from heaven!!!" and "God Almighty is at last brought into the scrape." He thought that rumor would soon report that these records were assembled in exact order "by streams of electrical fluid." The authorities could easily have secured, he wrote, "a pair of spectacles from any old woman" but they were tempted to risk "the fire of heaven" and hence preferred a lens. E. S. Thomas, writing forty-four years after the event, recalled that "I was in Georgia the next year,

The Yazoo Land Fraud   121

1796, when the new legislature . . . went in grand procession, with their respective officers at their head, and burnt, by the hands of the common hangman, the records . . ." of the 1795 act.

Two anonymous writers who sympathized with the Yazoo purchase reported their observations in a Charleston paper in 1796. One of them wrote:

Two old tar barrels, surrounded with half a cord of pine knots, were exhibited in front of the State-house for the funeral pile. A Negro drummer served to announce the approaching scene. . . . [At four o'clock in the afternoon] a small piece of paper was put into the hands of an ill looking person, who had put the lighted torch to the pile, and who from his inebriety and ignorance, appeared well suited to perform the function of high priest to such a sacrifice. There was no approval from the spectators, although the high priest called for it.

The other reported that the records of the sale were burned "very little to the satisfaction of the bystanders . . . with schoolboy inconsideration, and the heat and spirit of faction." He considered the Rescinding Act an *ex post facto* proceeding, for if the act of sale was unconstitutional then repealing it and burning the records were unnecessary.[11]

Early in 1797 the New England historian, the Reverend Jedidiah Morse, entered the controversy. After stating Georgia's claims to this land as voiced in the Rescinding Act, he added "Other and stronger ground seems to have been taken by the purchasers and their agents, ..." The affidavits secured by Jackson were under a strong bias of party and offered little proof of fraud, Morse said. If the purchasers were corrupt they could be condemned and the contracts annulled in a court. Referring to this criticism by Morse Jackson wrote Milledge of

. . . a motion to burn the . . . Mortgages, which I expect to be made to-morrow, & which I have no doubt will take place to convince the Union, that the annulling law of last Session was not the act of an individual, or the hasty ebullitions of a factious moment, as the infamous Geographer, Mr. Morse, has given room to suspect. What a prostitution of divinity!—If we had him in Georgia, we would burn his gown, if he wore one, as an appendage not compatible with a lying Historian. . . . This account of the records at Louisville is an infamous production, the Child of base information, & the Godchild of a venal pen. I have no doubt of Morse's being interested in the Yazoo, however his prostituted sanctity. . . .

You know as well as myself, that not a single record was touched, but those appertaining to that nefarious speculation on the rights of unborn Millions, which was begotten & matured by unexampled corruption. . . . Georgia will receive her full reward by the approbation of future ages. . . .

This letter indicates that after 1796 another resolution and one more burning were considered necessary before the evil spirit of corrupt speculation could be fully exorcised. This resolution called for the burning of the Yazoo mortgages and was enacted by the legislature on February 10, 1797.[12]

The rescinding of the Yazoo Act led many casual observers to believe that the controversy had come to an end, but there soon set in an era of bitterness which afflicted Georgia and the nation for the next eighteen years. This long controversy also brought to Jackson more physical and mental discomfort than any of his other turbulent experiences.

VIII

PERSECUTION AND PRAISE

THE PASSAGE of the Yazoo bill in 1795 led to vigorous efforts by both anti-Yazoo and pro-Yazoo citizens to punish their opponents. As soon as the report of the sale went abroad Jackson wrote that a large group of the people around Louisville came together and threatened to kill the majority of the lawmakers who had sold out to the land companies; but the minority of the lawmakers who had refused to be bribed came to the rescue of their bitter political enemies and prevented any bloodshed.

The signing of the bill by Governor Mathews "damnd him forever in the opinions of the Citizens of Georgia and he shortly after had to quit the State; indeed Georgia was a dangerous residence for all concerned in the Speculation. Senator Robards Thomas from Hancock County, to avoid being publicly tied up to a Sapling and whipped, fled to South Carolina but was followed and killed; most of the others, one or two Counties excepted, did not dare to appear in public. At this time the whole State was in a tumult." So wrote Jackson in his "Sketch of the Yazoo Speculation."[1]

About a month after the rescinding of the act of sale in 1796 the House passed a resolution affirming that Senator James Gunn had lost the confidence of the legislature. Six weeks later Gunn asserted in a public letter that the affidavits accusing him of attempting to bribe certain members of the Georgia legislature were not impartially obtained by questions on both sides but were solicited by a private committee headed by his enemy, James Jackson, and the committee omitted answers which favored Gunn. He welcomed an investigation, but it must be impartially conducted. Gunn then wrote Congressman Baldwin and demanded certain papers which according to rumor the members of the Georgia House had signed and sent to him. When this demand was refused Gunn named Frederick Frelinghuysen as his second and challenged Baldwin to a duel.

The matter was brought to the floor of the House. Madison was chairman of the committee on privileges, which was requested to report on the appropriate action to be taken. Gunn promptly wrote Speaker Jonathan Dayton that the conflict between himself and Baldwin was purely personal and that he had not intended a breach of the privileges of the House. Frelinghuysen also sent a letter of apology to Madison. The committee reported that the privileges of the House had been infringed but the two letters of apology had set matters at rest and no further action was taken.[2]

In March the Georgia legislature adjourned and Jackson returned to his home. But the frustrated ambitions and lacerated feelings of the Yazoo leaders would not let him rest. He wrote a friend that an attempt had been made on his life and that "daily attacks on my reputation appear from the Pandora's box of Georgia, the Augusta prints. . . . I am represented as wallowing in luxury obtained at my Country's expense. . . . There is . . . the secret satisfaction of integrity which no assassin can rob me of." A month later he again wrote this friend that he still suffered daily abuse from all quarters. "Thank God I am nearly callous. . . . I feel a little uneasy on the score of revenge. I could punish one or two, but where would it stop? They are all anxious to get me to Dueling, & would not quit until I was put out of the way. The Wife and five children . . . are powerful reasons . . ." for caution in this regard.

In 1796 many of the Yazoo men fled from the state to escape the anger of outraged citizens and from a safe distance attacked their opponents through the newspapers, chiefly the *Southern Sentinel* of Augusta. Jackson and his friends usually replied through the *Columbian Museum* of Savannah although all the papers of that era welcomed each side of a controversy as a means of increasing their circulation. The "paper war" of 1796 was especially bitter. In April the *Museum* prevailed upon John Wereat to make a public statement regarding a report that (his friend) Jackson had supported his offer to purchase the Yazoo lands. Wereat explained that his offer was made on behalf of Twiggs, Telfair, and Few and that Jackson had no connection with the group. He said that he also was accused by the *Sentinel* of having stated that "Gen-

Persecution and Praise

eral Jackson had authorized me to offer one million dollars, for the western lands, on his own account." He denied this and asked the *Museum* to insert an affidavit by him proving Jackson's innocence.

In a card in the same issue of the *Museum* "Ogeechee" charged that for reasons of humanity George Walton had taken Jackson as a youth into his law office and made him what he was but Jackson later deprived his benefactor of a seat in the United States Senate and a good job in Georgia, a harsh way to treat "an old and faithful servant." He also said that Jackson extorted large retainer's fees from widows, orphans, and others. When their cases were called he kept their fees but failed to appear for them in court. Jackson probably treated these accusations with "profound contempt." A few days later "Ogeechee" renewed his attack, accusing Jackson of admitting leniency towards the loyalists:

You next boast of having been the savior of many traitors, and that you did so knowingly—if so, are you not as bad as they are? Is it not as great a crime to conceal stolen goods, . . . as to steal them in the first instance? You are wrong to acknowledge that circumstance, for there are men living who are as foolish as to suppose, you never did wrong—

The *Museum* of May 10, 1796, contained a long list of articles written in defense of Jackson. He was accused of having been interested in one of the Yazoo companies in 1794. To answer this David Mitchell published an affidavit stating that in 1794 he took a walk on the bay with Jackson and Judge Pendleton. The judge took Jackson aside for ten minutes and then returned to the city. Later Jackson remarked that the judge urged him to take an interest in his land company. He replied that he had no money and had never engaged in such business. He added that he "had assisted in breaking down the Yazoo Act" of 1789, obtained by the South Carolina, Tennessee, and Virginia Yazoo companies. To change now "would create him enemies." The judge then told him that he did not want any money, only for Jackson to lend his name to the project. Jackson again declined. Mitchell added that the last conversation on the subject he had with Jackson was on the Savannah Bluff in company with Benjamin Maxwell. Judge Pendleton's proposal was again discussed "and Jackson pressed us Representatives in the Legislature to oppose the sale."

In the same issue Jackson added an article in his own defense.

He said he had been solicited twice to take an interest in the Yazoo sale but had declined both offers. He denied both the charge that he had written the House resolution censuring Gunn and that he was on the committee which brought in a resolution calling for Gunn's impeachment. In fact when his opinion had been asked he had said that the legislature could not impeach a member of the federal Senate and he moved an amendment that the resolution be altered to one of censure. The amended resolution was supported by all except Watkins and Randolph. He also claimed that the Rescinding Act was not his work but that of the legislature. A friend came to his rescue in a public letter which blended sarcasm with humor and spoke of Jackson alternately as a "Ram" and a "little blue headed boy [who] wore petticoats, ..."

A few days later an article in the same paper over the signature of "An Old Quaker" accused some "Major General" (possibly Twiggs) of having an armed force enter Augusta in January, 1795, with orders to compel the Senate to reject the Yazoo bill. When the "Major General" changed his mind and refused to lead them they "sneaked" out of town. He was supposedly one of the "select few" who made the "sham offer" of $800,000 to "disappoint" the first applicants and to await the "favorable moment when a *Cracker's* concurrence might be worth millions." Presumably the "Cracker" was Jackson.

In the fall of 1796 one of the Yazoo purchasers published a sacrilegious prayer in the *Chronicle*. In it he reminded God that Jackson, His "high priest," had set Him right on the ethics of speculation. "O Judge," it read, "let not the transgressions of the sons of Yazoo, formerly thy well beloved people, be remembered on thy *judgment seat.* . . . And call to mind the latter days, when thy zeal for this goodly heritage, made thee seal a covenant with the *Twiggites,* the *Wereatites* and the *Gibeonites,* . . . ." It went on, "We know, . . . that thou hast undergone the purification of the great Anti-Yazoo high priest, ... But our hope is that thou wilt yet remember mercy in thine anger. . . ."³

As though fighting this paper war was not enough Jackson fought several duels in 1796, each being in some way connected with Georgia's land policy. According to tradition he fought with James Seagrove, federal Indian agent, over the Coleraine Treaty of 1796. A. J. Pickett wrote that he had such a duel with Jackson but gave no details.

Tradition was equally vague in holding that Jackson exchanged

Persecution and Praise 127

a few shots with James Gunn. In an unsigned statement discussing the Senate debate of 1795 over the Yazoo sale Jackson wrote that "The two Georgia Senators came to high words." He also referred to Gunn in a personal letter when he wrote "I will fight him if he demands it. . . . I have set myself down for a very troublesome year & I expect to have firmness to go through with it."[4]

Although Colonel Robert Watkins of Augusta did not vote for the Yazoo sale he opposed Jackson's vigorous attacks upon the speculators. This controversy resulted in three fights and a serious duel between them. Concerning the first of these encounters Jackson wrote Milledge that Watkins and a group of his Yazoo friends, seeing that he was alone, and thinking him unarmed, "dogged" him to the state Capitol. There Watkins accused him of heading a "damned venal set or faction who have disgraced their Country," and Jackson "finely frapped him" three times with his small "lucas stick." The stick finally broke and Watkins struck Jackson a blow upon the head "which for the moment stunned me, & I fell. I rose and my blood rose with me—."

A man named Flournoy, a friend of the speculators, proposed a duel for the following morning but Jackson preferred to fight a "base assassin on the spot I met him," and fired a shot which he claimed would have killed Watkins if some one had not "knocked up" his hand. He threw his opponent twice when "a scoundrel" by the name of Woods turned Watkins on him and the "Assassin strove to gouge" him, or scoop out his eyeballs with his thumbs. Jackson bit Watkins' finger and suffered no injury other than "skinning my eye." Thwarted in this effort Watkins stabbed him repeatedly with a bayonet fastened to his pistol. One thrust struck his rib and another his collarbone. Jackson remarked that "Half an inch lower in the breast, the Doctors pronounced, would have finished my business. . . . I could whip two of him at any time, and notwithstanding my wound I was turning him the third time, when a few of my friends collected and tore me from him."

According to a press report Watkins, passing General Jackson on the street, asked him why he headed a "vile faction" which was injuring the people of Georgia. When Jackson angrily denied that he headed a faction Watkins called him a liar. Jackson then drew a pistol from his coat and fired a ball through the cape of Watkins' coat. Watkins knocked him down with his whip and only the timely interference of a man named Frazer prevented him from "killing the pygmy general." Watkins later recovered his whip and was "whaling the general when young Bostick interposed and rescued him. . . ." By this time Jackson was so weak that he was unable to drive his sulky from the scene.

About five weeks later there was a second skirmish between the two. Jackson stated in a letter that Watkins insulted him at the federal district court and "I at him" and received only "a small scratch of the face," but the people would have tarred and feathered Watkins if they could have found him. "We now stand I suppose for the third brush," he prophesied.

Both Watkins and Jackson were members of the Georgia Constituent Convention of 1798. Although Watkins was serving as lieutenant colonel of the Richmond County militia he not only fought the insertion of certain Yazoo clauses in the new Constitution but signed it reluctantly. He also later announced through "the public prints" that he would "never feel himself bound" by certain parts of that document. Brigadiers James Gunn and James Glascock also published in the press their criticisms of the inclusion of the Yazoo controversy in the fundamental law of the state.

In his message to the legislature the following January Governor James Jackson protested that if these state military officials could criticize two sections of the Constitution others could ridicule any section they wished. He had planned to bring the two brigadiers to a court-martial but because of preparations for an impending war with France he thought it unwise to call in the other brigadiers and fourteen field officers. He then asked whether the three who defied the state's Constitution should continue to hold commissions in its state militia. But since Jackson instigated no official charges against these men the legislature also failed to act against them.

In 1799 Georgia was sorely in need of an official digest of its laws and as Robert Watkins and his brother George had been working for some years on such a project the legislature offered them fifteen hundred dollars with which to complete it. The pair later reported that it would cost an additional five hundred dollars and the legislature agreed to raise their remuneration to two thousand dollars. When it was completed it contained the "obnoxious" Yazoo Act of 1795 with an explanation that it had been annulled. Jackson's wrath flamed forth again and he refused to sign a warrant in the Watkins brothers' favor.

Persecution and Praise   129

In his legislative message of November, 1800, he stated that the Watkins *Digest* reproduced the "Usurped Act" of 1795 which the legislature and the Convention had done their best to obliterate and that some inferior courts were using this work as an official document. He warned that if the legislators sanctioned the *Digest* by paying "the two thousand dollars ordered" the "Usurped Act" might be revived; he felt the treasury could afford another contract. The obedient legislature then decreed that any official digest must omit the Yazoo Sale Act.[5] The ill feeling between Jackson and Robert Watkins, quickened by this bitter controversy, lingered for a year and a half and finally resulted in a third "encounter" at Louisville on June 16, 1802. Friends quickly separated them and removed their pistols.

The bad blood between them eventually reached its climax in a duel. Captain Ralph Spence Philips, Watkins' second, sent the *Museum* a full report of "this very honorable conflict." According to this report it was shortly after the Louisville encounter that Philips waited on Jackson and demanded satisfaction. Thomas Collier, Jackson's second, then called on Philips to arrange the terms. Collier named a spot in Burke County on the main road to Waynesboro, one mile from that town and twenty-four miles from Louisville. Philips' suggestion of eleven o'clock in the morning was accepted. It was agreed that only seven persons were to be present—the two principals, their seconds, and surgeons Powell, Pugely, and White.

Jackson had expressed a preference for positions not more than ten steps apart and this was accepted by Philips. It was agreed that while in position the principals were to speak only through their seconds and that the command, "make ready, fire," was to be given in rotation by the seconds. It was also agreed that if either should withhold his fire he would be considered the loser. A flash would count as a shot and two shots were to be fired in each round. The seconds then cast lots to decide who should give the first command. Collier won. Meanwhile "the principals had entered into polite and general conversation; . . . not a word but what the strictest propriety would dictate."

In the first round Collier gave the command so rapidly that both balls struck the ground. Philips then slowly repeated the command and again both missed. The seconds retired to reload and the antagonists again joined each other in "polite converse." The second round was but a repeat of the first. During the recess "the General and Colonel vied with each other, in bravery, . . . coolness and deliberation, . . . liberality, politeness, generosity, gentlemanly conduct, . . . their souls seemed to rise superior to the passions of revenge and malice, and . . . they rested their cause on the issue of this very honorable conflict."

For the third round the men stepped briskly to their places and Collier directed "the fire for the fifth shot." Jackson missed but Watkins' ball entered the general's body "a little to the rear and above the right hip, passing through I suppose about five or eight inches; . . . ."

Jackson said, "Watkins, I believe I can give you another shot."

The colonel replied that he could do so then or later when he could better defend himself. Jackson said he had come to give him satisfaction and that he was determined to do so if he had to stay there an hour. Watkins then stated that he was satisfied. Philips said he thought the general should declare himself satisfied also and he did so. The duelists then shook hands and declared that their enmity had ended.

Jackson had grown weak from his wound. As he was laid upon the ground he remarked: "D—mit Watkins, I thought I could have given you another shot, but I find I am mistaken; thus evincing that his courage was the same, . . ." Jackson gratefully received the aid offered by Watkins and stated that if the outcome had been reversed he would have cheerfully done the same. Every act of friendship was therefore cordially offered and thankfully received. Jackson was then taken to the quarters which had been prepared.

At the wounded man's request Watkins called in Abraham Jackson, the general's brother. In the presence of this brother, Collier, and several others, Jackson remarked that "This has been a fair duel. Colonel Watkins has behaved like a gentleman, and a man of spirit, therefore it is my order to you and my friends, and it shall be my last dying request, should my wound prove mortal, that he is not to be prosecuted, nor any trouble whatever be given him on my account." Philips added that he and Collier had already mutually agreed that inasmuch as this duel had been predicated "upon five years of private and political animosity," there would be no prosecution.[6]

There was at least one occasion on which Jackson deliberately turned down a challenge to defend his honor. His opponent on this occasion was Jacob Waldburger. The story, tinged with pathos, is one of politics breaking up what promised to be a sincere and lifelong friendship. Jackson charged Waldburger with ingratitude and disloyalty and Waldburger wrote that Jackson was an "exotic" and a "foreigner." Each exhibited the most offensive facets of his personality and only the critical illness of Waldburger terminated a long, bitter correspondence which had not a valid reason for existence.

As a boy Waldburger had been placed in the law office of Jackson. Here he studied from 1783 to 1787, during the last two years living with Jackson's family. About the time he left this office Waldburger decided that Jackson's fighting temperament was driving away many friends and he formed an alliance with Jackson's enemies.

Jackson's influence had put Waldburger in the legislature and although the latter voted against the proposed Yazoo sale of 1794 he had nothing to do with the fraudulent sale of 1795. He later purchased some stock in one of the companies and promptly sold it at a good profit. The two at once entered into a very bitter newspaper controversy over the Rescinding Act. Writing under the name of "Civic" Waldburger was needlessly vituperative, and as "Gracchus" Jackson was equally caustic, calling up characters from ancient history and mythology to make pointed his sarcasm. Waldburger became incensed at some of these references and each of them then began to use his own name. Waldburger wrote that Jackson had added insult to injury by refusing a challenge through one "Lentulus." He then sent a Captain Robertson with a written and oral challenge to a duel. Since Jackson made no response other than to leave Robertson at the door and enter his house Waldburger, through the press, pronounced "General Jackson an *assassin of reputation* and a *coward*." To this Jackson replied:

I took you, sir, a little boy, and treated you with all the affection of a parent, and maintained you without reward, with the best my house afforded. . . . I believe previous to your leaving it, your leagues against me were formed, ... Did you not acknowledge this ingratitude to me, in the chair, coming from Governor Telfair's assuring me with tears in your eyes, that you esteemed me as your father—. . . . I shall not avoid any *proper invitation* [from a worthy opponent].

The controversy did not end here, however, for upon his return from Louisville Jackson wrote the press that Waldburger merely "excites in my breast, emotions of pity and contempt, instead of resentment. The story at Augusta, must be well remembered— ... the patience with which this hero bore the whip of Mr. Seagrove." Here Jackson was referring to the fact that a whipping had been substituted for a duel inasmuch as Seagrove considered Waldburger "no gentleman."

Waldburger required four columns for his review of the whole sorry story. He explained that Seagrove's assault occurred in 1788 "when I was really but a boy, altho' a member of the legislature." A letter from Seaborn Jones affirmed that he took a challenge from Waldburger to Seagrove which was declined and that Waldburger "posted" Seagrove in the customary manner. Waldburger asserted that Jackson "has the art of inducing the public to believe his private quarrels to be theirs. . . . (whenever he has exhausted his virulence upon his antagonist) . . . he whets his appetite for slander; . . . this marauder of private reputation." A few days later Jackson wrote, "I had . . . previously informed him I should treat him with pity and contempt. Whether fear, agitation, or what operated he that night burst a blood vessel, & I am told must die."

To both men 1796 was the most trying year of their lives, and unfortunately the strain under which they were living prevented each from tempering justice with mercy, for one was weighted by personal sorrow and the other by the cough of death. Referring to Jackson's recent loss of two children Waldburger wrote, "It would not be amiss how soon the Great Author of nature consigned him [Jackson] to his original condition." And Jackson, hearing that Waldburger had tuberculosis and his days were numbered, wrote, "Let him depart in peace, and I hope he will meet with more mercy at the tribunal [where] he is soon to appear than he had tenderness for my reputation." Waldburger sought relief for his affliction in the Bahamas where he died a few months later.[7]

The Yazoo controversy hounded Jackson down to the time of his death. In 1797 *Porcupine's Gazette* published "A Word for James Jackson" and this editorial was copied in the *Augusta Chronicle*. The writer stated:

Laws have been passed in one session to *convey property,* in another to *resume it,* and in a third to destroy every vestige of the contract. Threats have been published by influential characters, *to separate the Confederacy,* and to unite with a foreign nation. . . . Read your fate, ye Georgians, in the history of St. domingo. . . . Do you imagine, that when you have been adopted into the French Republic, which some of you meditate, that your seven hundred and fifty tyrants will relinquish their pretense of liberating the world. . . .

A certain Colonel Karr, an emigrant to the Natchez section under the Bourbon County Act of 1785, wrote Governor Jackson in 1798 for information as to whether Georgia or the Union could give him the better land titles. The governor advised the holders of grants from Georgia, Spain, Britain, and the Yazoo companies to "rely solely on . . . their Mother Country, Georgia, . . . until they have a Representative in Congress. . . ."

In the same year Jackson sought to unload some of his anxieties by writing Milledge that for his opposing the fraudulent land sale Jones "meets with universal suffrage, whilst you, Baldwin, & above *all myself,* meet for our service blackguard abuse. . . . As to popularity, my Friend, it is a shadow—here one moment, there another—as the sun of events changes its situation."

In an earlier letter to this friend Jackson laid aside his political cares long enough to repeat some gossip about his arch enemy, Senator James Gunn. The waiting maid had told "the females," who told it to Mrs. Jackson, who told it to her husband. He in turn cautioned Milledge "to be silent." According to this veritable grapevine report, "weary of life and the miseries she had endured," Mrs. Gunn had "put a period to her existence by a strong dose of poison which she had kept sometime by her. The deed . . . was hastened by his insisting to come into the same room where she had confined herself from the time of his arrival, declaring she would never bed with him again." Following this event Gunn retired to private life in Philadelphia where he died in 1801. Jackson informed the governor of Georgia that Gunn had left an estate of forty-five thousand dollars, all of which had been filched from innocent Yazoo purchasers "in every quarter of the Union."

This controversy soon added Judge George Walton to the growing list of Jackson's prominent enemies. Having contracted to sell most of the state's public domain Walton affirmed that the legislature erred in 1796 in annulling this action. In 1799 Jackson was still uneasy over his anti-Yazoo program and expressed a hope that Milledge, Tattnall, and Doctor Jones and Young would appear upon the floor of the Georgia House to block another possible effort by speculators to purchase the western lands.

The newspapers of Savannah and Augusta published Judge Walton's charges to the Screven and Montgomery county grand juries in which he cautioned them against being influenced by Governor Jackson to publish presentments praising the latter's administration. In an official statement in these papers Jackson accused Walton of trying to tear down his administration while pretending to do the opposite. The presentments were not the work "of a political faction" but reflected the feelings of most of the people in opposition to the Yazoo fraud. He hinted at the fact that during the trying days of 1779 Walton as governor had split the Georgia government into two factions. He also asserted that while holding the same office in 1789 Walton had signed warrants for 50,000 acres of public land to one man who was entitled to only 1,000.

Jackson said he would not need to blush when he compared his own administration with Walton's two—"the mock one of 1779, or the more expensive scene of 1789 . . . when I retire from public life, I shall do so with . . . satisfaction, . . . although not with the same exalted ideas of my former usefulness or importance." In his charge to the grand jury of Jefferson County Walton replied that on the spring circuit he had given charges showing the prevalence of a party spirit in the presentments of a number of county grand juries resulting in injury to the dignity of the jurors, but that Governor Jackson with "heat and indecorum" had publicly condemned his charges.

As an evidence of the conditions criticized Walton spoke of four of Jackson's supporters who were indicted in Richmond County on the charge of murdering a man accused of having stolen a slave. When the four men asked for bail a pro-Yazoo man in the courtroom objected and exclaimed that he was the foreman of the grand jury which indicted them. The four then cried out, "Yazoo and persecution." Judge William Few, another friend of Jackson, then granted them bail and during the trial allowed them "to go in and out in the face of the court." The same party spirit had prevented several grand juries from indicting some lynchers, Walton asserted. The governor had dragged in the Yazoo question on so many occasions that it had "been converted for too long a time into a popular hobby-horse" and loyalty to the anti-Yazoo philosophy had been substituted for "virtue, patriotism and talents."

The Yazoo question would eventually be settled by the courts

Persecution and Praise 135

but by arousing "pernicious animosities" and a "ferment in the government" Jackson's conduct had led to disorder and had driven several able men from office. Walton concluded with the hope that he soon would cease to hear such expressions as "lynch, anti-lynch, yazoo and anti-yazoo, ..."

The grand jury of Jefferson County took issue with Walton in the following presentment:

> We feel it our duty to dispense with the usual recommendation for the publication of his honor's charge, it being evidently calculated to produce the effects which he recommends us to avoid by our presentments, and aims unmerited censure at the heads of other departments, contrary to his own maxims.

In this controversy the bitter partisanship of the two politicians differed chiefly in degree. Walton perhaps deserved a little less criticism than Jackson.[8]

Among the few writers outside of the South who defended Jackson was Abraham Bishop of Hartford, Connecticut, a leader in the "Republican" Party. He asserted in a pamphlet that the Yazoo sale was null because Georgia had never possessed title in fee simple to its western lands and that[9]

> Those who have not cheated nor been cheated in this business, . . . calmly view the state of Georgia, exercising a sovereign right in a sovereign and righteous manner. . . . We hastened our bargains . . . ; and to crown all, after we knew the act was passed, . . . we cursed Jackson and his party, . . .—We then secretly employed lawyers to write treatises against the rescinding act, as their *voluntaries.*

Criticism of Jackson's vigorous leadership continued. Early in 1800 "Junius" affirmed in a public letter that he had opposed the Yazoo sale but he also condemned Jackson for inconsistency and oppression. Unfortunately the people still blindly supported him even though he was guilty of "repeated prostitution of executive dignity in scenes of turbulence and riot, over which, let the finger of humanity draw the veil." A few months later another public letter by "B" referred to the fact that one "Trumpeter" writing in a Louisville paper had asserted that the friends of Yazoo would not be safe above Little River; and "the Trumpeter" was asked if he planned to murder the editor. "B" had opposed the sale of 1795 but he thought Georgia ought to abide by the action of its agents.[10]

The difficulty Georgia experienced in organizing the proposed frontier counties of Houstoun and Bourbon, the realization that only Congress could extinguish Indian titles, and the determination of Congress to complete the organization of Mississippi Territory finally induced Georgia's leaders to favor ceding the Yazoo lands to the United States. In his message to the legislature in January, 1799, Governor Jackson stated that the cession was authorized by the Georgia Constitution of 1798 and it would be wise for Georgia to secure her lands east of the Chattahoochee River and sell the rest to the United States for a "moderate compensation."

He expressed himself more fully upon this subject in another message to the legislature in the following November. The proposed cession would "do away all contention for territory, and cause of uneasiness, between [Georgia and the United States] . . .—prove an immense fund for the reduction of the debt of the United States—and finally extinguish all latent hopes of grasping speculation, ..." For the first time Jackson now expressed some sympathy for the "innocent purchasers." There had been retained in the Georgia treasury $491.21 for expenses in "safe keeping" the Yazoo deposits. And, "in order that the State may do justice to the depositors which she is bound by law, the Constitution, honor and morality to do," the deposits should be "warily and cautiously" guarded.

He complained that, by its act of 1798 creating the Mississippi Territory, Congress had virtually endorsed the titles of the secondary Yazoo purchasers. In selecting Secretary of State Timothy Pickering, Secretary of the Treasury Oliver Wolcott, and Attorney General Samuel Sitgreaves as commissioners to carry out this act, President John Adams had named men who were in sympathy with the Yazoo sale. If Congress could set up a territory on the Yazoo it could erect one on the Altamaha and others in Glynn and Camden counties. The United States had claimed title to this western land but it should have harmonized this claim with that of Georgia before passing a bill for a territorial government, even though Georgia's claim to the soil had been left in abeyance by this act.

"Is it just, is it magnanimous in the United States, with the strong arm of power to thus evade the claims of Georgia?" Jackson asked. It was said that Georgia's rights were not endangered, but he held that the presence of a territorial government on its soil violated all state sovereignty. The majority in the Yazoo country claimed the protection of Georgia and he had heard that a petition from them was on the way to the legislature. A new federal administration would probably soon name another commission which would work in harmony with Georgia. In order that a cession might be obtained and harmony established between Georgia and the nation he urged the legislature to act with moderation as well as firmness.

The legislature responded to his appeal and in November sent Congress a mild protest against the setting up of a territory on Georgia's soil without the state's consent. In December, 1800, the legislature therefore named Abraham Baldwin, James Jones, and Benjamin Taliaferro as commissioners to deal with the cession of the Yazoo lands. In seeking to make a treaty with the Creeks and secure a cession of the western lands by Georgia the federal commissioners seemed to find no common ground with the Georgia commissioners and in the summer of 1800 Governor Jackson protested to the State Department that Georgia's claims to the Tallassee section were being ignored.[11]

Shortly after assuming the duties of the presidency Jefferson took under consideration the cession of the Yazoo lands. Since John Adams had named to the Yazoo commission the heads of three departments Jefferson named as a new commission his own appointees to these same cabinet positions—James Madison, Albert Gallatin, and Levi Lincoln. The Georgia legislature also named as a new commission Jackson, Baldwin, and Milledge. After prolonged deliberations on April 24, 1802, the terms for the cession were agreed upon by the two commissions. These terms were known as "The Georgia Compact" or "The Articles of Agreement and Cession." Georgia ceded 54,400,000 acres between the thirty-first and the thirty-fifth degrees of north latitude and west of a line based on the Chattahoochee and a line running north from the junction of this river with Uchee Creek to the junction of Nickajack Creek with the Tennessee River.

The United States guaranteed to Georgia title to all land east of this line and agreed to extinguish all Indian titles to this section at federal expense "as early as the same can be peaceably obtained, on reasonable terms." Georgia was promised $1,250,000 without interest from the first net proceeds of the land sales. Georgia reluctantly agreed that five million acres or the funds obtained from its sale could be used by the United States in adjusting the claims of secondary purchasers of the ceded territory. Georgia considered this a promise to give the state a title to lands which in the New York and Coleraine treaties the nation had guaranteed to the Indians.

Having settled with Georgia, the next task of Congress was to answer the petitions of some of the secondary purchasers who claimed title to the western two-thirds of this cession through the Yazoo Act of 1795. In February, 1803, the federal commission appointed to handle this matter reported to Congress that "the title of the claimants cannot be supported," but on the grounds of expediency recommended that the claimants be given either two and one half million dollars with interest at six per cent or five million dollars without interest. The claimants chose the latter terms and the deal was signed.[12]

Georgia's Congressional delegation opposed any compromise with these secondary purchasers, but Jackson was in the Senate where the debates were meagerly reported. Either he had little to say or his usual vehemence was partially tempered by the fact that he had agreed to an adjustment of these claims. The chief leader of the opposition in Congress was John Randolph of the House. As a youth of twenty-three he had visited his old friend Joseph Bryan in Georgia in 1796 when most of the Georgia people were seething with anger over the fraudulent sale. It was on this visit that he came to hate the Yazoo fraud and in Congress he was as violent against the purchasers as Jackson had been in Georgia. He failed to block the approval of the report of the federal commission in favor of adjusting the claims of the purchasers but for several years he prevented its terms from being carried out.

Randolph, Macon, and some other Southern members of Congress then proclaimed their loyalty to the "Old Republican School" and its state rights "principles of 1798" and began to desert the leadership of Jefferson. The title of "Quids" was given to this group. Jefferson and Madison, the fathers of "the principles of 1798," had very little to say in the Yazoo controversy but sought, for reasons of strategy, to hold the Northern Republicans in line. Jackson must have admired Randolph's violent opposition to the Yazoo fraud but he did not follow the Quids in breaking with the party leaders.

In 1803 Jackson wrote a friend[13] that some Congressional leaders were so weary with the Yazoo petitions that "At the President's" request they offered to give Georgia another million dollars if the state would assume the burden and settle with one female purchaser and the numerous male claimants.

This created a laugh round the Table, when Randolph asked if I would take Mrs. Morton with them. I told him that I would answer that the State of Georgia would take the Male Speculators into dealing, but I would have nothing to do with female sharpers. This created a roar. . . .

Zachariah Cox, one of the Yazoo leaders, sought revenge in 1803 by sending to the Georgia legislature some papers purporting to show that Jackson, while governor, had accepted a bribe in connection with the Yazoo deposits. These papers were examined by a select committee and a resolution was unanimously passed by each house declaring that Jackson "had been vilified by the said Cox; that his conduct was, during his administration, characterized with honesty and disinterestedness"; and that "his reputation stands too high in the opinion of this legislature, and his fellow citizens at large, to be affected by any malicious insinuations or assertions whatsoever." Governor Milledge sent Jackson a copy of this resolution and he replied that it had been published in the *National Intelligencer* where it had "effectually counteracted the nefarious intentions designed."

During 1803 most of Jackson's letters were quite cheerful, but that fall he wrote Daniel Sturges that in the recent "cruel" division of Jackson County, Georgia had ignored him while heaping honors upon the other members of its Yazoo Commission. A new county had been named in honor of Baldwin and the new state capital bore the name of Milledge. And another county was named in honor of Anthony Wayne. Since one county already was named for Jackson he thought that the capital should have been named Jacksonville and that Milledge instead of Wayne should have been honored in the second county.

Alluding to the cession of the West to the Union, also the securing for the state of the section between the Oconee and Chattahoochee through the Georgia Compact, Jackson said that *"God* knows and *they know* that the *whole business* was done by myself— . . . in future I shall be my own man—go to Congress when I please, . . . I shall collect all the proofs I can, to publish to the world the ingratitude of Georgia."[14]

In 1806 some of the secondary purchasers of the Yazoo scrip

persuaded Senator John Quincy Adams to present to the Senate two petitions seeking the government's aid in adjusting their claims against Georgia. Adams wrote that Senator Jackson answered with "a violent invective against the claims, without any specific object."[15] However, Congress did not make any settlement with the claimants until after Jackson's death. The last written statement from Jackson on this question was made in 1805 in his pamphlet *Facts in Reply to the Agents of the New England Land Company, by a Georgian*. Later that year the government reprinted this pamphlet in the [*Yazoo*] *Report from the [U. S.] Committee of Claims*.

Earlier in 1805 a memorial or petition addressed to Congress by the agents of the New England Mississippi Land Company had affirmed that in 1796 the company purchased for $1,138,000 the land which Georgia had sold to the Georgia Mississippi Company. To this Jackson replied that another New Englander, Abraham Bishop, in a pamphlet published in 1797 entitled *Georgia Speculation Unveiled* had questioned the titles of all the Yazoo land companies. He quoted Bishop as stating that some of the secondary purchasers paid their notes in full, others compromised by paying five per cent, most would never pay, and that both the sale of 1795 and the resale to purchasers in New England were "land bubbles."

In his *Facts* Jackson affirmed that the Georgia legislators sold public property to themselves contrary to the interests of the people. Therefore the sale was fraudulent in "the original contract and the transaction is void . . . in all its progress." He confirmed Abraham Bishop's assertion that inasmuch as the Rescinding Act had been promptly published in New England there were no innocent purchasers. Most of the purchasers indeed admitted that they were cheated by the fraud and since the Rescinding Act was fatal to their interests they would take any reasonable settlement by Congress. Jackson expressed regret that the New England Mississippi Land Company's chief agent, Postmaster General Gideon Granger, was a "Republican" lawyer and that he had censured Georgia and bullied Congress. Blackstone affirmed that "When it appears from the face of the grant that . . . [the legislature] is mistaken or deceived, . . . the grant is absolutely void. And to prevent deceits of the king . . . it is particularly provided by the statute of Henry I, chapter 6th, That no grant of his shall be good, unless . . . mention be made of the value of the lands."

Zachariah Cox, surveyor for the land companies, in 1794 informed the Georgia legislature that the sale involved 19,000,000 acres. He later laid a chart before Congress showing that it contained 29,000,000 acres and on a third occasion he asserted that the amount was 40,000,000 acres. Hence the sale was void. Jackson sought to justify the burning of the official state records by the fact that Georgia was "in duress, first by bribery, and next by bullying; . . . some members were tampered with to go home, and others intimidated." He recalled that Nathaniel Bacon, having rebelled against Virginia, in 1676 "coerced the legislature to pass certain laws"; later "the whole of the laws so passed were expunged from the public records—did Georgia do more?"

Emmerich von Vattel held that unless the people give the legislature power to alienate public lands the executive is powerless to execute an act of sale. There was nothing in the Georgia Constitution which justified the legislature in selling 35,000,000 acres "to a dozen speculators." Supreme Court Justice James Wilson was quoted as saying in the Pennsylvania Ratifying Convention of 1787 that "those who ordain and establish have the power if they think proper, to repeal." Jackson asserted that the New England Mississippi Land Company got its deed the very day the Rescinding Act was passed. The company's leaders had been assured of the act's passage six weeks previously; hence there was time for an express to reach Boston and as "Several New-England gentlemen were in the lobby of the Georgia legislature when it did pass . . . , it speaks strongly of antedating." It had been said that none of the money paid into the Georgia treasury by the Georgia Mississippi Company had been taken out; "very well, the agents and company are safe, let them go to the treasury of Georgia and take it out."

Governor Mathews had informed the legislature in January, 1796, that Georgia had already spent $100,000 of the Yazoo deposits. Jackson denied this. And Georgia had not impaired its contract, he said, because the Yazoo Act of 1795 contradicted the sovereignty of the state and was therefore null. The fact that the Georgia Convention placed the Rescinding Act in the Constitution of 1798 by an almost unanimous vote did not prove that this act was illegal. Instead it showed that it was the people who "consigned the Usurped Act of 1795 to eternal obloquy and nothingness." The people of New England must have been informed of the fraud because when the relationship of Georgia to the Creeks was before Congress during an extra session in June, 1795, the fraud was "in every member's mouth."

In a message to the Senate President Washington also hinted that the Yazoo Act might be invalid. He added that he had consented to treat with the Indians regarding a possible cession of some of their land to Georgia because

The views I have since taken, with information received, of a more pacific disposition on the part of the Creeks, have induced me now to accede to the request, *but with this explicit declaration, that neither my assent, nor the treaty which may be made, shall be considered as affecting any question which may arise upon the supplementary act, passed by the legislature of Georgia on the 7th of January, 1795, and upon which inquiries have been instituted, in pursuance of a resolution of the Senate and House of Representatives.*

The agents of the New England Mississippi Land Company insisted that during this controversy no one had been punished for bribery by the Georgia authorities but that among those who voted for the sale three—John King, Richard Carnes, and Lachlan McIntosh—subsequently were re-elected to the legislature. That body repeatedly named McIntosh and Archibald Gershal as judges. Stephen Heard was made justice of the peace; Ferdinand O'Neal was appointed a trustee of the University of Georgia; and O'Neal, Davis Gresham, and Luke Mann were several times sent to the Georgia Senate. These assertions were approximately correct and Jackson's efforts to contradict them were only partially successful. His explanation was that

Gunn, and Wilson and Pendleton were out of reach of the legislature of Georgia, and to catch the smallfry when the whales of speculation could not be punished, was too small an object, or Judge Stith, with many others would have been impeached; he was, . . . however dismissed from office, and . . . it is not true that he or any other interested in that speculation, retain the . . . confidence of . . . the people, or the government of Georgia . . . ; and I venture to assert, that if either of the Georgia senators or representatives, should even now be suspected of being partial to that speculation, they could never return to Congress. The great body of the Georgians are as feelingly alive as to that question, . . . as they were in 1795.

Georgia objected to submitting the Yazoo Act to the federal courts because federal Judges Wilson and Pendleton had helped persuade the legislature to make the sale. Jackson feared that Georgia would receive no justice in such courts. If the New Eng-

Persecution and Praise

land Land Company should receive any consideration, Jackson felt, it would be due to the compassion rather than the justice of Congress. He continued,[16] "One more single observation and I am done with this transaction forever—If the . . . Union stand prepared to give premiums for speculation, . . . I shall bow with submission to their decision; but . . . I shall ever lament the purchase of Louisiana, for it will assuredly become the prey of speculating harpies, who will beset the walls of Congress, as they did the legislature of Georgia, and with their vile means effect a similar event—for alas! poor human nature is every where the same. A Georgian."

In March, 1806, the federal House was debating a Senate bill favoring an adjustment of the Yazoo claims. In opposing the bill John Randolph said of Jackson, "will we, after following an illustrious patriot to his grave, sully the fairest page in his history by giving a sanction to this measure?" The bill was rejected by a vote of fifty-four to sixty-two. Then "Mr. J. Randolph moved that the House adjourn. He said that a few days ago the House had adjourned on account of the death of General Jackson. He hoped they would now adjourn on account of his resurrection. For he had told him, that if he could give a death-blow to the Yazoo business, he should die in peace." The motion for adjournment was carried.[17]

In the decision written by John Marshall in Fletcher v. Peck in 1810 the Supreme Court annulled the Rescinding Act on the ground that it violated the clause of the federal Constitution which forbids a state to make laws impairing the obligations of contracts. This decision was used by the Yazoo purchasers to strengthen their petitions and in 1814, when Randolph was not in the House, a bill awarding them approximately five million dollars was enacted into law.

In 1814 the Creeks ceded to Georgia most of their lands within the present boundaries of the state and in 1819 the Cherokees did likewise. By 1838 all the Indians in Georgia except about 14,000 Cherokees who had concealed themselves in some caves in north Georgia were settled in the Indian territory west of the Mississippi.

And so the long drawn out Yazoo controversy was brought to a close.[18] This controversy did not destroy Jackson, as many of his friends, as well as his enemies, prophesied. On the contrary it assisted in elevating him to the governorship and brought him other high political honors.

IX

PARTY BOSS AND GOVERNOR, 1795-1806

IN MOST of the newly-united states during the administrations of our first three presidents, the aristocrats rallied to the Federalists and the common people to the "Republicans" but local conditions in Georgia caused this alignment to be reversed. Wealthy James Jackson was elected to the governorship as head of the "Jackson Party," later called the "Jackson-Crawford-Troup Party." In national politics this group affiliated with the Jeffersonian or Republican Party. The state's leaders admired Washington's character and leadership in the Revolution but few of them saw eye to eye with him about the Indians. As the Federalist and Republican parties began to take shape during the administrations of Washington and John Adams some of the wealthy Georgians who had participated in the fraudulent Pine Barren and Yazoo land speculations turned against Jackson and his supporters.

In 1794 and 1795 wealthy John and Elijah Clarke the younger were in league with the Yazoo land companies. Since Jackson headed the Republican Party, these frontier leaders temporarily found shelter among the Federalists. But while a few of the Georgia Federalists were educated and wealthy the majority were the poor backwoods cattle raisers who had emigrated from North Carolina. On the other hand the Jackson or Jeffersonian group was built around the wealthy, aristocratic citizens who came from the British Isles to the coastal plain or from the Virginia and Carolina plantations to the Little River and Broad River sections of east central Georgia.

In the presidential election of 1796 the Federalists carried only four of the state's twenty-one counties although their defeat was by a slim margin in two other counties. Georgia gave its entire electoral vote three times to Jefferson, once to William H. Crawford, and twice each to James Madison, James Monroe, and Andrew Jackson. Thus on national issues there was an "era of good feeling" in Georgia earlier than in the rest of the nation. From 1796 to 1806 many of the former Federalists and Yazoo men continued with the Clarke faction because of their hatred for Jackson but most of them gradually drifted into the Jeffersonian group.[1]

From 1795 until his death in 1806 Jackson was the recognized leader of the Jeffersonian Party in Georgia. His enemies charged that his resignation from the Senate and his vehement fight against the Yazoo fraud were motivated more by a desire to build up his political machine than to enhance Georgia's financial resources. Whichever was his primary motive—and his enemies' charges were never proved—both results were realized in generous measure. After 1796 land frauds ceased to plague the state.

By controlling the legislature Jackson's party named the federal senators, the governors, and most of the state and county officials. In order to build up his political machine in the middle and upper counties Jackson sought to line up young men of ability and character. One of these was William H. Crawford, who had come to Georgia from Virginia as a boy. He studied at Waddel's Academy in South Carolina and taught at Richmond Academy in Augusta. After beginning the practice of law he moved to the frontier town of Lexington, Georgia. Jackson wrote a friend that he needed a leader "from the Westward. . . . I have mentioned the name of William H. Crawford, Barret's nephew, as a Candidate for the C. Judgeship. . . . Crawford will satisfy them all—Early and a few Yazoo lawyers excepted—and we must take some of those Friendly Young Men by the hand."

Another young protege of Jackson was George M. Troup. He was born in the Indian country in what is now Alabama. After graduating from Princeton he began the practice of law in Savannah and promptly aligned himself with the Jeffersonians. He attracted attention by a series of able political newspaper articles under the name of "Z." Jackson placed him on his staff as aide and gave him the title of "colonel." Another Savannah youth who filled an active place in Jackson's party was Thomas U. P. Charlton, his aide-de-camp during the Revolution. Charlton later began a two-volume biography of Jackson but for some reason completed only half of it. David B. Mitchell and Governor Josiah Tattnall were other brilliant lawyers whom Jackson enlisted.

While claiming to be independent of Jefferson in national politics Jackson looked upon him as a personal friend. Their friendship, both political and personal, is revealed in Jackson's writing Baldwin in 1800 that the Georgia legislature was "purely Republican" and that Jefferson never had so many friends in any assembly, Virginia not excepted; "in comparison to the number on the floor, there being but six or seven Adamites in both branches . . . neither Mr. Adams nor Mr. Pinckney will have a vote. . . . Present my respects & best wishes to Mr. Jefferson. The State of Georgia prays for his success. I received under cover his . . . note; & for which mark of attention I thank him; more so as he honord [sic] me as a Friend."

After Jackson's death the leadership of his party fell to Crawford and later Crawford became so involved in national and international affairs that he gave way to Troup.[2]

Jackson served as governor for one full term of two years and a little over half of a second term—from January 12, 1798, to March 3, 1801. He was first elected by the legislature on January 11, 1798, and qualified the following day. Problems of his governorship included the establishment of a state university, the rounding out of his political party, making a new state Constitution, ceding the Yazoo lands to the Union, revising the system of tax collections, controlling the foreign slave trade, developing the new revolutionary cotton gin, and Indian relations.

As chief executive Jackson continued the interest he had shown in education as a state legislator. In a letter to Baldwin in 1801 he denied a report that he was the author of "the University Act" of 1800, but added, "It is my sincere wish to promote the institution and I think it is on as good a footing as before. . . ." Although he did not give the measure his full approval and considered vetoing it at one time he did reluctantly sign the bill, believing it to be the best attainable at the time.

In 1800 he wrote Professor Josiah Meigs of Yale University that he had been extended a unanimous call by the Board of Trustees to the position of "presiding professor" of the new university at an annual salary of $1,500. Elijah Clarke the younger, a student at Yale, and Abraham Baldwin had assured the Board that they were pleased with his "amiable & qualified character" and every member of the Senatus Academicus wished to commit the youths of Georgia to his instruction. In another letter to Meigs he wrote that the last legislature had passed a new act regarding the University Board and that "the new appointments are myself, Genl Twiggs Genl [John] Clarke brother to the gentleman now studying in your College Colo Tattnall Mr. Milledge. . . . The board of visitors is composed of the Governor, the Judges of the Superior Courts," and others.

When the university opened in 1801 Jackson's two oldest sons, William Henry and James, were enrolled in the small group of students. In September of this year he wrote Milledge that he would soon "Post off with the boys . . . to see them settled" at Athens. In still another letter, this time in 1803, Jackson wrote Milledge, "I expect Mr. Mays has sent down for my Boys. If you should be in Augusta when they arrive in the state & will advise them as to getting along, you will much oblige me. They will have money to hire horses." This letter was mailed from Washington while the Senate was in session and if the sons were with him this is the only evidence we have that he ever took any member of his family with him to any of our three national capitals.

When the first class was graduated from the University in 1804 Jackson's two sons were among those receiving their degrees.

Much later, in 1845, President Alonzo Church of the University wrote that Jackson's and Baldwin's convictions that the state should become an efficient patron of learning would "add a bright chaplet to their fame."[3]

When the Georgia Convention met at Louisville from May 8 to 28, 1798, Chatham County was represented by James Jackson, James Jones, and George Jones. Instead of revising the old Constitution, according to its instructions, this body produced a new document four times as long as that of 1789. Although it later received twenty-three amendments it was destined to last until 1861. Jackson wrote the first section of the third article, revising the state's judicial system. He also wrote sections twenty-three and twenty-four of the first article which declared the Yazoo Sale Act "null and void" and decreed that henceforth "no . . . order shall pass the General Assembly, granting a donation or gratuity in favor of any person whatever, but by the concurrence of two-thirds" of that body. The press carried this terse report of the convention:

Louisville, June 1, 1798. On Wednesday last, the Constitution of this state being revised, amended and fairly engrossed on parchment, . . .

governor Jackson announced it to the citizens under a discharge of sixteen rounds of artillery. The governor having invited the members of the convention, the citizens and strangers in Louisville to celebrate the event, it was pleasing to [see former enemies sit down together] to a handsome dinner provided by his excellency for the occasion.

Jackson sent a message of appreciation to Captain Shellman, his subordinate officers, and the privates of the Louisville Artillery Company for their soldierly bearing and "firing admirable" in celebrating the completion of the work of the Convention.

Four days after adjournment Jackson wrote Secretary of War James McHenry that the new Constitution was signed on May 28 "amidst the acclamations of the attending Citizens" and expressed a personal pride in the fact that his leadership had caused this document to authorize the cession of the Yazoo lands to the United States.

It will afford me and I can assure you, it will the Great Body of . . . this State, more happiness than I, or they, ever experienced on any public occasion, in which our local interest was concerned;—if the United States should prove as much disposed to accommodate as the State of Georgia in this great object. It will effectually rivet the affections of the people of Georgia to the General Government, and as effectually destroy those fatal party influences, so much to be dreaded at this crisis.

After a delay of three months McHenry replied, congratulating him upon the completion of the Constitution and expressing his appreciation of the favorable attitude shown by Georgia on the question of ceding its western lands. The national government promised that at the proper time it would offer "fair, just and honorable terms."[4]

Jackson's annual salary as governor was $2,000 and he discussed the question of salaries in a special legislative message on March 3, 1801. Since he was leaving office he could speak freely. He said that a "$2,000 salary for the Governor does not bear any proportion" to his expenses, "whilst his neglect of his private to attend public concerns adds to the injury of his own finances, ..." Salaries of $1,500 for a judge and $1,000 for a state treasurer were also too low, he felt. The state should command the ablest men as its official servants and this would be impossible without adequate salaries. In an earlier letter he had complained of the crowded conditions in Louisville where the legislators were forced to live "eight or ten in a room." No changes in salaries or improvement in housing were made for some years, however.

Jackson dealt with the state tax system in two messages to the legislature. In January of 1798 he urged the appointment of an inspector of revenues to check on the county tax collectors and receivers, to check the amount and returns of land grants, and "to attend to filling of vacancies by notifying the Executive as they happen, ..." Some collectors had sold the property of defaulters and "pocketed" the money, he said. He recommended that fixed salaries replace the fee system for collectors and receivers. When a sheriff or collector defaulted, the courts should leave this problem to the state treasurer. In an executive order he required William Norment, collector for Chatham County, to send in his digest for 1797, and the state treasurer was ordered to obtain a list of the digests from the counties that had not been sent in for that year.

In Jackson's legislative message of January, 1799, he announced that he had found it necessary to check a fraudulent practice of certain sheriffs. When citizens were in arrears in their taxes the law required that their property be sold, but some sheriffs were allowing the owners to bid in their land for one half of the taxes thus depriving the state of its full revenues from that source. In such a sale in Camden County Governor Jackson had this word of praise for Sheriff R. Gillis for bidding in a piece of property for the state: "I think it proper . . . for you . . . to bid to the amount thereof . . .—I have had to take this step before in Franklin, whither I sent the Treasurer to bid."

In a special message to the legislature in February, 1798,[5] he conveyed the joyous news of the unanimous ratification of the eleventh amendment to the federal Constitution, which prohibits a lawsuit against a state by a person who is not one of its citizens. "I . . . congratulate you on the event—The State relieved from this oppressive part of the Constitution will have a more perfect right of extending her perogative [sic] of Justice to herself, and benevolence to individuals, whose claims will now depend upon her equity alone."

Jackson's governorship covered the last three years of the administration of President John Adams. During this period the United States engaged in an undeclared naval war against France. The authorities at Washington handled foreign affairs, but the governor, acting as commander-in-chief of his state's militia, could greatly hinder or help the nation's effort. Jackson proved most loyal to the administration during this crisis. He wrote to a friend in 1798:

As to Foreign influence I believe the eastern States possess an abundance more of it than Georgia, tho' theirs may be the current of the day. I will venture to assert that our Citizens would fight any power at war with the United States, but I fear all to the North of North River would hesitate, if that war were with Great Britain.

In a special message in January, 1798, he found it necessary to deal with foreign affairs. He notified the legislature that America's commissioners to France had returned without settling the points at issue and that

war suspended by a thread seems to threaten the peace of the United States, and to involve us in the horrors and compel us to share the scenes of the European Convulsions. . . . Georgia the Southern Boundary of the United States ought peculiarly to be prepared, she is exposed to a line of Sea Coast with a multiplicity of Inlets, and in case of war when there might be a necessity for the removal of the Troops on our frontier to some other part to oppose the Common Enemy, she would have her South, South West and North West frontiers fully exposed to the Creek and Cherokee Nations of Indians.

The legislature instructed the governor to have the militia more effectively trained and held in readiness for war as provided by an act of Congress.

Early in 1798 he ordered the officers in each county to see that their men were carefully drilled and the brigade inspector and the adjutant general of each unit to review their troops and to report to him and to the war department. He warned that all defaulting officers and men would be prosecuted. The brigadiers were to stimulate volunteering for a troop of cavalry in each county, each being equipped and made ready for the field. In the eastern division he ordered the first brigade to be ready to defend the coast, the second should support the first, and the third should support the second.

Jackson had been pro-French until the late 1790s but during his governorship he showed no pronounced love for either France or Britain. He once wrote a friend that "You have not surprised me about the Post Master [Habersham of Georgia], I have long since discovered that Ca Ira was turning into God save the K—g, . . . and Orations Francaise into damn-d French buj-s. Wonderful, wonderful human creatures! . . . . Place the most Frenchifyed Jacobin in the Offices of the United States, and he immediately signs hallulejah [sic] to . . . Great Britain. Monroe is an exception, and he smarts for it."

In May, 1798, Washington wrote Hamilton that he was disturbed by the troubles with France but he had "learnt from a very intelligent Gentleman just returned from . . . [Georgia], that the people of that State . . . seem to be actuated by one spirit, *and that,* a very friendly one to the General Government. I have likewise heard, that the present governor . . . , professes to be strongly attached to it."

In two messages to the legislature in 1799 Jackson defended Georgia against the criticism of lukewarmness towards the Union. Early in the year he prophesied that if war, "that worst of all human scourges," should come, "Georgians would meet it with firmness in defense of their "common Country." In November he stated that he yearned for peace but if war came he wanted his state to "hand down to posterity unimpaired those invaluable blessings of freedom, and independence, for which our fathers fought, and bled to secure." He felt that Jay's Treaty of 1795 secured more for Britain than for the United States, and although France violated our commerce, Britain did worse with less excuse.

Georgia's relations with Spain were also disturbing. The state suspected that its fugitive slaves were allowed refuge in East Florida and felt that Spain's ships interfered with its commerce. In May, 1798, Major Samuel Wright of the state militia wrote from St. Simons Island that the Spanish of East Florida were fitting out privateers and that as soon as possible they probably would attempt to capture American vessels bound for British ports "as do the French." He said the citizens of that island would probably have fled had he not drafted its thirty-nine militiamen as guards.

Three months later trouble again threatened over an incident at Savannah. In a proclamation the governor publicized a report by John Habersham, federal collector of customs for the Port of Savannah, that about midnight on the fourth of August certain unknown men boarded the Spanish schooner *Maria* of about twelve tons "burthen," entered from St. Augustine, secured the crew, carried the vessel about a mile up the river, and burned it. As these men violated Thomas Pinckney's Treaty of San Lorenzo el Real of 1795 with Spain, Jackson ordered all military officers to arrest them, offering a reward of four hundred dollars for information leading to successful prosecution.

He also wrote a friend that Savannah had requested an appropriation for defense against the Spanish privateers but he felt that it would be wiser for the state to confine its protection to weaker and more exposed sections. In order that the city might be properly fortified Jackson offered a personal contribution of one hundred dollars and advised each of the large planters along the Savannah River to make a similar gift.[6]

Another problem which kept the governor busy was the foreign slave trade. The federal government was not permitted by the Constitution to block this business until 1808. Although the importation of slaves was forbidden by Georgia in the Constitution of 1798 and a legislative act of that year, Jackson found it necessary to use his executive powers to the full to effectually stop this trade. When in 1798 some Negroes were smuggled into Savannah and the town's authorities sheltered them, the governor wrote Mayor John Glen rebuking the city corporation for harboring thirty-five slaves taken from the "Ship General Nichols." Some of the citizens of Savannah had erred in asserting that these men were brigands from Grenada; they were probably being brought from Africa for sale in some Atlantic port. The governor said that he would order them sold according to the tax act, the proceeds to be divided between the town and the state.

Later in the month James Norment, Tax Collector for Chatham County, reported to the governor that both the Savannah council and the jailor had refused to deliver the slaves to him. Norment had sold them anyway for five hundred dollars but had not yet received payment. Jackson then wrote the mayor that while the attitude of the council was respectful its actions were illegal. He was inclined to suspend the council but rather than punish all the citizens of the town he would refer the matter to the legislature. The town authorities finally decided to comply with the law and wrote Jackson of their joy over his election to the governorship and his return to the city. He thanked them and declared that he had done his duty.

Later in the spring the governor heard that some slaves from the insurrection centers in the West Indies were being shipped to Georgia and South Carolina. He issued a proclamation calling attention to the fact that Georgia's laws forbade the admission of any "negroe, mustee, mulatto, freeman, . . . or slave" from any of these turbulent islands. He ordered the civil and military authorities to apprehend such Negroes and take them before the corporation of Savannah or any three justices of the peace and have them exported at the expense of the importer. In the fall of 1798 the secretary of war congratulated him on his vigorous measures in preventing the landing of some brigands with seditious tenets from Port Au Prince, Haiti, and assured him that the United States had ordered the construction of some "gallies" for the protection of its southern coasts.[7]

Jackson's letters of this period show that at times he would have preferred to abandon politics. He wrote Milledge that the term "Your Excellency" had a pleasing sound but it caused him to "look around me to find the person it is addressed to, when pop comes into my head the big chair." He also expressed a nostalgic desire to live again the life of the planter, "snuffing the oderiferous air of the rice swamps."

The year 1798 was second only to 1796 in the bitterness of the conflicts between Jackson and his enemies. In August of that year he gave voice to his troubled state of mind in another letter to Milledge:

They set me down for a Proteus—an Englishman—skip Jack—from Oliver Cromwell they metamorphose my Presbyterian Countenance into Jean Frenchman, and as suddenly change Robespierre, one & indivisible of course Federal, into a wicked Anti Federalist who wishes to support State Governments. Lord help us, what will they make of me next?

The controversy referred to was reported at some length by William Cobbett in his *Gazette* and later reprinted in his *Porcupine's Works*. The fight was a three-cornered one among some Georgia grand juries, Alexander McMillan, publisher of the *Southern Sentinel,* and Governor Jackson. Cobbett stated:

*Republican Liberty.—Augusta, October 20.—October Term, 1798. The following are the presentments of the Grand Jury of the county of Jefferson.—*We present as a public nuisance the Augusta Southern Sentinel, and as *a public grievance,* the editor and printer thereof; for suffering to be inserted therein, anonymous and scurrilous pieces against the chief magistrate of this state; . . . whose services have done honor to his country, and, on whose integrity and conduct, we have the most perfect reliance.—Moreover such scurrilous publications appear to be intended to *take away the confidence of the people in the* *government of our country;* which, when avowed publications, much less anonymous scribblers, are permitted to do, it is no longer the liberty, but the licentiousness of the press. And we conceive the said printer to have been *tantalizing* the inhabitants of this country, and *insulting the* public in *general.* . . .

In the same volume Cobbett printed an editorial entitled *"Liberty of the Press!"* It asserted that the "excellent" *Sentinel* of Augusta was "almost the only federal paper in that country . . . ; but, the bold and useful truths, which . . . appeared in his paper, drew on . . . [McMillan] not a prosecution from the governor (the noted Jackson) but his *dark* and *despot-like* revenge." It complained that Jackson worked indirectly through several grand juries of the state and that "The Governor's brother, *Abraham Jackson,* . . . *his Secretary of State,"* sent a message and a petition in a letter through one Caldwell to certain members of the Burke County Grand Jury, of which he was a member. Caldwell got drunk and lost the letter in the home of a man with whom he spent the night and his host mailed it to the *Sentinel.*

According to that paper the letter stated that Caldwell was requested to show the petition to those jurors "who can be relied on" and to procure from the grand jury a presentment against McMillan. Cobbett also reprinted an editorial by McMillan which stated that the letter Caldwell conveyed was an insult to the grand juries of Georgia and tempted them to perjure themselves to provide "a momentary gratification" for the governor. He acknowledged that he had published certain criticisms of Jackson but if they were false his friends could correct them through the *Sentinel.* He warned that if Jackson should prevent public criticism liberty would die. He was honored to be told that he represented a party of most intelligent and honorable men who were opposed to the chief executive.

Jackson replied through the *Louisville Gazette and Republican Trumpet* in a letter which Cobbett quoted:

to meet the abuse of the dirty editor of the Southern Sentinel, has been . . . the lot of every chief magistrate of this state. . . . I . . . solemnly deny, that ever my brother was ordered or desired by me to write to Mr. Caldwell . . . , and I hope that my standing among my fellow-citizens for twenty-six years past, will at least stamp a credit on my word equal to the assertion of Mr. M'Millan. . . . Such authors . . . strive to break down the very *pillars of federalism,* the state governments—which if not checked, must . . . settle us down into a government similar to France, *one and indivisible . . . so very . . . unsuitable to our interests.*

McMillan replied that Jackson's letter further lessened his dignity but he would not copy his "Own very flowery and *elegant* stile." The governor used freely such expressions, as "Dirt, dung, and Cloacina," McMillan said, and his thought and diction were comparable to the oratory of a "Parisian fish-woman," bearing out an assertion by a recent writer that *"when the political pot boils the scum rises to the top."* He also accused Jackson of disloyalty to the federal government, which disloyalty "designates the political hypocrit, not the independent patriot. A man, who has once declared *that he would join the French, if ever they landed in this country,* is entitled to little confidence from the community."

Cobbett added that Jackson's letter was "Shuffling, base and blackguard." He then exclaimed with this sarcastic, rhetorical flourish:[8] "BRITONS, when some precious knave shall again call on you to *reform* your monarchy into a *representative government,* hollow in his ear the name of JACKSON, and strike the villain dumb."

During the period of Jackson's political prominence the public authorities of Georgia gave little attention to the question of health other than endeavoring to check the ravages of dangerous contagious diseases. In the fall of 1798 Doctor Michael Burke, health officer for Savannah, informed the governor that he had learned of the return of yellow fever to Philadelphia. Jackson replied that while the quarantine law was not effectively enforced in any American city he would issue a proclamation on the subject if the corporation of Savannah should request it. In the meantime any justice of the peace could legally impose a fine of fifty pounds on any person who disembarked from a ship infected with a contagious disease. In 1800 smallpox became prevalent in several Georgia counties and in a proclamation the governor sought to control the disease through the civil and military authorities. He would have the troops called out in Chatham and Bryan counties and the state treasurer, Edwin Mounger, would pay the daily legal remuneration.

The governor's reputation for firmness discouraged applications for clemency on the part of convicted criminals and he declined to interfere in most of the cases reported. Judge Carnes sent him a petition requesting the pardon of one John Salter who had been convicted of violating the "Gouging Act." In a fight Salter had pulled out his enemy's eye with his thumb. In reply Jackson asked for more particulars and notified the judge that he would not set the man free because such "barbarous" conduct required an example but he might possibly commute his sentence by "taking off a part." But if the sentence should not be commuted the law required that the culprit stand in the pillory for an hour and if by that time he had not paid the fine of one hundred pounds he should receive one hundred lashes.[9]

In January, 1799, he sent the legislature a message of thirty-one pages. He promised to discharge his obligations "as far as my small ability will permit." This assumption of modesty, in striking contrast to his usual air of self-assurance, doubtless amused most of the legislature.

He again discussed the charge of several of the nation's newspapers that Georgia was halfhearted in its allegiance to the Union. The state was obviously in an exposed position, he said, and needed the Union; therefore a policy of half-hearted support would be contrary to duty and interest. The state was "one of the pillars of the federal fabric, whilst we watch with a vigilant eye over our own constitutional rights, command our exertions, . . . to preserve the confederation, and to remember . . . that however individually we may differ in sentiment on some points of domestic arrangement, . . . I conceive it the unbounden duty of every Citizen to protect, with his life and fortune, the independence of his . . . Country, ..." It was the part of wisdom, however, to avoid being "entangled in European politics . . . if there be encroachments on our rights, let us patiently wait for Constitutional means of removing them."[10]

Governor Jackson thought that Georgia's chief dependence for wealth was agriculture and he faced the future with optimism. In January, 1799, he reminded the legislature that with continued health and peace Georgia might soon become America's most wealthy and important state. He thought that the increase of cotton and tobacco "was big with promise" for the state's commerce. He also stated in his legislative message of November that "cotton, . . . is rapidly advancing to the head of American exports . . . a staple, which deserves the fostering hand of the Union, ..."

Georgia was the first state to prove the value of this export but foreign merchants had begun to complain that the quality of its cotton was inferior to that indicated by the stamp. He thought that the exports of all the states ought to be supervised and he regretted that Georgia's inspection law of 1796 had been repealed the following year. Of those who exported cotton under false labels he said, "such infamous practices tend to stamp on our character, as a people, a total want of honor, justice and morality; which, I feel convinced, you will deem it your duty to prevent."

In 1793 Eli Whitney, of Connecticut, with his partner, Phineas Miller, began manufacturing the cotton gin which he had invented on Mrs. Nathanael Greene's Georgia plantation. In a 1799 legislative message Jackson condemned the "cruel extortion of the gin holders" by which Georgia and South Carolina had been made tributary to Whitney and Miller. He had been told that the partners were demanding two hundred dollars for the mere privilege of using a gin.

According to a Louisville merchant when the patentees first distributed their product they "reserved the right of property of it," and two-thirds of the net proceeds arising from the gin. The expense of working was to be "joint between" the patentees and the ginner. Finding a defect in the patent law "they determined to sell the machines, together with the right vested in them, for five hundred dollars [or] a person to build and work one at his own expense four hundred—" They discovered that the defect in the patent law was generally known and, failing to get redress in the courts, they lowered the price until in 1800 it was only two hundred dollars.

Others began to introduce improvements and it was estimated that two new patentees who had appropriated certain features of these inventions would realize one hundred thousand dollars in Georgia and South Carolina alone. Jackson said that Coke, "the great law meteor," declared that monopolies were contrary to the common law and the fundamental law of England and Adam Smith held that they were always bolstered by oppressive laws. The dockets of the federal courts were filled with suits between artificers and planters for making or vending the machines without licenses and Jackson suggested that Georgia, the Carolinas, and Tennessee petition Congress for relief.

A few weeks later Whitney and Miller published a joint statement concerning "this public instance of persecution and slander." The governor had accused them of conducting a monopoly but Whitney, in perfecting his invention, had spent a number of years with heavy expenses and no profits. In order to stimulate ingenuity the patent law allowed large profits for a few years, after which the invention belonged to the public. Jackson was accused of giving publicity to idle tales. The patentees claimed that they had no pioneer to blaze the trail and all the improvements that others had made had been foreseen by them. They concluded with a wish that Jackson would not again bring their private concerns into public notice and force them to make a further defense.

Two months later Jackson learned through Arthur Fort that the inventors had threatened to prosecute the government of Georgia. He replied, "I would willingly try the experiment if state Sovereignties are inferior to created petty corporations of the United States. . . ." This statement brought the controversy to an end. Whitney finally abandoned his interests in the cotton gin and began to manufacture arms for the federal government.

In 1799 Jackson brought to the attention of the legislators the controversy between the United States and Britain over executing the Treaty of 1783. In 1781 and 1782 Georgia had confiscated the properties of a number of loyalists and sold them or given them to the state's Revolutionary soldiers. The Treaty of 1783 stipulated that Congress would endeavor to persuade the thirteen states to return such confiscated property to its original owners but the states had refused to do so.

During November of 1798 the federal district court sitting at Augusta had handed down two decrees in favor of certain British subjects against four "Citizens of this State holding landed property under the title of our confiscation Act," namely—Mrs. George Kincaid, James Mossman, William Mein, and Alex Wylly.

"As those decrees if not reversed will produce endless lawsuits, a confusion of titles & in short shake the whole confiscation Act," Jackson asked if it would not be wise for Georgia to appropriate money for defending its citizens. He suggested the following defense: 1—when its Confiscation Act was passed Georgia was a sovereign state; 2—by referring to the thirteen states the Treaty of 1783 recognized Georgia's right to pass its own laws; 3—Secretary of State Jefferson convinced Britain that Congress had no power over property confiscated by the states and Britain had already compensated its loyalists; 4—the official correspondence of John Adams, Benjamin Franklin, and John Jay also convinced the British that the United States had no authority over individual states; 5—as a bar to the restitution of confiscated property, Franklin's letter of November 26, 1782, to Richard Oswald cited a Congressional resolution of the previous September, instructing the secretary for foreign affairs to report to the peace commissioners the number of slaves taken from the states by the British; 6—the Constitution states that "nothing in this Constitution shall be so construed as to prejudice any claims . . . of any particular State" and "the claim or title of the State is affected by those decrees, by prejudicing the claim of those holding under her"; 7—the naturalization laws of the Union provide "That no person heretofore proscribed by any State, or who has been legally convicted of having joined the Army of Great Britain during the late War, shall be admitted a Citizen as aforesaid without the consent of the Legislature of the State in which such person was proscribed"; 8—these two decrees virtually were destroying the eleventh amendment; 9—the tenth amendment reserves to the states powers not delegated to the Union, and the people of Georgia have not thus delegated the power of destroying their Confiscation Act; and—10—finally, in compensating the loyalists Britain had relieved them of their debts to the American patriots and many of those debts had been paid by the state from the sale of confiscated property, this being true of all of Kincaid's estate and of much of Wylly's, and if Georgia should be forced to refund the sums demanded by the British she would rest under the burden of a double confiscation.

The legislature authorized the governor to employ attorneys to defend the citizens holding confiscated land. In a legislative message in 1800 Jackson stated that he had employed the firm of Dallas and Ingersoll and that, on an appeal from the federal District Court in Georgia, the federal Supreme Court had sustained Georgia's Confiscation Act.[11]

As Jackson's first term was to expire in the fall of 1799 the legislature re-elected him on November 7 of that year by a vote of fifty-three to fourteen and he qualified the following day. One of the first legislative bills passed during his second term called for the naming of presidential electors in the general election planned for the first Monday in October. Jackson vetoed this measure on the ground that it violated a federal law which required that the election be held within thirty days of the first Wednesday in December.

Shortly after disapproving this bill he received the sad news of Washington's death on December 14, 1799. In January of the following year Jackson issued a proclamation which called upon the citizens to wear for six weeks the customary sign of mourning as an expression of their "grateful respect," affection, veneration, and deep affliction for that "once great man, and the father of his country," whose leadership had procured for them freedom and independence.[12]

Of Jackson's numerous legislative messages the one of November 4, 1800, aroused the most bitter discussion. The publication of this message and the resultant debate upon it by six writers required eight issues of Savannah's *Columbian Museum*. The subscribers who failed to read the message could have gotten a fair idea of its contents from the positions taken in the discussion.

The governor had rebuked the corporation of Savannah for not promptly notifying him of the appearance of smallpox in the city. One writer, "Anti-Dictator," replied that the law required that when the city placed a quarantine it should report the number of cases to the governor, whose duty it would then be to issue a proclamation calling upon the city to obey the state health regulations for such situations. He added that the corporation was not accountable to the chief executive and, as the people suspected, when his "Liquor Merchant" and his confidential officer notified him of the depletion of his liquid stores Jackson "raised the siege."

"Un bon Citoyen" wrote of Jackson as *"high admiral"* of Georgia and as one who "always sported the *bloody flag*, in commemoration of his matchless prowess and never-to-be-enough-talked-of feats in our late glorious revolution!!!—I wonder he was not drowned *wading through such oceans* of blood as he talks so much about!" One signing himself "Super-Dictator" took as the text of his article Jackson's statement that the richest European monarch was too poor to purchase his principles. It was evidently proper for a man to *"think, praise* and *speak* of nothing but *himself. . . .* I have long been in quest of popularity without obtaining it—I now design to follow the governor's good example—I . . . will at once plainly and candidly tell the world that I am the best and greatest man in it. I shall without doubt, be believed, and be made . . . , nothing less than a *governor. . . . Who's afraid?"*

George M. Troup, writing for the defense under the name of "Z," favored freedom of the press but not licentiousness, scurrility, scandal, and intemperance. In another article Troup commended Jackson's message for stating that "it is asserted, and with some color of authority, that an influence exists in America, partial to British rule, and ready for a monarch; . . . ." President John Adams wrote to Tenche Coxe that he knew of intrigue and suspected much British influence in his administration. Troup affirmed that Hamilton was the "mover of this party" and inferred that Jackson's enemies were following Hamilton's love for Britain and his advocacy of a powerful hereditary chief executive.

Taking up his pen again "Anti-Dictator" accused Jackson of rebuking Miller, Whitney, Watkins, and Berrien, the former state treasurer, because they would not "cringe" to the governor. Jackson praised Scheuber, the late tax collector, the writer said, because Scheuber condemned the national government and worked for Jackson's election. Jackson claimed to support democracy and yet assumed all power. The legislature would give him any law he requested and even allowed him to serve as governor while actively campaigning for the United States Senate.

"An American Soldier" ridiculed the assertion that the governor's principles were "instilled in the trying hours of 1776." If by "principles" Jackson meant having and expressing opinions then his experience went further back than 1776 to his native England where its citizens boast that they speak of the government "as they please." And when they become American citizens, with what wonderful facility "these Englishmen will assume a participation in the inheritance of Americans! They will speak of *our rights* which were purchased at the expense of oceans of the blood of *our fathers!* when perhaps, *their* fathers never saw America; nor did their sons ever spill a drop of blood in its cause."

"A" next came to Jackson's defense by opposing the "nonsense —and disappointed envy" and the "billingsgate phillippics" of those who were unable to travel in "the peaceful track of gentle ratiocination," because they must trail after the Federalists who were attacking the Republican governor. Near the end of the year Troup returned to the argument. He affirmed that during the past three years no one had been more vilified in the press than James Jackson. "How shall we apologize to generations, who succeed us, for this vulgar, this despicable and unmerited abuse of a first magistrate—I will tell you, sirs, the history of our own times will plead the apology, . . . that British *influence,* . . . had infused itself into our sentiments." The governor had done well to say that he was loyal to the principles of 1776 and that no one could buy his principles. He should have added that some of his enemies had sold their principles. But Jackson had never betrayed the confidence of the people.

The governor's sensitivity to criticism is indicated in this letter to Colonel Andrew Burns:[13]

You are not Sir, to Judge for me in my Official capacity nor has the Legislature as yet assigned me a Guardian—until that period, I shall undertake to Judge for myself and act as I conceive the interest and advantage of the State may require . . . & am resolved never to be forced by any threats or menace.

At frequent intervals during his public life Jackson became involved in Georgia's relations with the Creek Indians. Some of the bitterness he had felt during the Coleraine conference carried over into his governorship. Early in his first term he wrote Secretary of War James McHenry that Georgia had purchased the Tallassee section from the Creeks but the contract had been abrogated by the federal treaties of New York and Coleraine. He felt that some members of Congress were advocating savages' rights in preference to those of their own civilized citizens. These federal treaties gave too much attention to Indians and too little to the frontier Georgia citizens, he said. Since he had become governor the Indians had taken the initiative by shooting across the Oconee but the Georgians had crossed the river and punished by actions rather than words.

A few days later Jackson notified Benjamin Hawkins, federal Indian Agent, that the Creeks had murdered several white people and also had committed some robberies, and that he might have to declare it an invasion "which must be expensive to the United States, . . . for the Citizens of Georgia are as much the Citizens of the United States & entitled to have protection as any other Citizens. . . ."

In another letter to McHenry he asked, "If Congress cannot send Regulars to protect us, ought they not to permit us to defend ourselves, and they bear the expense—Where Georgia has cost the Union one shilling many others have cost it one pound." He complained that the war department was a year behind in sending the funds appropriated for the Georgia militia and that insufficient regulars had been sent to Georgia. He also requested that a federal galley be used in preventing Spanish vessels from removing the state's slaves to East Florida.

When in 1799 certain citizens of Montgomery County stole two horses from the Cheehaw King, Jackson wrote the justices of the peace of that county that "No man has a right to make law for himself. . . . It is in vain for us to expect redress from the Union . . . if persons are with impunity to . . . disgrace the State. . . ." He also wrote the Cheehaw King that he was angry with his own people, that one of the horses had been captured and would be sent on to the king and Georgia also would pay him for the other one.

In the spring of the following year Jackson became very much perturbed over the actions of William Augustus Bowles, the white adventurer among the Creeks. Bowles read in the papers that the governor had been called a "Jacobin" or French radical and immediately concluded that he was disloyal to the Union. He therefore wrote Jackson that "On being re-elected Director Genl. of Muscogee" he had ordered the Creeks not to fight Georgia and the United States and as a result order had been restored between the two races. In a more quiet time he hoped for a "friendly correspondence." He also had induced the Creeks to declare war on Spain, he claimed, and since Colonel Hawkins had tried to create trouble between the governor and Bowles the latter should have ordered Hawkins shot.

Jackson answered through a proclamation that since Bowles had invited him to enlist against the Spanish it should be ascertained whether Bowles had violated a federal law against enlisting in the services of a foreign power. Unless the accused turned state's evidence within thirty days this law demanded a penalty of not over a thousand dollars or imprisonment for three years. Regardless of whether or not he had violated this law Bowles had threatened the life of a prominent American and should be considered "in no other light than a common plunderer and vagabond and common disturber of the peace of nations." A few days later John King wrote the governor that Bowles had placed spies, recruited from the old Tories, along the St. Mary's River. Fugitive slaves and criminals from Georgia also were collecting in that region, he said, and two Negroes were repeating a rumor that Bowles had letters from Jackson.

Jackson thought it proper to report the situation to the federal state department and he enclosed two letters written by Bowles. One was a general statement which had been circulated in the southern part of Georgia and the other was a personal letter to

Jackson. The governor felt certain that he temporarily had Bowles in check, but the latter might later arouse the Indians against the frontier counties of Camden and Montgomery. Although he would exercise care in the matter, naturally he might need to call out the militia.[14]

In dealing with the Indians Jackson's policy was to prevent bloodshed, to obtain federal aid in extinguishing the Creek titles to the Oconee, Ocmulgee, and Tallassee sections and to cede to the Union the land west of the Chattahoochee on terms favorable to Georgia. With the exception of an occasional brush between the two races Jackson succeeded in keeping the peace and paved the way for the fulfillment of the remainder of the program after his governorship ended.

Some of the secondary writers correctly refer to Jackson as a friend of public education. But like the other governors of his era he recommended little on the subject. In his message to the legislature in January, 1799, he stated that education and literature were at a low ebb in Georgia but he made no specific recommendations for the advancement of either. He expressed regret that Georgia had never had a "classical historian." Although in proportion to its population Georgia lost more wealth and shed more blood in the Revolution than any other state many of its achievements were credited to South Carolina by the historians of that state.[15]

This message also contained a brief criticism of the Alien and Sedition Acts which were passed during the administration of President John Adams but expressed no opinion of the Virginia and Kentucky resolutions which condemned these acts. However, at the request of the governor of Kentucky, Jackson transmitted to the Georgia legislature Jefferson's Kentucky Resolutions.

On Friday, November 22, 1799, the Georgia Senate by a vote of sixteen to four accepted the report of a committee, expressing the hope that the Alien and Sedition Acts would be repealed by Congress so that the legislature would not need to pass any "violent resolutions against them." The committee report further declared that "if the American government had no greater hold upon the people's allegiance and fidelity than those acts it would not rest on that firm foundation which the committee hope and trust it does, and ever will, on the affections of the citizens over whom it presides, rivetted by the acts of a wise administration; . . . ."[16]

On December 4 the House slightly altered the wording of the

resolution and approved it by a vote of twenty-one to sixteen. On the following day the Senate approved the House action.[17]

In November, 1800, Jackson was elected by the legislature to the national Senate by a vote of fifty-eight to nine. He was to succeed James Gunn, whose term would expire the following March.

Jackson's attitude toward public office at this time is indicated in a letter to Baldwin:[18]

You will also have perceived that I have been elected to the Senate . . . , against my will. . . . They all agreed to make way for me if I would offer. This I would not do . . . our Democratic and Antiyazoo Friends determined to run me whether or not, and elected me, 58 votes out of 67. . . .

He finally decided to continue in the governorship until the following March. Early in January, before he surrendered the office, a "respectable number of Republicans" gave him a banquet at Gunn's Savannah Tavern. At this meeting Major William Brown, Colonel Josiah Tattnall, Major Harden, William Bulloch, and Messrs. Glass and Shaffer offered a resolution which was adopted by all present. It declared that the governor had discharged the duties of his trust in "a faithful and upright manner," and defended him against recent criticisms in the press.

Jackson replied that he would have treated his enemies "with silent and most profound contempt" but the "cordial and affectionate manner" in which the committee had praised his administration would induce him to make a reply to "the lowest of Billingsgate abuse" of himself and the legislature. An editorial in the *Museum* commented that such merited expressions of appreciation must stimulate future public servants to realize that "faithful performance of public duty brings the approbation and applaudits of a free and enlightened people."

On the day after the banquet "W" explained in the press that in the previous year "A" and "Z" had defended Jackson because he rewarded each with "a regimental coat and a pair of epaulets." In a later issue of this paper "Anti-Dictator" wrote that he had heard that there were only eighty present at "the very numerous meeting" when Major Brown's committee made its report. Jackson was addressed alternately as governor, major general, and senator and seemed quite willing to fill all three positions simultaneously. "Anti-Dictator" declaimed further,

Do you not wish to play the tyrant, to injure and insult those who dare to differ from you in opinion? . . . Does not your excellency's republicanism consist in opposing every measure of the federal government, both when in and out of congress? . . . perhaps few monarchs ever had more absolute control over a people—You have ascended a giddy height indeed, a dangerous one to republicanism . . . you do not openly tell the people your favorite measures *must* be carried—no, you have only to project the measure, set your engines to work, keep behind the curtain, and let others father the whole.

Criticism of Jackson also had reverberations in the national capital. According to a caustic editorial in the partisan Washington *Federalist,* the governor's legislative message of November, 1800,

. . . is one of the most violent and indecent attacks on the government of the United States, that has ever disgraced this country. . . . It is said the good governor, for some time past, has been laboring under a mental derangement; whether a jury of that state would return him *non compos* it is hard to say.

In answering the criticism of Jackson for refusing to pay the Watkins brothers for their *Digest* of the state laws, "A" sent the press a better defense than Jackson had made. He explained that this *Digest* had printed after each of the other obsolete laws the words "repealed by the act of," giving the year. But the Yazoo Act of 1795 was followed by the statement that "This act has been declared null and void, and the original record thereof directed to be burnt by an act of the legislature, passed on the 13th of February, 1796." Their *Digest* gave only titles of other repealed acts but the Yazoo Act was given in full. "A" concluded that the explanations printed in connection with the two acts were intended to "leave it very problematical, whether that act [of 1796] had a repealing effect or not."

Early in December, 1800, Jackson's thoughts were turning to the completion of his work at the state capital. He stated in an intimate letter to Baldwin:

on the 2 day of March next I shall leave a Government which has occasioned me Waggon loads of abuse—and which Thank God & good Fortune has procured me the approbation of my State and the regard— a few Aristocrats excepted of her Citizens at large—do not suppose it vaunting when I friendly inform you that I know not how I shall leave this place—The tear of gratitude is frequently forced from my eye—

The poor gather round me in crowds—and with the apellation of Father ask me why I desert them—my sweet little Charlotte & my dear lost John rush on my mind too distressed for utterance and I hurry from them wishing myself from the spot or in Uncle Tobys language asleep—I can give them no answer—I do not take this merit to my self alone—My dear partner in the walks of life deserves perhaps the better share—possessed of real and useful—not splendid talents—she does not act the Pharisee; but as privately as she can, indulges her generous turn & disposition—In three Years administration, at least one half my salary has been given & bestowed, between us, on those Objects.

David Emanuel, president of the Georgia Senate, assumed the governorship on March 3, 1801, and on the same day Jackson signed his last official legislative message. As the legislature was not in session at the time it was not read to its members until they assembled again the following November. He expressed to them his gratitude for the many "signal marks" of confidence Georgia had shown him in his military and civil career and he would "leave those honorable testimonies to my children as my last best legacy. . . ."[19]

During his governorship he strengthened his domination of the "Republican" Party in Georgia and defended the sovereignty of the state against the encroachments of President John Adams' administration. He advanced plans for ceding the western lands. An effort was begun to secure less expensive cotton gins and for a revival of inspection laws for the shipment of cotton.

He also secured a victory for certain Georgians over some British loyalists in suits for the recovery of their confiscated estates. The foreign slave trade was prohibited and the state was protected against the illegal entrance of Negroes from Africa and the French Islands. In the troubles with France and Great Britain the state militia was placed on a war footing and the national administration was assured of Georgia's loyal support.

Difficulties with Spain in East Florida were successfully handled with firmness and tact. By a judicious, firm policy he kept the Indians relatively quiet. A new Constitution and a new state seal were adopted. An official digest of the laws was secured. Tax collections were improved. And plans were completed for opening the state university. All in all, Jackson probably rendered greater public service while in the governorship than in any other office.

X

JACKSON'S SWAN SONG IN THE SENATE, 1801-1806

THE NATIONAL government was transferred from Philadelphia to the new village of Washington during the summer of 1800 and President John Adams moved his family into the new White House.

James Jackson resigned the governorship too late to witness the inauguration of President Thomas Jefferson in the new capital on March 4, 1801. The nine months which intervened before he was scheduled to assume his senatorial duties in December were spent at his Cedar Hill plantation. During this time he was the recipient of toasts at banquets held by the Savannah Hibernian Fusileers and by informal groups in Chatham and Bryan counties.

He probably had never visited Washington. In September he wrote to John Milledge (now a House member), who had expressed a wish of "our being together." Jackson suggested that the first one to arrive in Washington should provide lodgings for the other. "Do you carry Mrs. Milledge?" he asked. "The Doctors have forbid my conveying of Mrs. Jackson, and have advised her being on or near the Sea Islands for the Winter."

He took his seat on December 7th, Abraham Baldwin being Georgia's other senator. The new administration of Jefferson seemed to look to Jackson as its chief supporter in Georgia. As a recent historian has expressed it: "There were small farms, . . . and the debtors' suspicions of concentrated wealth. . . . And there to lead them was James Jackson, the idol of the people. . . . He . . . was to strike Titan blows in the cause that Jefferson nationally led."[1]

The patronage was the first task to engage Jackson's attention. In the spring of 1801 he had written Secretary of State James

Madison, reminding him of the fact that they had served together in the lower House and of Jackson's recent election to the Senate "in which I flatter myself our political opinions will not more materially differ than they formerly have done." Hence he felt free to mention matters relating to the politics of his state. Near the close of his term President John Adams had proposed for federal offices certain "corrupt Yazoo men" who were obnoxious to the people of Georgia, the most objectionable being Thomas Gibbons, proposed for the federal district judgeship. This arrogant "old Tory—a British Commissary" would be unable to secure the endorsement of fifty Georgians. Jackson considered the national Judiciary Act of 1801 as "in a state of abeyance, . . . until the next Congress meet. . . ." Jackson recommended William Stephens for either circuit or district judge but opposed the applications of George Walker and Stith for these positions.

On Jackson's recommendation Jefferson appointed David B. Mitchell of Savannah as federal district attorney in Georgia. In 1801 Jefferson wrote Jackson concerning a severe criticism of Mitchell in the Washington *Federalist*. Jackson was an intimate friend of the Mitchell family and he said that the malicious gossip was probably due to the fact that some years previously a young woman living in the home "had a child & his enemies say his but his friends say one of several youths who were often at his house. Mrs. Mitchell has continued loyal and affectionate. . . ." Since the birth of this child Mitchell had served "as mayor, judge of the superior court, and as a member of the Georgia Senate. . . ." A few days later Jefferson replied that he had investigated the matter and was satisfied that Mitchell was worthy of the appointment.

Early in 1803 the *Federalist* also criticized William Stephens, whom Jackson had persuaded Jefferson to name as a federal district judge in Georgia. It also had accused Jackson's friend John Milledge of treason. The sources do not give the bases of these charges but Jackson's defense of them appeared in one of the Washington papers. He also published a presentment by the grand jury of the "sixth circuit court for the district of Georgia," upholding the character of Judge Stephens. He did not know what proof the *Federalist* had of Milledge's treason but he did know that during the Revolution the British confiscated his property as a "rebel counsellor" and that Milledge was with him in the storming of Savannah and in the final campaign under Wayne in Georgia.

Jackson seems to have felt that his leadership of the Jeffersonian Party in Georgia also entitled him to advise the administration upon the general problem of patronage. He wrote Jefferson that "Senator General" Stephen R. Bradley had been called home by the illness of his wife and he hoped the important appointments would be held up until the Vermonter's return so that his influence might be used to line up the doubtful senators for the President's program.[2]

In the spring of 1801 the Georgia press announced that Jackson and Milledge had pushed through Congress a bill to appropriate four thousand dollars for the erection of a lighthouse on the St. Mary's River. Jackson was also deeply interested in obtaining federal aid toward building a southeastern national highway from Danville, Kentucky, to Augusta. Early in 1803 he wrote Governor Milledge that the legislatures of Kentucky, Tennessee, and Georgia had laid before Jefferson resolutions favoring such a road "& he assured me on Saturday when I laid your last dispatches before him, that the Road would be procured, which will prove of immense advantage to our State." Such a road was completed in 1815 but its southern terminus was Athens, Georgia.[3]

In 1801 Jackson was offered the position of "president, pro tempore," of the Senate but he declined the honor in order to render what he considered a more important service in the debates upon the floor. Baldwin was then elected to this position.[4]

Considerable excitement was aroused early in December, 1802, by Jackson's very dramatic departure from Savannah for the next meeting of the Senate. The editor of the now hostile *Museum* rebuked a group whom he sarcastically designated as "exclusive republicans" for desecrating the Sabbath which most citizens look upon as "a day set apart for the honoring of God instead of man." The previous Sunday all had been delighted with the display of the flags of all nations from the ship *Minerva*, moored in the harbor with several cannon on board. But this

> was the signal to begin this Republican and Sunday *fete*. The ship Comet was next seen drifting from the wharf, when the Minerva immediately commenced a . . . cannonading, . . . ; but the ship no sooner discontinued its firing, than another was opened by the revenue cutter, . . . which was equally severe and tremendous. By the time the cutter had exhausted her quantum of the United States powder, . . . they

were surprised by the piercing *moans* of a field piece . . . ; the occasion of this impious breach of the Sabbath . . . was in honor of Gen. JAMES JACKSON, our Senator in Congress, who had taken his passage . . . on . . . the ship Comet for Baltimore. . . .

A second editorial of the *Museum* complained that

the jacobin "Republican," . . . accuse [sic] us of *seeking* a subject for caviling in exposing the absurd proceedings of last Sunday! It is so indeed,—when men of . . . *illustrious fame* which gen. Jackson holds, openly violate those laws which they have been themselves the guardians of—But it is ridiculous to assert that "he was by no means desirous of receiving" such marks of *"honorable regard,"* . . . [when with a look he could] have dispersed the crowd. . . .

The same editor again attacked him in the fall of 1803. Sturges, the state's surveyor-general, had published one of Jackson's personal letters complaining that henceforth he would look after his own interests instead of sacrificing for the public. Jackson's friends had tried to shield him by blaming Sturges for publishing a letter written in confidence while the two were friends and making a selfish use of it when they became estranged. But the editor held that this was the sole means by which Sturges could defend himself against Jackson's accusations of misconduct in office.

He wrote regarding Jackson that "The interests of the state, as well as those of his particular friends, lose their importance with him, the moment they cease to be governed by his will." Men must rise above prejudice or "the post of honor" becomes indeed "a private station." A still later editorial in the *Museum* complained that[5]

It is unfortunate for our great men, who associate themselves on the side of democracy, that there should exist such a diversity of sentiment among them as to make their opinions, when brought face to face, the subject of ridicule for each other. General Jackson says, "*Republics are always ungrateful*" . . . the *National Intelligencer* . . . [says] that republics are "*ungrateful but to those who use them ungratefully.*"

Even in Washington Jackson could not cease thinking of his Georgia enemies. In 1803 he wrote Milledge:[6]

So I have been once more dead in Georgia. My enemies are again deceived, for I am alive & never more hearty. Brown tells me I have been dead in Kentucky; Green of the Mississippi that I was dead there; and Ross that I was dead at Pittsburg; and all stared to see me alive & on the floor. In all the Atlantic States I have also been dead, & I find by a London paper I have been dead in England. I begin to think I am somewhat beyond the Cat's nine lives.

Among Jackson's warmest friends in Georgia were John Milledge and Abraham Baldwin. His correspondence also reveals some intimacy with certain members of Congress, particularly Colonel Parker, Giles of Virginia, Grove, Macon, and Ashe of North Carolina, and Findley, Gregg, Neister, Grey, Weyman, Stein, and Wager.

One of the most heated debates of this Congress was over the repeal of the Judiciary Act of 1801 for reorganizing and enlarging the federal courts.[7] It had been passed about three weeks before the term of John Adams expired. The law, followed by certain "midnight appointments" of Adams just as he was leaving office, added to the national courts several justices, federal attorneys, marshals, and clerks.

Senator Gouverneur Morris of New York spoke in defense of the act. In reply Jackson asserted that he had greater fear of judges than soldiers because soldiers served two-year enlistments, while judges, who could deprive us of our very liberties, served as long as they maintained good behavior. The people had already been burdened by judges under the federal Sedition Law, he felt, and one citizen had been imprisoned for "wishing that the wadding of a gun had been lodged in a certain Presidential part." Fortunately this law had expired with the administration of Adams, and Jackson hoped that it would not be renewed under the "virtuous Jefferson." If it should be renewed the justices could place one half of the people in irons, he claimed, and a Senator had truly said that it had "converted the judges into post-boys."

He also thanked God that "we are not now under the influence of an intolerant clergy" but that church leaders were able to do nothing worse than abuse the President. He also rejoiced that the country was no longer in fear of the judges, their maximum domination in 1801 being limited to attacks upon Secretary of State Madison because he refused to give their credentials to some of the new appointees. Let us not tolerate religious persecution by the clergy nor political violence by the judges, Jackson said. The Constitution merely provides that Congress should establish a Supreme Court but the creation of inferior federal courts is optional. The national circuit and district courts were creatures of Congress and hence it could undo the act which had enlarged them. Surely the creator can control his creatures.

When reactionary Gouverneur Morris dramatically declared that the Senators were expected to "save the people from themselves" Jackson exclaimed, "Good God! Is it possible that I have heard such a sentiment in this body! Rather should I have expected to have heard it sounded from the despots of Turkey, or the deserts of Siberia, ..."

The Federalists suggested that the Jeffersonians seek to remove the judges Congress had added by securing an amendment to the Constitution but Jackson thought that if two thirds of Congress could not agree upon such a revision how could three fourths of the states agree upon it? If the English judges rode the circuit our Supreme Court judges could do the same. How could six judges spend their entire time in Washington and then pass on matters involving a knowledge of each of the states?

The new positions created under Adams made Jackson fear that an army of judges might soon follow. While he admired the private character of Mr. Adams, the trend of his acts was to "attach all powers to a particular person or favorite family." The gentleman from Massachusetts then stated that litigation would increase and there would be need for more judges, but Jackson thought that an increase of courts tempted to litigation. He believed that more business of the inferior federal courts should be referred to the state courts. He vowed that if he thought the repeal of the Judiciary Act would be a victory over the Constitution, as the Federalists had asserted, "I would cut off my hand or cut out my tongue" rather than vote for it, for he loved and respected the Constitution.

The bill repealing the Judiciary Act passed the Senate by a majority of one vote and the House by a majority of twenty-seven. Some of the minor officials who were displaced by the repeal of this act promptly petitioned Congress to restore their offices. A committee to whom the matter was referred recommended that the President have the attorney general take the matter to the courts by filing a "quo warranto" against Richard Bassett, one of the petitioners for the purpose of deciding judicially on their claims. Jackson replied that such action would dishonor the Senate and that the court had no control over the executive or the legislature. "I contend that they are not judges. Their office was taken away and given to others, who are now in the exercise of it," he said. "Let them take their seat upon the bench and see if the Marshall will obey them." By petitioning Congress they proved that that body had the right to decide the matter. The motion to have the matter brought before the court lost by a vote of thirteen to fifteen.

One of the last official acts of President John Adams was the naming of William Marbury, J. P. Hooe, and a man named Ramsay as justices of the peace for "the counties of Washington and Alexandria, in the Territory of Columbia, ..." When Madison, the new secretary of state, refused to sign their commissions Marbury took his case directly to the Supreme Court. The Federalists then sponsored a resolution to give these men a copy of the Senate proceedings of March 2 and 3 relating to their nominations. Jackson spoke of this as an attack upon the Executive. Since the applicants had appealed to the Supreme Court let them make the most of it. He favored surrendering the Senate records only if the House impeached Madison. If this should be done the Senate would serve as the court and he thought it unwise for prospective judges to give out evidence in advance. The petition was denied by another vote of thirteen to fifteen.

Later Marbury lost his case before the Court, its justices deciding that as the Constitution did not give them original jurisdiction in such cases they would kill that clause in the Judiciary Act which permitted the new appointees to approach the Court directly. This was the first federal, or state, act which the Supreme Court declared unconstitutional.

Jackson was chairman of a committee which was instructed to inquire into the expediency of extending the transportation of the public mail by stages. In a public letter to Postmaster General Gideon Granger he asked whether the act to alter and extend the post roads had been carried out and if not, what circumstances caused its failure. He also asked if the carriage of the mail had been of public utility both as to the mail and the conveyance of the traveling citizens. He also wished to know if at the expiration of the present contract it would be the policy of the government to arrange for stages and covered wagons to carry the mail at the owner's expense, if the intercourse would support it, if it was expedient to extend to other roads the carriage of the mail, and whether private or public control was preferable.

Granger replied in two public letters. He advised an extension of mail contracts an additional seven years instead of the five allowed him by law. He also advised doubling the cost instead of increasing it by the lawful one-third. He had asked for bids on two routes from Fayetteville, North Carolina, one through Charleston to Savannah and another through Columbia and Augusta to Louisville, Georgia. The bids received would carry out this plan except that it would be impossible to get the mail to Louisville. He wrote that the increasing number of newspapers added to the volume of the mail but the combination of mail and passengers was profitable to the owners of the stages and a convenience to the traveling public.[8]

During the five years of his second term in the Senate Jackson differed with the Executive on the question of removing the Indians from the Southeast. Jefferson sought to do with persuasion what Jackson wanted done by force. However, the latter showed considerable patience in dealing with the President in this matter. Early in 1802 he stated on the Senate floor that "as a political person, I am no more for Thomas Jefferson than for John Adams. When he acts, according to my opinion, right, I will support him; when wrong, oppose him; . . . ."

In an address to the Senate late in 1803 he said that the exalted character and good deeds of Jefferson defied the "shallow railings and little-minded attacks of his enemies" and "rendered him dear to his fellow citizens," making them "the happiest people that ever existed." The people had "the man of their choice; . . . . And small and obscure as the *little corner* called Georgia is," it was willing to go to war in defense of the Constitution. In another Senate debate he referred to Jefferson as a great and good man. He complained that under John Adams' administration Georgia's rights were violated: while Governor of Georgia he could hardly get an answer from Secretary of State Timothy Pickering; state rights were disregarded and the principles of the Revolution were topics of reproach. But "We looked to the author of the Declaration of Independence—he has not disappointed us." In another speech he stated that he was happy and trusted all were happy while Jefferson was President. "But . . . we may have a Buonaparte, ..."

He was on sufficiently intimate terms with the President in 1805 to make him a loan or sell him some property, for he wrote,[9]

Genl Jackson begs leave to remind the President of the United States of the bill drawn on him for $194—some cents and given the President last Saturday—as the hurry of the session and no doubt increased business of the President may tend to prevent attention to such small matters without improper interruption. . . .

In planning to reduce the national debt while foregoing the revenue from the excise Jefferson was fortunate in naming Albert Gallatin as secretary of the treasury. Jackson supported Gallatin's moves for economy and was named chairman of one of the military committees. Early in 1805 he reported a bill on the military peace establishment. Several amendments were offered but most of them were lost and on a motion by Jackson the others were referred to a special committee composed of Samuel White, Robert Wright, and John Quincy Adams. The latter wrote of this debate that

It was impossible to attempt any amendments without raising General Jackson's temper. For he, having been chairman of the former committee, naturally concluded that it had come from their hands with the last polish of perfection, and would of course feel irritated at any presumption of improving it further. . . . [I had] to encounter this tempest, or suffer the bill to pass . . . into the world with all its imperfections on its head.

When the bill became a law it reduced the total military budget although provision was made for a military academy at West Point. Jackson later claimed that by reducing the military forces Jefferson and Gallatin saved the treasury nine hundred thousand dollars a year.[10]

In March, 1802, he spoke in support of a bill to repeal the excise. He felt that this form of taxation was impolitic and impious, claiming that it was sectional, for New England made no cider and hence was not taxed while an excise was placed on all the peach orchards to the southward. He believed that the recommendation of the virtuous Jefferson was sufficient ground for repeal and if the revenue proved inadequate bank and other stock could be taxed. Tracy replied that when New England's cider was turned into brandy it was subject to the excise. The excise was repealed by a strict party vote.[11]

Jackson did not see a dangerous disunity in the country unless it were the Whigs against the Tories. He was amused at the stress on the various struggles of Federalists versus Republicans, large versus small states, Eastern versus Southern states, and Eastern versus Western states. He thought that some might even wish to speak of "the rats against the anti-rats." In another speech he sought to calm the fears of the small states, saying that the large states probably had too many differences among themselves ever to get together on any program. On account of its large public domain Georgia had usually voted with the large states but it had never asked the nation to consider one of its men for the presidency.

Jackson supported a bill to amend the Constitution with a view to limiting the presidency to eight years but it failed to pass the Senate. In the debate over this bill there were occasional expressions of jealousy over the alleged dictatorship of Virginia. He demanded to know the reasons for jealousy of Virginia, claiming that it was to Virginia the country owed the Revolution, for it acted first in a resolve for freedom. Virginia gave us George Washington, Thomas Jefferson, and the Constitution. It also took the initiative in calling the Constitutional Convention, he reminded the Senators.

Some light is thrown upon Jackson's influence in the Senate by a statement to that body by Senator Jonathan Dayton who thought it unrealistic to expect all the members to ignore the distinction between the large and small states. Jackson could do this because he had obtained from Congress more than one million dollars for Georgia, Dayton claimed. If there was a single member who had more warmly, ably, perseveringly, and successfully contended for the rights and interests of his particular state than all the others Jackson was that person. He replied to Dayton that he had only intended to vote, "but the profusion of compliments heaped upon him for merely discharging his duty, demanded some return." He explained that any success he had attained was largely due to the fact that he conscientiously acted on the understanding that he was sent to Congress to watch the interests of his state.[12]

He supported Jefferson to the full on the purchase and government of Louisiana. When Spain in 1802 withdrew from American ships the right of deposit at the mouth of the Mississippi granted in the Treaty of 1795, the Federalists urged violent action but the President preferred the more patient plan of diplomatic exchange. Jackson's speeches in 1803 revealed his active displeasure over the lofty spirit in which Federalists James Ross and Samuel White boasted that during the first twelve years of the new Union no injury to the nation was endured without energetic opposition by Presidents Washington and John Adams. To this statement Jackson queried, "did not France capture our vessels and imprison our seamen? Did Washington appeal to arms? No, sir. Mr. Adams then came into the administration. Did he appeal to arms? No, sir, he sent a new set of Ministers who were received and who made the memorable treaty which was ratified."

Jackson had experienced enough of the frontier life to understand the violent opposition of the West to the changed attitude of Spain. Early in 1803 he made this report to Governor Milledge of Georgia:

Mr. Munroe was appointed Minister extraordinary to France and Spain on the New Orleans business, and to purchase the Floridas if possible. Negotiation will be first tried in every State to preserve peace; if it fails, what must ensue I need not tell you. The Western people are resolved & prepared to force a free passage of the Mississippi.

He spoke successfully against a Senate resolution which would have authorized the President to call out the militia to force Spain to renew the right of deposit. His sympathy was with the Mississippi and Ohio people but he felt sure that war at New Orleans would spread to the St. Mary's and he thought peaceful means should have a fair trial. He then quoted a letter from Georgia approving James Monroe's appointment to iron out the matter. He insisted that the ships of the United States were still using the mouth of the Mississippi.

He sought wisdom in this problem from a custom followed by ancient Rome. Before declaring war its Senators through religious ceremonies sought to learn whether the cause was just. If it was found to be just they next decided whether it was good policy. Unless both justice and policy called for war their decision was for peace. On the question of deposits justice favored America but policy taught that there was no immediate necessity for force, Jackson said. Through patience common ground could be found and the United States and Spain would remain at peace. But "God and nature have destined New Orleans and the Floridas to belong to this great and rising empire." In this matter he wished our government to show prudence as our advance guard and determination as our rear guard.

Jackson did not share the feeling of many that the West would revolt over the issue of deposits. He assured the Senate that neither Georgia nor the West would make an alliance with France under a despotic Napoleon, with "freedom-lacking," decadent Spain, nor with England burdened with debt. Our Revolutionary veterans would remain loyal and there were more of them in the West than in the coastal states combined. He was certain that Spain would eventually renew the right of deposit and that it would not support any violence on the part of its citizens in Louisiana.

In another speech Jackson declared "Our bond of union has been styled by the politicians of Europe, a rope of sand; . . ." and we never ought to lose sight of an old Revolutionary motto on our "rattlesnake" money, "United We Stand, Divided We Fall." The bill calling for force in regaining the right of deposit was defeated by a margin of four votes.

When it was announced in 1803 that Napoleon had agreed to sell the whole of Louisiana the Federalists who in 1802 had wanted America to use violence against Spain now suddenly became sensitive to Spanish rights. "Spain considers herself injured by this treaty," Samuel White asserted. Others questioned whether Spain had given France a legal title to Louisiana. The Louisiana Treaty was ratified by substantial majorities in each house in October of 1803 and as chairman of the "Louisiana Committee," Jackson reported an appropriation bill which proposed to "create a stock" of $11,250,000 to carry into effect the treaty. In supporting this proposal he asked, "Is not, I ask, the King of Spain's proclamation, declaring the cession of Louisiana to France, and his orders to his Governor . . . to deliver it to France, a title?" This appropriation bill passed the Senate by a vote of twenty-six to five.

Jackson reported a successful bill entitled "An act making provision for the payment of claims of citizens of the United States on the Government of France, ..." Also, he voted with the majority for bills applying the tariff to Louisiana and authorizing Jefferson to take over the government of that territory. Later some of the Federalists vainly sought to have Congress postpone the date for setting up a territorial government in Louisiana but Jackson took the position that since Congress had already decided to purchase this territory, delay in setting up a government might reveal that the French were sick of their bargain and might give them an opportunity to break it altogether. The frontier people would listen to reason and respect the laws of their country, he said. If Spain could be kept amicable the Indians might be persuaded to move to Louisiana, especially since ploughs and looms had no charms for them.

Fortunately England had officially approved the treaty and therefore could not interfere. If Jefferson had forcibly taken the territory in 1802 we would have spent ten times fifteen million dollars in a war with Spain and if Spain in 1803 should fight us over the Louisiana Purchase we would win the Floridas. The people of the Floridas, most of whom were Irish and Creoles, "pant for" the freedom enjoyed in the United States. The Irish were disaffected and the Creoles were the dregs of mankind. A war with Spain would open for us the road to Mexico but he hoped that Spain would "behave" and this road would be closed to America for all time. Furthermore this was an executive matter and should be left to the President.

Europeans would probably flock to the United States, Jackson predicted, and the country would soon be well populated all the way to the Mississippi and in the southern part of the Louisiana Purchase. Many of these would settle between the Chattahoochee and Mississippi rivers. He disagreed with those who thought that Louisiana would remain a howling wilderness where no civilized foot would ever tread and he prophesied that it would eventually become the seat of science and civilization.[13] In 1804 a law was enacted by the government to prohibit the importation of slaves into Louisiana Territory. Jackson passionately and vociferously opposed this measure. According to Senator John Quincy Adams,[14] "The discussion of this question has developed characters. Jackson has opposed the section *totis viribus,* in all its shapes, and was very angry when the question was taken—called twice for an adjournment, in which they would not indulge him, and complained of unfairness."

Early in 1804 many of the senators became so dissatisfied with their lack of domestic comforts and social intercourse that an unsuccessful bill was introduced to remove the capital to Baltimore. Jackson opposed this bill "in terms of appropriate energy." The compromise which had originally brought the capital to the Potomac had cost the assumption and funding at par of state debts amounting to twenty-one million dollars and the proposed removal would necessitate indemnifying the property holders of Washington for two and a half million dollars spent upon public improvements. After meeting for a year and a half in New York

City, Congress in July of 1790 had decided upon Philadelphia as a temporary site for the capital. This was with the understanding that in 1800 a permanent site would be selected.

"It was not then imagined that the government ought to be travelling about from post to pillar, according to the prevalence of this or that party or faction. All the ideas of that day were hostile to this wheelbarrow kind of Government. . . ." Jackson hoped that his children's children would not live to see it happen but after some centuries the country's population would probably extend beyond the Mississippi and the seat of government would then be moved to its banks.[15]

In December, 1805, Jackson made his last speech in Congress. He seconded and spoke on a bill which proposed an embargo on our trade with Santo Domingo as long as it was in rebellion against France. During the latter part of John Adams' administration our freighters were armed in order to protect our profitable carrying trade with all the West Indian islands of France, Spain, and England. In 1800 the United States promised France that we would cease forcing our trade upon its rebellious colonies but in 1805 certain of our shippers were ignoring this agreement, particularly in Santo Domingo. Jackson prefaced his remarks on the embargo bill against our trade with Santo Domingo by a general statement on international relations. He then accused certain Americans of having aided the French under General Charles Victor Leclerc in crushing the rebellion in Haiti and Santo Domingo in 1802. He reported that "in a private company" at his boarding house a French general had remarked that plans had been made, based on the expectation of French victory, to send the rebellious slaves to the southern parts of the United States.

"This was a melancholy subject for South Carolina and Georgia," he continued, "and one of those brigands introduced into the Southern States was worse than an hundred . . . blacks from Africa, and more dangerous to the United States." He had seen a whole fleet of vessels at Newcastle, Delaware, "bound to St. Domingo, to force a trade which even captains of vessels, true Americans, cried shame on." We should first stop our vessels from injuring other nations, he said. Then we could strike at others who insulted us by committing depredations on our commerce. He had seen an unofficial letter from General Marie Louis Ferrand, "governor" of Santo Domingo, which complained to the French government and indirectly laid the blame upon the United States for allowing our vessels to force an exchange of goods upon his rebellious colony. This situation was "a serious bugbear" to Jackson and he felt that if we even indirectly recognized the Negro insurrectionists in Haiti we should logically recognize the independence of the hundreds of Negro refugees from Georgia and South Carolina in the Okefenokee Swamp of southern Georgia.

The bill, as finally enacted in February, 1806, merely required American shipowners to give bond that they would use their arms solely in self-defense and in getting their ships back home. Jackson's failure to vote was probably due to illness. He missed a few committee meetings during the latter part of 1805 and after December 20 he did not attend the Senate sessions.

After an illness of three months, and in his forty-ninth year, he died in Washington as the spring day was breaking on the nineteenth of March, 1806.[16]

XI

HIS PROPER NICHE IN HISTORY

❖ • ❖ • ❖ • ❖ • ❖ • ❖ • ❖ • ❖ • ❖ • ❖ • ❖ • ❖ • ❖ • ❖ • ❖ • ❖ • ❖

ON MARCH 19, 1806, John Quincy Adams made this notation in his *Memoirs*: "Mr. Jackson, one of the Senators from the State of Georgia, died this morning about four o'clock. His disorder was the dropsy. Immediately on the meeting of the Senate this morning, his colleague, Mr. Baldwin, with tears in his eyes, gave notice of the event, and expressed his hope that the Senate would take the orders usual on such occasions."

Thomas Hart Benton stated that it was not customary at this time for Congress to pronounce

> funeral eulogiums over deceased members. . . . Attending the funeral, and wearing the badge of mourning, were deemed the adequate honor; and well worthy was General James Jackson of it. He was a man of marked character, . . . brave—hating tyranny, oppression, and meanness in every form; the bold denouncer of crime in high as well as in low places; a ready speaker, and as ready with his pistol as his tongue, and involved in many duels on account of his hot opposition to criminal measures. The defeat of the Yazoo fraud was the most signal act of his legislative life, for which he paid the penalty of his life—dying of wounds received in the last of the many duels which his undaunted attacks upon that measure brought upon him.

The Senate and House passed resolutions of esteem and voted to attend the funeral, wear the badge of mourning for one month, and pay the funeral expenses.

The following day Jackson was buried at Rock Creek Cemetery, four miles from the national capital. A Washington paper spoke of the procession of the military, the Masons, the members of Congress and the executive department, and the citizens. The inscription on the marble slab was written by John Randolph, who in the plastic years of his youth had formed a high regard for the character of Jackson. After five years of association with him in Congress he was reported to have said that in some degree his own life had its model in Jackson's. In 1832 Jackson's ashes were reinterred in the Congressional Cemetery in Washington.[1]

Georgia was not to be outdone in expressing its appreciation of Jackson. Senator Baldwin expressed his admiration in a letter to Governor Milledge and Brigadier General David B. Mitchell of the first brigade of the Georgia militia ordered his subordinate officers to wear the symbols of mourning for three months. The regimental corps of the Chatham County Regiment was also ordered to assemble on May 10 and participate in appropriate military ceremonies. The Savannah City Council resolved to dress in mourning for one month and to attend the funeral in a body. The Georgia Grand Lodge of Masons ordered all the members of its Savannah lodges to meet in their room in the Filature on April 10 and to march in Masonic procession to the historic Presbyterian Church for the purpose of honoring the memory of "our deceased late *Right Worshipful Grand Master,* Brother General James Jackson."

Only the families of John Wereat and Samuel Farley could have been expected to remember the quiet entry into Savannah, thirty-two years previously, of the lad James Jackson. But many remembered that twenty-four years earlier they had cheered the dashing young lieutenant colonel as he led the advance into the city with his ragged, victorious veterans hard upon the heels of the departing British. These and others now joined the family in the slow, solemn procession to the church to do him the last honors as neighbor, Revolutionary leader, major general of militia, state legislator, congressman, senator, governor, and political reformer.

Thomas U. P. Charlton had already begun to assemble material for a biography of his close friend. Who then could more appropriately deliver the "eulogium"? While Charlton noted with pleasure the presence of some former enemies of Jackson, he was "apprehensive of awakening feelings, which ought to slumber on this occasion, ..." The audience was also reminded of the attendance of many of Jackson's Revolutionary veterans who were still "willing to go to the world's end with him." The address was remarkably free from extravagant praise, both the vices and virtues of the deceased being noted, although the virtues naturally received greater emphasis.

Following the memorial exercises at the church, "the procession moved to the Burial Ground, and the Funeral Service being performed by The Revd. Doctor Best, the Coffin was committed to the Earth with Masonic Rites, and the Usual Military Honors." There is no explanation as to why a coffin and the formal committal service were used when the body was not present.

Extravagantly eulogistic statements were made by Governor Milledge, the Savannah press, the editor of the *National Intelligencer*, the legislature, and the Tammany Society of Savannah.[2] Our best authority on this period, the late Dr. Ulrich Bonnell Phillips,[3] wrote that "His principles were high and his convictions strong. Like many men of his temperament, he could see only one side of a question. . . . And yet withal Jackson was a most attractive man to those with whom he held friendly intercourse. . . . And above all he was a Georgian with his whole heart. His traits of character are important because from conscious imitation or from the . . . influence of the same environment the same traits were possessed in large degree by the successive leaders in Georgia for decades after his death."

The witnesses to Jackson's will were Thomas Whitefield, Ebenezer Stark, and Archibald Mackay. It probably pleased the ladies by stating in part, "I . . . desire that my Wife . . . [marry], if she can meet an honest, worthy man, deserving of her regard; . . . ." The beneficiaries were his wife; his four sons; "my Dear Brother Doctor Henry Jackson," who received a "child's part"; his mother-in-law, Mrs. Sophia Young; his wards, Thomas, George, and William Whitefield; and "my Friend Thomas de Mattos Johnson." Others mentioned were his "Father in law, the late honble William Young," and his late brother-in-law, "Doctor James Box Young . . . , The only trace of their, or either of their blood, being to be found in my family—"

Jackson ordered that his estate be kept undivided for three years after his death. He also asked that the Cedar Hill plantation be kept intact until the death of his wife or until 1817 if she died before that year, at which time he wished it sold in lots of from one half to five acres at a "Public outcry."[4]

If some indication of a state's evaluation of its public men is seen in the memorials which perpetuate their memory then historically minded Savannah seems to have largely forgotten its own son. Jackson's name is not associated with any object within the city. Three miles below the city, however, on the south side of the Savannah River the federal government in 1808 began the erection of Fort Jackson, named in honor of James Jackson. Between 1815 and 1848 Congress made several appropriations for this work and in the latter year a sum of twenty thousand dollars was set aside for its completion. When Georgia seceded from the Union a group of Savannah men seized this fort but it was of no service to the Confederacy or to Georgia and was evacuated when Sherman took the city late in 1864. It was never fully completed and in 1921 the war department recommended its disposal. On June 9, 1925, it was sold to the city of Savannah "for park purposes only."

Other Georgia memorials to Jackson are Jackson County, the General James Jackson Chapter of the Daughters of the American Revolution in Valdosta; and the town of Jackson, the county seat of Butts County; and as Georgia's citizens have "never been slow to appreciate worth or to render grateful homage to the greatness of her sons," in 1858 the governor complied with a request of the legislature and had "a competent artist," John Maien, paint a full-length portrait of Jackson which is now on display in the rotunda of the state Capitol in Atlanta.[5]

A difficult responsibility devolves upon the author of this work of placing Jackson in his proper niche in history.

During his Revolutionary service Jackson was a good soldier. Among his handicaps during the Revolution were his extreme youth, the fact that his service was in the state militia, and the fact that Georgia was the youngest, poorest, and most exposed of the states. His courage, alertness, initiative, inspiring leadership, and steadfastness won the high regard of his superiors—Pickens, Morgan, Wayne, and Greene. His rapid rise in six years from the rank of private to that of lieutenant colonel at the age of twenty-four gave him some right to be "pleased with myself." He never at one time had more than a few hundred men under his command but in the limited sphere to which he was assigned he made an excellent record, especially in the battles of Blackstock, Cowpens, Augusta, and Ogeechee.

Because of prolonged absences from home his success as a planter was not phenomenal. But the financial returns indicate that his legal career was brilliant and unexcelled by any Georgian of his time. He was also a "prince of duelists." His enemies and some of his friends thought him conceited but those who favored his policies believed that his performance atoned for his high self-regard.

He was too close to the Indian problem to have anything other than a local view. He possibly justified bribery, trickery, and force in getting the Indians to surrender their lands. The only time he showed any marked moderation in dealing with the Indians was during his governorship. Roger Williams, William Penn and all the Quakers, Oglethorpe, Washington, John Adams, Jefferson, and some others treated the Indians as human beings but they were the exception to the general rule in the colonial and early national periods. Most of those who criticized Jackson's inhumanity were no longer exposed to the menace of Indian attacks.

Jackson's political stature gradually grew from the time of his entrance into the legislature. During the last decade of his life his enemies grudgingly conceded that his will was the political will of Georgia. However, he was not a dictator, but a dominant popular leader. The elaborate memorial service in Savannah, three weeks after his death, was only one among many evidences that a very large majority in the state endorsed his forthright public measures.

In Congress his very early advocacy of democratic simplicity, strict construction of the Constitution, state rights, a low tariff, and the welfare of the common man helped erect the foundations upon which Jefferson later built the Republican or Democratic Party. He was the pioneer Jeffersonian in the House. While his sectionalism was pronounced it was not unique.

When Jefferson inaugurated the "Republican" regime in 1801 Jackson was a member of the majority party. He expressed pride in the fact that Jefferson treated him as a friend. He was a "great admirer" of the President and remarked that Jefferson's "exalted character" needed no defense. He believed others shared his happiness under the rule of "the virtuous Jefferson." Now that the country had an executive who was devoted to the interests of all the people and fairly just towards the rights of the states the Georgia people were willing to go to war in defense of the country, he felt.

The national administration considered Jackson a strong, loyal Jeffersonian. Since he dominated the politial affairs of Georgia from 1796 to 1806 Jefferson looked chiefly to him to keep the Georgia leaders in line with his national program. The few political appointments made by the administration in Georgia during this period were based partly on Jackson's recommendations. In the repeal of the Judiciary Act of 1801 he rendered constructive service to the administration. His support for the building of "the Southeastern Road" and several lighthouses shows that he supported the principle of internal improvements.

Jefferson's program for expanding the national domain also received his enthusiastic support. He did active committee work and participated at length in the Senate debates in connection with the purchase and government of Louisiana. There were no clashes between Jackson and Jefferson except in their proposals for expelling the Creeks and Cherokees and in disposing of Georgia's western lands. Even on these issues Georgia's leaders were much more harmonious with Jefferson than they had been with Washington and John Adams. Nothing ever so aroused Jackson's prejudice as the Yazoo fraud and those who knew best his bitterness on this subject were astonished when in 1802 he consented to the use of approximately a tenth of the Yazoo lands to satisfy the claims of "the innocent purchasers."

When John Randolph of Roanoke broke with Jefferson over compromising the Yazoo claims and other issues involving extreme state rights Jackson never wavered in his loyalty to the President. Jefferson's appeasement of the Northern Yazoo purchasers involved nothing more than a tactful effort to strengthen his party in the North and while Jackson never approved the compromise proposed by the administration he left much of the opposition to other Georgians and to Randolph.

Jackson heartily disliked the Alien and Sedition Acts passed when John Adams was President; but we find no suggestion anywhere that he ever approved, even as anti-Federalist propaganda, the radical state rights "principles of '98" expressed in Madison's "Virginia Resolutions" and Jefferson's "Kentucky Resolutions," and later in Randolph's "Quids." During the Republican era Jackson had far more sympathy for the rights of the states than Hamilton and John Adams had shown, but with Jefferson in the presidency he gave hearty support to that statesman's moderately nationalistic program.

In the excise debate he manifested a blind loyalty to his chief. The embargo issue did not receive serious consideration until after Jackson's death. During the "Republican" era Jackson considered

His Proper Niche in History 189

himself a free lance but since their policies were so nearly alike it was easy for him to affirm independence of Jefferson.

A review of his entire political life shows that in the Confederation period, 1781-1789, Jackson was a conservative, mild nationalist. During 1789, one of the twelve years of Federalist domination, he welcomed the strong powers enjoyed by the President and Congress but Washington's friendliness to the Indians and the persecution of certain Republicans by the courts during John Adams' administration aroused in him a fear that the Federalists planned to establish a centralized autocracy. During the rest of the Federalist era, 1790 to 1801, he assumed a strong state rights position. From 1798 to 1801 he used his powers as governor to support the administration of Adams in its hostility towards France but sought to protect Georgia's sovereignty from the encroachments of the national government. Then in 1801 when the President of his choice took over the national government he resumed the attitude of a mild nationalist.

Jackson's chief achievement was the rescinding of the Yazoo sale. Most of the American newspapers and some in Europe discussed this controversy. Jackson was given most of the credit or most of the blame for the action of the 1796 legislature. Cutting out the fraudulent Yazoo transactions from the state's official records and publicly burning them were undignified acts of rashness and Jackson kept the issue alive too long after it had been settled.

According to the loose-construction view of the national Constitution held by the Federalist Supreme Court of his day, Jackson erred in persuading the legislature of 1796 to pass an "unconstitutional" act "impairing the obligation of contracts." But in this phrase limiting the powers of the states, the Constitutional fathers probably never intended to bolster a fraudulent legislative contract. The evils they were seeking to avoid were the enactment of debtor and stay laws, whereby mortgages and other honest pledges would be bypassed. The Federalist justices of the national courts, however, minimized human rights when they conflicted with property rights, regardless of the ethics of the legislative contracts by which legal titles were obtained.

If a contract between individuals is proved fraudulent the courts pronounce it void. Unless there are innocent purchasers involved the same practice should hold in legislative contracts. Having promptly published the fraudulent character of the Yazoo sale the Georgia legislature felt ethically justified in annulling it. Some of the secondary purchasers of the Yazoo scrip petitioned Congress for aid as "innocent purchasers" but a Congressional committee reported that the title of the claimants could not be supported.[6] Since their scrip plainly stated that no legal titles to the lands were guaranteed there were no "innocent purchasers." The purchasers were speculators and deserved no protection. Hence Congress should have replied that the only remuneration they deserved or would receive was the money originally paid and this Georgia had offered to refund.

The only persons in this controversy who deserved sympathy were the innocent sufferers, the Georgia people. Jackson believed that the prejudiced Federalist jurists would "construe" the Constitution as legalizing the fraudulent Yazoo sale and he took the only course which could secure justice—the rescinding of the sale by another legislature.

As many worthy Americans during the great depression of the 1930s justified certain emergency state laws which postponed the foreclosure of mortgages until honest debtors could give and receive justice, so the rescinding of the Yazoo sale may be ethically justified as an imperative act of justice and public honor. Since in 1796 the Supreme Court had not yet decided that the fraudulent Yazoo sale was a legal contract and that even fraudulent legislative contracts are inviolable, some legal justification may be asserted for Jackson's advocacy of the Rescinding Act. In ceding to the Union approximately fifty million acres in 1802 Georgia received more than twice the amount paid by the Yazoo companies in 1795 and eventual freedom from the state's Indian controversies. Hence Jackson was justified in reluctantly conceding that the United States might grant part of this land to the secondary purchasers.

His position in this controversy proves false the cynical opinion continuously relayed from generation to generation that every politician has his price. If honesty of purpose in political action is a reality, no one can rob Jackson of the credit of seeking the public welfare when he resigned the highest office his state could give to fight the Yazoo fraud. The struggle over rescinding the sale would either make or break him and his stand called for the highest degree of physical and moral courage. Only a virile personality can turn political suicide into political triumph and transform the terms "integrity" and "good politics" from antonyms into synonyms. His stamina put fear into the hearts of un-

His Proper Niche in History

principled politicians and there was relatively little corruption in the state's public life while his example remained green in the memory of its citizens. The unanimous voices of tradition and some Georgia historians affirm that in oratorical powers, keenness of mind, political leadership, and integrity Jackson was not surpassed by any Georgian of his era. But some of these voices do no violence to the sources in admitting his sensitivity, egotism, arrogance, turbulence, sectionalism, and intolerance. His contemporary critics were chiefly the corrupt Yazoo men and the aristocratic Federalists. In his numerous Congressional addresses he often was too emotional and too blunt, but the facts that his opponents sought to answer him and that most of the historians who deal at length with our national history from 1789 to 1806 refer to his speeches indicate that he was an active, colorful, and effective member of Congress.

Although most of the reactionary, aristocratic writers who deal with his era react unfavorably to his eccentricities and decided democratic views, most of the objective historians overlook or are amused by his erratic, overbearing temperament. The interpretation of most historians and more particularly the records of Congress show that he probably had sufficient influence to merit a place just without the inner circle of the most important statesmen in the administrations of Washington, John Adams, and Jefferson.

Since it does no violence to the opinions of either the friends or the foes who knew him best perhaps it would be accurate and just to take him at his own estimate in the very strange statements in the closing paragraph of his autobiography. In this passage Jackson judicially weighed his vices and virtues and through imagination stood on the far side of death and declared in the third person approximately what others would write in his obituaries:

"In public life he was patriotic and zealous for the preservation of those liberties America had so perseveringly obtained—Strenuous against the least invasion of the people [sic] rights and totally opposed to any measure of either Titles or otherwise which might endanger true Republicanism—In private life he was affectionate to his Family and kind to his servants; his slaves lived & were clothed much better than those of most of his Neighbors—The Mechanics loved him for his punctuality in payment and the poor were never dismissed from his door empty handed—He had however (& where is the Mortal without them) his Foibles—He had a sensibility to extreme and frequently took amiss from even his Friends what was never intended as such—which rendered him frequently unhappy in his disposition and he gave too much way to violent passions which for the moment led him too far—Reason however soon resumed her sway & his natural good temper returned with all but himself with himself he would be angry for having been so with others.—On the whole we may safely conclude that his good qualities far exceeded those of a contrary tendency and that he is a real loss to the community who sincerely lament him."

NOTES

CHAPTER I

1. Thomas U. P. Charlton, *The Life of Major General James Jackson,* Part I, 43, 44n., hereinafter referred to as Charlton, *Jackson*. Clement and Honor Jackson, the great-great-grandparents of James Jackson, were the parents of Abraham, who was born August 8, 1678. Abraham married Rebecca and on October 2, 1700, to them was born Jabez. Jabez married Sarah Waldron and on September 1, 1730, they became the parents of James the elder. On August 30, 1755, James the elder married Mary Webber and they became the parents of James Jackson, the subject of this sketch. Jackson's brothers were John, Abraham, and Henry. Henry Jackson taught at the University of Georgia. "A Genealogical Chart . . .," a page preceding the title-page, Charlton, *Jackson*.
2. "Character of J. J. drawn by Himself," *Georgia Historical Quarterly,* XXXVII (1953), 156, hereinafter referred to as Jackson, *Autobiography*. This magazine has published the papers of Jackson. Unless otherwise indicated, the author of this work used the original Jackson papers which may be seen in the Georgia Historical Society Library at Savannah.
3. Sophia Lee Foster, comp., *Revolutionary Reader,* 79; W. J. Northen, *Men of Mark in Georgia,* I, 190.
4. E. Merton Coulter, *A Short History of Georgia,* 112, 113, hereinafter referred to as Coulter, *History*. Cf. Allen D. Candler, ed., *The Revolutionary Records of the State of Georgia,* I, 119, 127, 137, 277, II, 13, 23, hereinafter referred to as *Rev. Rec. of Ga.;* Biographical Directory of the American Congress, 1774-1927, 1142; George White, *Statistics of the State of Georgia,* 336, 337, hereinafter referred to as White, *Statistics*.
5. William Bordley Clarke, *Early and Historic Freemasonry of Georgia,* 66.
6. William Bacon Stevens, *A History of Georgia,* II, 133-36, hereinafter referred to as Stevens, *History*.
7. Charlton, *Jackson,* 72; "Communication," *Columbian Museum,* April 9, 1806, hereinafter referred to as *Museum*.
8. Stevens, *History,* II, 163-67.
9. Charles C. Jones, Jr., *The History of Georgia,* II, 307, hereinafter referred to as Jones, *History*. Cf. Stevens, *History,* II, 171, 172.
10. Charlton, *Jackson,* 13-16; Jackson, *Autobiography;* White, *Statistics,* 337; A. H. Chappell, *Miscellanies of Georgia, Historical, Biographical, Descriptive,* Part III, 7; O. A. Park, *History of Georgia,* 67.
11. Charlton, *Jackson,* 16, 17; Jackson, *Autobiography;* Annals of Congress, 7th Cong., 2 sess., 149, hereinafter referred to as *Annals*.

12. "Miscellaneous Papers of James Jackson, 1781-1798," *Ga. Hist. Quar.*, XXXVII (1953), 68, 69; Coulter, *History*, 144-47; Thomas Gamble, *Annals of Savannah*, 39, 40, hereinafter referred to as Gamble, *Annals*.
13. Edward McCrady, *History of South Carolina in the Revolution, 1775-1780*, 820-23.
14. B. J. Lossing, *The Pictorial Field-Book of the Revolution*, II, 652, 653n; L. L. Mackall, "Edward Langworthy," *Ga. Hist. Quar.*, VII (1923), 15; J. W. Fortescue, *History of the British Army*, III, 363; C. Stedman, *The History of the Origin, Progress, and Termination of the American War*, II, 229, 230.
15. Hammond, "The Battle of Blackstocks," Joseph Johnson, in *Traditions and Reminiscences Chiefly of the American Revolution in the South*, 503, 524.
16. McCrady, *Hist. of S. C. in the Rev., 1775-1780*, 831-33.
17. Charlton, *Jackson*, 24, 25n.; R. W. Gibbes, comp., *Documentary History of the American Revolution. . . .*, 17; Lieut.-Col. [Sir Banastre] Tarleton, *History of the Campaigns of 1780 and 1781. . . .*, 215-22; C. Stedman, *History of the Origin, Progress, and Termination of the American War*, 323, 324; J. W. Fortescue, *A History of the British Army*, III, 369; David Ramsay, *The History of the Revolution of South Carolina. . . .*, II, 473.
18. W. A. Courtenay, *Proceedings at the Unveiling of the Battle Monument in . . . the Centennial of the Battle of Cowpens*, 132; Adiel Sherwood, *A Gazetteer of the State of Georgia*, 3rd ed., 288-90; Jones, *History*, II, 471; James Graham, comp., *The Life of General Daniel Morgan . . .*, 472, 473; McCrady, *Hist. of S. C. in the Rev.*, 35, quoted from William Johnson, comp., *Sketches of the Life and Correspondence of Greene*, I, 375, 376; Charlton, *Jackson*, 24-26; Pickens to Lee, Aug. 28, 1811, D. M., IVV 107, Draper Collection, University of Wisconsin.
19. L. L. Mackall, "Edward Langworthy," *Ga. Hist. Quar.*, VII (1923), 8, 9, 17; *Georgia Gazette* (Savannah), May 12, 26, June 2, July 14, 21, 1791; Jackson to Langworthy, January 28, 1795, James Jackson MSS., Duke University.
20. James Graham, *Life of General Daniel Morgan . . .*, 348, 349; Charlton, *Jackson*, 26, 28; Jones, *History*, II, 26; William Johnson, comp., *Sketches of the Life and Correspondence of Nathanael Greene . . .*, I, 453; J. H. Wheeler, *Historical Sketches of North Carolina . . .*, II, 381.
21. Charlton, *Jackson*, 26, 27, 31-34; A. L. Pickens, *Skyagunsta . . ., Andrew Pickens (1739-1817)*, 95; Jones, *History*, II, 493.

CHAPTER II

1. Charlton, *Jackson*, 49; *Museum*, May 13, 1796; Mabel F. Lafar and Caroline P. Wilson, comps., *Genealogical Publications*, No. 6 (1936), 47, 90, 161, 162, 169, 173; *Rev. Rec. of Ga.*, II, 774.
2. James Jackson MSS., Duke University; *Augusta Chronicle*, Mar. 27, 1790, hereinafter referred to as *Chronicle*.
3. James Jackson MSS.; Allen D. Candler, ed., *The Colonial Records of Georgia*, XIX, Part 1, 287, hereinafter referred to as *Col. Rec. of Ga.*; Jones, *History*, II, 177, 183; *Historical Collections of the Joseph Habersham Chapter, D. A. R.*, I, 246; *S. C. Weekly Gazette* (Charleston), Jan. 20, 1785; Carolyn Price Wilson, comp., *Annals of Georgia . . .*, III, 248, hereinafter referred to as Wilson, *Annals*.
4. Charlton, *Jackson*, 182, 183, 209, 210; Wilson, *Annals*, III, 248; Mrs. H. H. McCall, comp., "McCall's Collections, D.A.C.," I, 20; M. M. Elliott,

Notes

"A Sketch of the Life of James Jackson, 1757-1806," 23, M. A. Thesis (1935), Univ. of Ga.; W. J. Northen, ed., *Men of Mark in Georgia*, III, 449; Lucian Lamar Knight, "Genealogy of the Knight, Walton, Cobb, . . . Jackson . . . and other Georgia families"; Governors' Letter-Books, 1800-1801, 48; *Museum*, Aug. 29, 1800.

5. *Gazette of the State of Georgia* (Savannah), March 27, 1788; Charlton, *Jackson*, 138-215; *Savannah Morning News*, Jan. 19, 1930. In 1824 Gibbons was involved in the New Jersey case of Gibbons v. Ogden, in which the U. S. Supreme Court first established the right of Congress to control interstate commerce.
6. *Georgia State Gazette or Independent Register* (Augusta), Oct. 4, 1788; White, *Statistics*, 348.
7. *Rev. Rec. of Ga.*, I, 438, 532, 603, II, 270, III, 516; Coulter, *History*, 149; *Museum*, Nov. 27, 1798, and May 10, 1796, and Nov. 5, 23, 1803; House Journals of Georgia, 1784-1786, 419; A. S. Clayton, *A Compilation of the Laws of the State of Georgia*, 196; Gov. Letter-Books, 1800-1801, 171, 172 and 1795-1798. 260-62; Stevens, *History*, II, 358, 359; S. G. McLendon, *History of the Public Domain of Georgia*, 178-80; Coulter, *History*, 181; Executive Department Minutes of Georgia, 1796-1797, 31; *Ga. Gazette* (Savannah), Feb. 7, 1793; Ruth Blair, comp. and ed., *Some Early Tax Digests of Georgia*, 21; Charlton, *Jackson*, 178, 179, 186, 211.
8. W. B. Clarke, *Early and Historic Freemasonry of Georgia* . . ., 94-96, 133; R. and G. Watkins, comps., *A Digest of the Laws of Georgia*, 571, 572, hereinafter referred to as Watkins, *Digest*.

CHAPTER III

1. Charlton, *Jackson*, 53; House Journals of Ga., 1784-1786, 531; *Museum*, May 10, 1796; *Chronicle*, Dec. 12, 1792.
2. *Ga. Hist. Quar.*, XXI (1937), 148, 149; *American State Papers, Indian Affairs*, I, 17, hereinafter referred to as A.S.P., *Indian Affairs*; Executive Council Journals of Georgia, 1785-1786, 122.
3. *Rev. Rec. of Ga.*, III, 109, 228; Charlton, *Jackson*, 134; A. H. Chappell, *Miscellanies* . . ., Part II, 101, 102; Harry Emerson Wildes, *Anthony Wayne, Trouble Shooter of the American Revolution*, 290, 312; F. D. Lee and J. L. Agnew, *Historical Record of the City of Savannah*, 68, 69.
4. McLendon, *Hist. of Public Domain of Ga.*, 9-15; J. W. Caughey, *McGillivray of the Creeks*, 121, 122; House Journals of Ga., 1784-1786, 471, 473, 475, 483, 484, 503, 504, 523; J. W. Rabun, "Georgia and the Creek Indians," M. A. Thesis (1937), Univ. of N. C.
5. *Museum*, May 10, 13, 1796.
6. *Ga. Hist. Quar.*, XXI (1937), 155-57; Gov. Letter-Books, 1787-1789, 46, 56, 57 and 1786-1789, 61-68, 95; Gunn to Jackson, May 5, 1787, Jackson MSS.
7. *Ga. State Gazette or Independent Register* (Augusta), Sept. 29, 1787; Gov. Letter-Books, 1786-1789, 115, 116; A.S.P., *Indian Affairs*, I, 76, 77.
8. Ulrich B. Phillips, *Georgia and State Rights* . . ., 21; Jonathan Elliot, comp., *The Debates in the Several State Conventions* . . ., I, 355, 356.
9. Jackson to Handley, Feb. 20, Oct. 3, 1788, and Jackson to Walton, March 20, 1789, Jackson MSS., State Archives, Atlanta; Gov. Letter-Books, 1786-1789, 138, 140, 174, 175; Stevens, *History*, II, 434.
10. Jackson to Walton, Mar. 28, April 29, 1789, Jackson MSS., State Archives, Atlanta; Exec. Dept. Min. of Ga., 1789, 164, 177, 178.
11. Lear to Jackson, July 22, 1789, J. C. Fitzpatrick, ed., *The Writings of*

George Washington, XXX, 358; *Annals*, 1st Cong., 1 sess., 65, 696-701, 721-23; *A.S.P., Indian Affairs*, I, 75-81.

12. J. C. Fitzpatrick, ed., *The Diaries of Washington*, IV, 103; *Annals*, 1st Cong., 2 sess., 1646, 1647.
13. Charles J. Kappler, comp. and ed., *Indian Affairs, Laws and Treaties*, II, 25-29, hereinafter referred to as Kappler, *Indian Affairs*; *A.S.P., Indian Affairs*, I, 80-82, 127, II, 790, 791; J. D. Richardson, comp., *A Compilation of the Messages and Papers of the Presidents, 1789-1908*, I, 78, 79; *Annals*, 1st Cong., 3 sess., 1792, 1793 and 8th Cong., 1 sess., 113; *Ga. Gazette* (Savannah), Jan. 13, 1791.
14. Fitzpatrick, ed., *Diaries of Washington*, IV, 196; Exec. Dept. Min. of Ga., 1791-1792, 24, 25; Coulter, *History*, 170.
15. *Ga. Gazette* (Savannah), May 23, 1793; Jackson to Telfair, May 27, 1793, Jackson MSS., State Archives, Atlanta; *A.S.P., Indian Affairs*, I, 364, 365, 370, 371, 411, 412. Seagrove also appears as Seagroves and Seagrave.
16. Jackson to Seagrove, Sept. 11, 1793; Jackson MSS.; Jackson to Carr, Sept. 28, 1793, Carr Papers, Univ. of Ga.
17. *Annals*, 3rd Cong., 1 sess., 123; Coulter, *History*, 185; Jackson to Armstrong, July 24, 1794, Jackson MSS.,

Duke University; Richard Hildreth, *The History of the United States of America*, IV, 438, 439, 477.

18. Jackson to Mathews, Sept., 1794, Jackson MSS., State Archives, Atlanta; *Annals*, 3rd Cong., 2 sess., 838, 839, 849, 850.
19. Gov. Letter-Books, 1795-1796, 12; *Annals*, 3rd Cong., 2 sess., 866, 867; *A.S.P., Indian Affairs*, I, 587-612; Exec. Dept. Min. of Ga., 1793-1796, 676, 684; Kappler, *Indian Affairs*, 46, 50; *A.S.P., Indian Affairs*. I, 587-612; A. J. Pickett, *History of Alabama, . . . Georgia and Mississippi . . .*, II, 166, 167.
20. *A.S.P., Indian Affairs*, II, 613-15; *Museum*, Aug. 5, 12, 1796; *Chronicle*, Aug. 7, 12, 27, 1796; Kappler, *Indian Affairs*, II, 46n.; *Annals*, 5th Cong., 1 sess., 475, 656; 2 sess., 1582; 3 sess., 2547, 2548, 2551, 2816.
21. Charlton, *Jackson*, 166-68; McLendon, *Hist. of Public Domain of Ga.*, 14-17.
22. *Ga. Gazette* (Savannah), May 19, 1791.
23. *Rev. Rec. of Ga.*, III, 140; "Petition," Jackson MSS.; *Museum*, May 10, 13, 1796; Nov. 5, 1803; Charlton, *Jackson*, 150, 151, 196, 197.
24. Exec. Dept. Min. of Ga., 1796-1797, 43, 138; 1800-1802, 545; House Journals of Ga., 1796-1797, 336; White, *Statistics*, 170; Jedidiah Morse, *The American Gazetteer . . .*, 481.

CHAPTER IV

1. Lee and Agnew, *Historical Record of the City of Savannah*, 68; *Rev. Rec. of Ga.*, III, 7, 15, 23, 34, 41, 118, 122, 136.
2. *Gazette of the State of Ga.* (Savannah), Dec. 27, 1787; House Journals of Ga., 1787-1788, 266, 293; 1784-1786, 297, 309; *Ga. Gazette* (Savannah), Dec. 18, 1788; *Ga. Hist. Quar.*, XX (1937), 93; *Rev. Rec. of Ga.*, III, 10, 43, 47, 50, 191.
3. House Journals of Ga., 1784-1786, 182, 215-19, 261, 268, 269, 286; 1789, 5, 20, 89; 1796-1797, 1, 35-55, 98; *Rev. Rec. of Ga.*, III, 58; Allan Nevins, *American States During and After the Revolution; 1775-1789*, 524, 542.
4. *Rev. Rec. of Ga.*, III, 50, 51, 59-61, 78, 215-19, 259, 261, 286; Watkins, *Digest . . .*, 291, 293; *Col. Rec. of Ga.*, XIX, Part II, 363-69; Horatio Marbury and Wm. H. Crawford, comps., *Digest of the Laws of . . . Georgia . . .*, 563, 566; House Journals of Ga., 1784-1786, 301; "University Act," Baldwin Papers, Univ. of Ga.; *Ga. Hist. Quar.*, XXXVII (1953), 147-49; I (1917), 108-11; *Ga. Gazette* (Savannah), Jan. 19, 1792.

Notes

5. House Journals of Ga., 1784-1786, 181, 290; 1787-1788, 44, 45, 129, 290; 1789, 89, 520; *Ga. Gazette* (Savannah), Dec. 18, 1788; *Ga. Hist. Quar.*, XX (1937), 93; Coulter, *History*, 157; Charlton, *Jackson*, 84.
6. *Col. Rec. of Ga.*, XIX, Part II, 348-59; House Journals of Ga., 1784-1786, 167, 170, 284; Coulter, *History*, 139, 175, 176.
7. House Journals of Ga., 1784-1786, 297, 309, 480-89, 505; 1787-1788, 44, 45, 334; *Museum*, May 10, 1796; *Ga. Hist. Quar.*, II (1918), 202-23; Stevens, *History*, II, 370.
8. Exec. Dept. Min. of Ga., 1796-1797, 29, 30; House Journals of Ga., 1796-1797, 179; *Ga. Gazette* (Savannah), Nov. 10, 1797; *Museum*, Nov. 8, Dec. 6, 1796.
9. Niles, quoted by Coulter, *History*, 226; Nevins, *American States . . .*, 195, 196, 411, 418; Stevens, *History*, II, 406, 407; Fletcher M. Green, *Constitutional Development in the South Atlantic States . . .*, 233-40; Thomas Gamble, "Ga.'s 1st Contested Election," *Savannah Morning News*, Feb. 23, 1930; Ulrich B. Phillips, *Georgia and State Rights . . .*, 93; Jackson to Baldwin, Baldwin Papers, Univ. of Ga.

CHAPTER V

1. *Ga. State Gazette* (Augusta), Jan. 31, 1789; House Journals of Ga., 1789, 33, 34; Stevens, *History*, II, 394; Exec. Dept. Min. of Ga., 1789, 101, 111-30.
2. *Annals*, 1st Cong., 1 sess., 170, 322, 531, 532; A. J. Beveridge, *Life of John Marshall*, III, 55n., quoting Wm. Smith in Johnson, *Union and Democracy*, 105, 106; Claude G. Bowers, *Jefferson and Hamilton. . .*, 45, 46; Charlton, *Jackson*, 153, 154; A. P. Whitaker, "Jackson, James," *Dictionary of American Biography*, IX, 544, 545.
3. *Annals*, 1st Cong., 1 sess., 322, 553, 1223; Seth Ames, ed., *Works of Fisher Ames . . .*, I, 87; J. H. Preston, *A Gentleman Rebel, Mad Anthony Wayne*, 271.
4. J. C. Fitzpatrick, ed., *Diaries of Washington*, IV, 72, 105; *Annals*, 1st Cong., 1 sess., 374, 486, 489, 591, 614, 1075, 1079; 2 sess., 1476.
5. *Annals*, 1st Cong., 1 sess., 407, 408, 829; 7th Cong., 1 sess., 182, 245; Charlton, *Jackson*, 172.
6. *Annals*, 1st Cong., 1 sess., 733, 777.
7. *Ibid.*, 210, 211, 231, 243, 244, 256, 257, 281-90, 356, 357; 2 sess., 1565; Thomas Hart Benton, ed., *Abridgement of Debates of Congress from 1789 to 1856 . . .*, I, 44, hereinafter referred to as Benton, *Abridgement*.
8. Seth Ames, ed., *Works of Fisher Ames . . .*, I, 92; Joseph Gales, Sr., comp., *The Debates and Proceedings in the Congress of the United States, 1789-1791*, II, 1890; "Jackson's Speech," *Chronicle*, Mar. 5, 12, 1791; *Annals*, 1st Cong., 3 sess., 1842, 1843, 1884.
9. *Annals*, 1st Cong., 1 sess., 802, 803, 814, 830, 894.
10. *Ibid.*, 2 sess., 1094-1103, 1140-43, 1224-27, 1298; *Chronicle*, April 17, 1790.
11. *Annals*, 1st Cong., 2 sess., 1379-82, 1507, 1510; 3 sess., 1689-93, 1710, 1711, 1723; Richard Hildreth, *History of the United States of America*, IV, 170-73, 214.
12. *Annals*, 1st Cong., 1 sess., 844, 845, 878, 881-86, 911.
13. *Ibid.*, 1st Cong., 2 sess., 1114, 1122, 1125, 1412; 3 sess., 1806-13, 1822, 1823, 1917-19, 1960; Benton, *Abridgement*, I, 285-87.
14. *Annals*, 1st Cong., 1 sess., 645, 646, 652, 657, 658, 899-903; Richard Hildreth, *History . . .*, IV, 125, 126.
15. *Annals*, 1st Cong., 2 sess., 1200, 1465, 1500; *Ga. Gazette* (Savannah), Apr. 29, May 6, 1790; Ulrich B. Phillips, *The Course of the South to Secession*, 28n. For Franklin's criticism of Jackson, cf. appendix of this work.

CHAPTER VI

1. H. E. Wildes, *Anthony Wayne*, 329; Exec. Dept. Min. of Ga., 1790, 32, 33; "Mad A. Wayne," *Savannah Morning News*, Dec. 8, 1929.
2. *Ga. Gazette* (Savannah), April 7, July 28, 1791; Thomas Gamble, *Savannah Morning News*, Feb. 23, 1930; *Museum*, May 10, 1796.
3. H. E. Wildes, *Anthony Wayne* . . ., 337-38; Senate Journals of Ga., 1790-1791, 161-67, 195, 252, 253.
4. Senate Journals of Ga., 1791-1792, 30, 31; *Museum*, May 10, 1796; Thomas Gamble, *Savannah Morning News*, Feb. 23, 1930.
5. "To J. Jackson," *Chronicle*, Nov. 5, 1791.
6. *Proceedings in the House of Representatives of the United States of America, Respecting the Contested Election for the Eastern District of the State of Georgia*, 1-58; *Annals*, 2nd Cong., 1 sess., 458-79; M. St. Clair Clarke, comp., *Cases of Contested Elections in Congress* . . ., 49, 50.
7. *Chronicle*, May 26, 1792.
8. "J. to Sturgess," *Museum*, Nov. 5, 1803; *Constitution of Georgia, 1798*, Article IV, Sec. 8.
9. Gamble, *Annals*, 41, 44.
10. Charlton, *Jackson*, 140, 204; Senate Journals of Ga., 1791-1792, 163; Exec. Dept. Min. of Ga., 1792-1793, 9; Benton, *Abridgement* . . ., I, 445.
11. Charlton, *Jackson*, 145-47; *Annals*, 3rd Cong., 1 sess., 114-16; 3rd Cong., spec. sess., 854-64; S. M. Hamilton, ed., *The Writings of James Monroe* . . ., I, 293.
12. Charlton, *Jackson*, 146, 147; Benton, *Abridgement* . . ., 446; *Annals*, 3rd Cong., 1 sess., 47, 57, 96, 103, 106; Richard Hildreth, *History* . . ., IV, 497.
13. *Annals*, 3rd Cong., 2 sess., 45, 57, 74, 82, 86, 784, 794, 820, 833.
14. *Ga. Hist. Quar.*, VII (1923), 183; Hildreth, *History* . . ., IV, 538; Jackson to Mathews, Exec. Dept. Min. of Ga., 1793-1796, 318.
15. Jackson to Madison, Nov. 17, 1795, Madison Papers, Library of Congress.

CHAPTER VII

1. William Priest, *Travels in the United States of America* . . ., 132, 133.
2. Jackson to Bird, Exec. Dept. Min. of Ga., 1799, 122; [Jackson], *Facts in Reply . . . by a Georgian*, 23; House Journals of Ga., 1784-1786, 524, 540; *A.S.P., Public Lands*, I, 100; "Sketch of the Yazoo Speculation in Jackson's Hand," *Ga. Hist. Quar.*, XXXVII (1953), 153.
3. Stevens, *History*, II, 463; Coulter, *History*, 186-87; A. M. Sakolski, *The Great American Land Bubble* . . ., 132, 133; C. H. Haskins, *The Yazoo Land Companies*, 81n.; [Jackson], *Facts in Reply . . . by a Georgian*, 23; *Ga. Hist. Quar.*, XXXVII (1953) 152-55; Amanda Johnson, *Georgia as Colony and State*, 178.
4. *Annals*, 3rd Cong., 2 sess., 826, 838; J. B. McMaster, *A History of the People of the United States* . . ., III, 128; [United States], *A Report of the Attorney General* [Charles Lee] *to Congress.* . . .
5. Amanda Johnson, *Georgia as Colony and State*, 177-80; C. H. Haskins, *The Yazoo Land Companies*, 88-103; White, *Statistics*, 49; Charlton, *Jackson*, 154, 207, 208; *Ga. Hist. Quar.*, VII (1923), 14; XXXVII (1953), 154, 155; J. B. McMaster, *A History of the People of the United States* . . ., II, 223; *Federal Intelligencer*, Aug. 14, 1795.
6. *Chronicle*, Nov. 14, 1795; *City Gazette and Daily Advertiser* (Charleston), Nov. 14, 1795; "Jackson to Madison, Nov. 17, 1795," Madison Papers, Library of Congress.
7. [James Jackson], *Letters of Sicilius to Citizens of Georgia*, 1-26; *Chronicle*, Oct. 24, Nov. 7, 28, 1795.
8. Stevens, *History*, II, 408, 409; *Chronicle*, Nov. 14, 1795; House

Notes 199

Journals of Ga., 1796-1797, 10-13, 26, 27; McLendon, *Hist. of Public Domain of Ga.*, 75-98; [Yazoo] *Report from the Committee of Claims,* 24; *A.S.P., Public Lands,* I, 144.
9. Marbury and Crawford, *Digest* . . ., 581; *Ga. Hist. Quar.,* XVI (1932), 281-83; *A.S.P., Public Lands,* I, 142-58.
10. Stevens, *History,* II, 491-94.
11. E. S. Thomas, *Reminiscences* . . ., I, 59; *City Gazette and Daily Advertiser* (Charleston), Mar. 1, 8, 1796.
12. Jedidiah Morse, *American Gazetteer,* 185, 188n., 614; Charlton, *Jackson,* 167-70; Marbury and Crawford, *Digest* . . ., 581.

CHAPTER VIII

1. *Ga. Hist. Quar.,* XXXVII (1953), 154.
2. "Extract from Minutes of Ga. House," *North Carolina Minerva* (Fayetteville), March 31, 1796; *Museum,* May 13, 1796; *Federal Gazette and Baltimore Daily Advertiser,* March 21, 23, 1796.
3. Charlton, *Jackson,* 159-64; *Museum,* Apr. 26, 29, May 20, 24, 1796; "A Yazoo Prayer," *Chronicle,* Oct. 29, 1796.
4. A. J. Pickett, *History of Alabama, Georgia and Mississippi* . . ., II, 167; *Ga. Hist. Quar.,* XXXVII (1953), 154; Charlton, *Jackson,* 165; Gamble, *Annals,* 45.
5. Charlton, *Jackson,* 157-73; "Extract of a Letter," *Federal Gazette and Baltimore Daily Advertiser,* March 19, 1796; "Governor's Message," *Museum,* Jan. 25, 1799; Nov. 21, 1800; O. A. Park, *History of Georgia,* 135.
6. *Museum,* June 22, July 2, 9, 1802; Gamble, *Annals,* 51.
7. *Museum,* July 9, 1802; April 29, May 3, 10, 1796; Charlton, *Jackson,* 151, 158; Gamble, *Annals,* 53, 54, 56; Marbury and Crawford, *Digest* . . ., 565.
8. *Chronicle,* Apr. 15, 1797; Exec. Dept. Min. of Ga., 1797-1798, 133, 134; Charlton, *Jackson,* 160, 177,
180, 212-14; *Museum,* Apr. 9, 23, 1799.
9. Abraham Bishop, *Georgia Speculation Unveiled* . . ., 6, 14, 17, 18.
10. "Letter by Junius," *Augusta Herald,* Jan. 8, July 9, 1800.
11. Exec. Dept. Min. of Ga., 1798-1799, 333-64; 1800-1802, 382-87; *Journal of the House of Representatives of Ga., 1800,* 54-60; House Journals of Ga., 1799-1802, 7-14.
12. Oliver H. Prince, comp., *A Digest of the Laws of the State of Georgia,* 151; *A.S.P., Public Lands,* I, 125-35.
13. Hugh A. Garland, *The Life of John Randolph of Roanoke,* I, 67; Charlton, *Jackson,* 194-95.
14. Charlton, *Jackson,* 88, 202; *Museum,* Nov. 5, 1803.
15. *Memoirs,* I, 381, quoted in Beveridge, *Life of John Marshall,* III, 583.
16. James Jackson, *Facts in Reply* . . . *by a Georgian,* 1-20; *Memorial of Agents of the New England Mississippi Land Company,* 86; Stevens, *History,* II, 490.
17. *Annals,* 9th Cong., 1 sess., 910, 921.
18. Phillips, *Georgia and State Rights,* 36; *U. S. Statutes at Large,* III, 117, quoted in Beveridge, *Life of John Marshall,* III, 601, 602; Payson Jackson Treat, *The National Land System, 1785-1820,* 404; Phillips, *Georgia and State Rights,* 86.

CHAPTER IX

1. Phillips, *Georgia & State Rights,* 93, 94, 108-10, 140, 145; Paul Murray, "The Whig Party in Georgia, 1825-1853," iv, v, 2, 10, 21, unpublished Doctoral Dissertation (1940), Univ. of N. C.
2. Charlton, *Jackson,* 184; E. J. Harden, *Life of George M. Troup,* 2, 3, 10, 11. Crawford was later a candidate for the presidency; cf. "Louisville, Nov. 26, 1800," Baldwin Papers, Univ. of Ga.

3. Exec. Dept. Min. of Ga., 1798-1799, 63, 64; "Jan. 13, 1801," Baldwin Papers, Univ. of Ga.; "To Meigs, Dec. 7, 1800," Henry Jackson Papers, Univ. of Ga.; Gov. Letter-Books, 1800-1801, 153, 154; Charlton, *Jackson*, 183, 188, 189; W. G. Cooper, *Story of Georgia*, II, 91; White, *Statistics*, 67, 70.

4. Knight, *Georgia's Landmarks* . . ., 821; Walter McElreath, *A Treatise on the Constitution of Georgia*, 97; "Augusta, June 9," *Chronicle*, June 9, 1798; Exec. Dept. Min. of Ga., 1797-1798, 333, 339, 340; *Museum*, Oct. 16, 1798.

5. Exec. Dept. Min. of Ga., 1797-1798, 70, 122, 265; 1798-1799, 333; 1800-1802, 148; Gov. Letter-Books, 1795, 1798, 73-75, 124, 280.

6. Charlton, *Jackson*, 141, 142, 175; Exec. Dept. Min. of Ga., 1797-1798, 97, 144-47, 268, 328, 329, 363.

7. Exec. Dept. Min. of Ga., 1797-1798, 105, 120, 121, 185, 186, 241-43, 272, 273, 300-03; "To Governor," *Museum*, Oct. 16, 1798.

8. Charlton, *Jackson*, 140, 141, 175; W. Cobbett, *Porcupine's Works*, X, 9, 22-31; Exec. Dept. Min. of Ga., 1799-1800, 396; Gov. Letter-Books, 1795-1798, 290, 291.

9. Exec. Dept. Min. of Ga., 1799-1800, 396; Gov. Letter-Books, 1795-1798, 290, 291, 315, 317; 1800-1801, 75.

10. Exec. Dept. Min. of Ga., 1798-1799, 333, 349; 1800-1802, 151; Gov. Letter-Books, 1799, 10, 11.

11. *Museum*, Jan. 29, Nov. 19, Dec. 10, 1799; Nov. 21, Dec. 23, 1800; Gov. Letter-Books, 1800-1801, 172; 1799, 18-24.

12. Exec. Dept. Min. of Ga., 1799-1800, 2; *Chronicle*, Nov. 9, 1799; "Proclamation," *Museum*, Jan. 28, 1800.

13. House Journals of Ga., 1800, 2, 3; *Museum*, Nov. 21, 28, Dec. 2, 5, 9, 19, 23, 30, 1800; Gov. Letter-Books, 1799, 63-67.

14. Gov. Letter-Books, 1795-1798, 104-07, 121, 122, 1799, 43, 44, 63-67; Exec. Dept. Min. of Ga., 1797-1798, 112, 161, 1799-1800, 371-87; Stevens, *History*, II, 446-54; Georgia, East Florida, and West Florida Yazoo Land Sales, 122, 127, 128.

15. "Governor's Message," *Museum*, Jan. 29, 1799.

16. Exec. Dept. Min. of Ga., 1798-1799, 357, 358; Phillips, *Georgia and State Rights*, 92; *Journal of the Senate of the State of Georgia, Nov.-Dec., 1799*, 18, 19.

Recent research by the author of this work makes it necessary to correct a statement by Professor Ulrich Bonnell Phillips that "The journals of the legislative houses of Georgia for 1799 do not now exist." He thought that they were probably among the papers destroyed by Sherman's army during the invasion of the state in 1864. Doctor Phillips learned from a manuscript index to the House Journal that some action was taken by that body on the Alien and Sedition Laws passed by Congress but he concluded that "What that action was no one can say." The journal for the Georgia Senate for 1799 may now be seen in the State Library at the Capitol in Atlanta. The action taken by the House may be seen in the *House Journal* for 1799 at the State Archives, Atlanta.

17. *Ga. House Journal, Nov.-Dec., 1799*, 48-50, State Archives, Atlanta; *Journal of the Senate of Ga., Nov.-Dec., 1799*, State Library, Capitol, Atlanta.

18. Exec. Dept. Min. of Ga., 1800-1802, 25; "Nov. 26, 1800," Baldwin Papers, Univ. of Ga.

19. *Chronicle*, Jan. 17, 1801; *Museum*, Jan. 9, 13, 1801, Feb. 7, 13, 1801; "Dec. 5, 1800," Baldwin Papers, Univ. of Ga.; Exec. Dept. Min. of Ga., 1800-1802, 147, 152.

CHAPTER X

1. Claude G. Bowers, *Jefferson and Hamilton*, 150; Charlton, *Jackson*, 183, 184; *Museum*, Mar. 20, 31, April 7, 1801.

Notes

2. May 15, 1801, Madison Papers, Library of Congress; May 1, 4, 1802 and Dec. 28, 1801, Jefferson Papers, Library of Congress; *National Intelligencer and Washington Advertiser*, Jan. 18, 1803.
3. *Ga. Gazette* (Savannah), May 6, 1802; Charlton, *Jackson*, 198; Coulter, *History*, 236.
4. Charlton, *Jackson*, 198; *Annals*, 7th Cong., 1 sess., 9.
5. *Museum*, Dec. 7, 10, 1802, Nov. 9, 12, 1803.
6. *Georgia Republican and State Intelligencer* (Savannah), June 23, 1803; Charlton, *Jackson*, 138-215.
7. *Annals*, 7th Cong., 1 sess., 47-51, 183; *ibid.*, 2 sess., 34-78.
8. *Ibid.*, 8th Cong., 2 sess., 270; *National Intelligencer and Washington Advertiser*, Jan. 18, 25, 1804.
9. *Annals*, 7th Cong., 1 sess., 50; 8th Cong., 1 sess., 157-200; Mar. 1, 1805, Jefferson Papers, Library of Congress.
10. Charles F. Adams, ed., *Memoirs of John Quincy Adams* . . ., I, 292; *Annals*, 7th Cong., 1 sess., 195, 245, 1312.
11. *Annals*, 7th Cong., 1 sess., 244, 250.
12. *Ibid.*, 8th Cong., I sess, 91, 109-13, 114, 124, 157, 158, 214, 268, 271, 278.
13. Richard Hildreth, *History* . . ., V, 470; Claude G. Bowers, *Jefferson in Power*, 117; Charlton, *Jackson*, 189; *Annals*, 7th Cong., 2 sess., 147-50, 243-46; 8th Cong., 1 sess., 29, 32, 37-41, 73, 230, 231.
14. Charles F. Adams, ed., *Memoirs of John Quincy Adams* . . ., I, 292.
15. *Annals*, 8th Cong., 1 sess., 282-88.
16. *Ibid.*, 9th Cong., 1 sess., 30-37, 138; *National Intelligencer and Washington Advertiser*, Mar. 21, 1806.

CHAPTER XI

1. Charles F. Adams, *Memoirs of John Quincy Adams* . . ., I, 422; Benton, *Abridgement* . . ., III, 372, 465, 465n; *Annals*, 9th Cong., 1 sess., 238; *National Intelligencer and Washington Advertiser*, Mar. 21, 1806; Charlton, *Jackson*, 89; *Biographical Directory of the American Congress, 1774-1927*, 1142, 1143. The inscription on his monument states that he was "the determined foe of foreign tyranny, the scourge and terror of corruption at home." White, *Statistics*, 348.
2. *Museum*, April 9, 12, 16, May 3, 1806; Charlton, *Jackson*, 57-69; according to Charlton's "Eulogium" Jackson was "impatient under contradictions" but "his enemies were always apprized of his points of attack" and "the smallest advances to reconciliation buried his resentments." Also "it was his favorite wish that if after death his heart could be opened, Georgia would be legibly read there." Cf. S. F. Miller, *The Bench and Bar of Georgia*, I, 219.
3. Phillips, *Georgia and State Rights*, 94.
4. Mabel F. Lafar and Caroline P. Wilson, "Abstracts of Wills, Chatham County, Georgia, 1773-1817," *Genealogical Publications of the National Genealogical Society*, No. 6 (1936), 74, 75. Among the executors of Jackson's will were Thomas de Mattos Johnson and David B. Mitchell.
5. Wm. Tittamin, "Forts Jackson, Lee, and Barton," typed MS., Ga. Hist. Soc.; White, *Statistics*, 161, 335; White, *Historical Collections of Georgia*, 336; *Acts of the General Assembly of the State of Georgia, Nov. and Dec., 1858*, 197. Cf. *Reports 1850-1860; Comptroller General of Georgia*, 74.
6. Henry Adams, *History of the U. S. of America During the Administrations of Jefferson and Madison*, 305; A. J. Beveridge, *Life of John Marshall*, III, 557, 558n.

BIBLIOGRAPHY

I. PRIMARY SOURCES

A. Manuscripts

1. *Public Archives*

    Executive Council Journals of Georgia, 1778-1783, 1783-1785, 1785-1786, 1786, 1787, 1788, 1789. Georgia Department of Archives and History, Atlanta. The Journals of 1778-1785 are printed in the *Revolutionary Records of Georgia*, II, 1-799.

    Executive Department Minutes of Georgia, 1789-1802. Georgia Department of Archives and History, Atlanta. The official decisions of the governors and other business of the executive department are found in these documents.

    Georgia. East Florida—West Florida and Yazoo Land Sales, 1764-1850. Georgia Department of Archives and History, Atlanta. Copied, indexed, and bound in one typed volume. Contains newspaper articles, letters, and documents, 1764 to 1850, relating to boundaries, lands, and border conflicts between the Spanish and Georgia authorities.

    Governors' Letter-Books, 1786-1806. State Archives, Atlanta.

    House Journals of Georgia, 1781-1808. Georgia Department of Archives and History, Atlanta. Pages 1-126 of the Journals, January 21, 1784, to August 15, 1786, have been published in the *Revolutionary Records of Georgia*, III, 1-574.

    Senate Journals of Georgia, 1789-1790, 1790-1791, 1791-1792, 1799, 1800-1802, 1803, 1804, 1805. Georgia Department of Archives and History, Atlanta. The Executive Council was replaced by the Senate in 1789.

2. *Historical Correspondence, Writings, etc.*

    Baldwin Papers. University of Georgia. Four letters from James Jackson to Abraham Baldwin and one from Baldwin to Jackson.

Bibliography

Carr Papers. University of Georgia. Two letters from James Jackson to Thomas Carr.

Draper Collection, D. M., IVV 107. University of Wisconsin.

Henry Jackson Papers. University of Georgia. One letter from James Jackson to Henry Jackson.

James Jackson Manuscripts. Georgia Department of Archives and History, 1782-1806. Approximately fifty letters.

James Jackson Manuscripts. Duke University. Thirteen letters, 1782-1798.

James Jackson Manuscripts. Georgia Historical Society Library, Savannah. "Character of J. J. by himself," ten pages of autobiography in Jackson's own handwriting. As it does not refer to his first election to the United States Senate or to any event after 1793, the autobiography must have been written before that time. Letters and records.

Jefferson Papers. Library of Congress.

McCall, Mrs. Howard H., comp., McCall's Collections. Daughters of American Colonists, 6 vols., 1938, 1939. Georgia Department of Archives and History, Atlanta. These bound volumes are typed and indexed. The records of wills, marriages, and deaths were obtained from family Bibles and cemetery and county records in several Georgia communities.

Madison Papers. Library of Congress.

Will of James Jackson. Record of Chatham County Wills, Book D., 1801-1807, 217-224, Savannah.

B. Printed

1. *Public Archives*

    Acts of the General Assembly of the State of Georgia, Passed in Milledgeville, at an Annual Session in November and December, 1858. Columbus, Georgia, 1858.

    American State Papers, Documents, Executive and Legislative . . ., 38 vols., 1789-1814. The eight volumes on *Public Lands* and two on *Indian Affairs* have many valuable state and federal documents and reports bearing on the Yazoo fraud and Indian controversies.

    Annals of Congress, 1789-1814.

    Benton, Thomas Hart, ed., *Abridgement of the Debates of Congress from 1789 to 1856 . . .* , 17 vols. New York, 1857-1860.

    Candler, Allen D., ed., *The Colonial Records of the State of Georgia*, 26 vols. Atlanta, 1904-1916.

    Candler, Allen D., ed., *The Revolutionary Records of the State of Georgia*, 3 vols. Atlanta, 1908.

Clayton, Augustin Smith, comp., *A Compilation of the Laws of the State of Georgia, 1800-1810.* Augusta, 1812.

Constitution of the State of Georgia, 1798.

Elliot, Jonathan, comp., *The Debates in the Several State Conventions, on the Adoption of the Federal Constitution* . . . , 4 vols. Washington, 1836.

Gales, Joseph, Sr., comp., *The Debates and Proceedings in the Congress of the United States* . . . , *1789-1791,* 2 vols. Washington 1834.

Georgia House Journal, 1799, Augusta, 1800.

Journal of the House of Representatives, of the State of Georgia, 1800. Louisville, 1801.

Journal of the Senate of the State of Georgia, 1799, Nov.-Dec., Augusta, [1800].

Kappler, Charles J., comp. and ed., *Indian Affairs, Laws and Treaties,* 4 vols. Washington, 1904. Senate Document no. 319, 58th Congress, 2 sess.

Marbury, Horatio and Crawford, William H., comps., *Digest of the Laws of the State of Georgia, from its Settlement as a British Province, in 1755, to the Session of the General Assembly in 1800, Inclusive.* Savannah, 1802.

"Official Letters of Governor John Martin, 1782-1783," *Georgia Historical Quarterly,* I (1917), 281-335.

Prince, Oliver H., comp., *A Digest of the Laws of the State of Georgia:* . . . . Milledgeville, 1822.

Proceedings in the House of Representatives of the United States of America, Respecting the Contested Election for the Eastern District of the State of Georgia. Philadelphia, 1792. This anonymous pamphlet gives Jackson's petition and speeches to the House in full; and also testimony presented to the Georgia legislature (but ruled out in the hearing by the Federal House) regarding corruption in the election of Wayne to Congress.

Reports 1850-1860; Comptroller General of Georgia. Atlanta, 1861.

Richardson, James D., comp., *A Compilation of the Messages and Papers of the Presidents, 1789-1908,* 10 vols. Washington, 1899.

[United States.] *A Report of the Attorney General* [Charles Lee] *to Congress; Containing a Collection of Charters, Treaties, and Other Documents, Relative to* . . . *the Land Situated in the South Western Parts of the United States;* . . . . Philadelphia, 1796.

Watkins, Robert and George, comps., *A Digest of the Laws of the State of Georgia, From its First Establishment as a British Province Down to the Year 1798, inclusive* . . . . Philadelphia, 1800.

[Yazoo]. *Report from the* [U. S.] *Committee of Claims, to Whom*

Were Referred the Representation and Memorials of Sundry Citizens of Massachusetts, Purchasers Under the Georgia Company; of the Agents for the New England Land Company, Purchasers Under the Georgia and Mississippi Company; and the Agent for Sundry Citizens of South Carolina, Purchasers Under the Upper Mississippi Company. Washington, 1805. The several memorials are presented under their separate title pages, each paged separately.

2. *Historical Correspondence, Writings, etc.*

Adams, John Quincy, *Memoirs of John Quincy Adams, . . . ,* edited by Charles Francis Adams, 12 vols. Philadelphia, 1874-1877.

Ames, Seth, ed., *Works of Fisher Ames. With a Selection from his Speeches and Correspondence,* 2 vols. Boston, 1854.

Bishop, Abraham, *Georgia Speculation Unveiled; in Two Numbers.* Hartford, 1797. Written in answer to a pamphlet put out by four Yazoo companies in defense of their action, entitled *State of Facts.*

Blair, Ruth, comp. and ed., *Some Early Tax Digests of Georgia.* [Atlanta], 1926.

Case of the Georgia Sales on the Mississippi Considered. Philadelphia, 1799. An anonymous pamphlet, probably by Harper, Robert G.

Cobbett, William, *Porcupine's Works; Containing Various Writings and Selections, Exhibiting a Faithful Picture of the United States of America . . . ,* 12 vols. London, 1801.

Fitzpatrick, John C., ed., *The Diaries of George Washington, 1748-1799,* 4 vols. Regents' ed. Boston, 1925.

Fitzpatrick, John C., ed., *The Writings of George Washington from the Original Manuscript Sources, 1745-1799,* 39 vols. Bicentennial ed. Washington, 1939.

Gibbes, R. W., comp., *Documentary History of the American Revolution: . . . , 1776-1782.* New York, 1857.

Gibbes, R. W., comp., *Documentary History of the American Revolution . . . , Chiefly in South Carolina, in 1781 and 1782, ...* Columbia, S. C., 1853.

Hamilton, Stanislaus Murray, ed., *The Writings of James Monroe . . . ,* 7 vols. New York and London, 1898-1903.

Hawes, Lilla M., ed., "Miscellaneous Papers of James Jackson, 1781-1798," *Ga. Hist. Quar.,* XXXVII (1953), 54-80, 147-60, 220-48, 299-329.

Historical Collections of the Joseph Habersham Chapter, Daughters of the American Revolution, 3 vols. Dalton, Georgia, 1902.

[Jackson, James], *Facts in Reply to the Agents of the New England*

Land Company, by a Georgian. Washington, 1805. This pamphlet was later reprinted in the [Yazoo] *Report of the Committee of Claims.*

[Jackson, James], *The Letters of Sicilius, to the Citizens of the State of Georgia, on the Constitutionality, the Policy, and the Legality of the Late Sale of Western Lands, in the State of Georgia, Considered in a Series of Numbers, By a Citizen of that State.* N. p., August, 1795. These letters, after appearing in certain Georgia papers, were published anonymously in pamphlet form in 1795.

Janson, Charles William, *The Stranger in America, 1793-1806.* New York, 1935.

Johnson, Joseph, *Traditions and Reminiscences Chiefly of the American Revolution in the South,* . . . Charleston, 1851.

King, Charles R., ed., *The Life and Correspondence of Rufus King* . . . , 6 vols. New York, 1894-1900.

Lafar, Mabel Freeman and Wilson, Caroline Price, comps., "Abstracts of Wills, Chatham County, Georgia, 1773-1817," *Genealogical Publications of the National Genealogical Society,* no. 6, 1-176. Washington, 1936.

Memorial of the Agents of the New England Mississippi Land Company to Congress, with a Vindication of their Title at Law Annexed. Washington, 1805.

Priest, William, *Travels in the United States of America; Commencing in the Year 1793, and Ending in 1797* . . . . London, 1802.

Sherwood, Adiel, *A Gazetteer of the State of Georgia:* . . . , *Greatly Enlarged and Improved.* 3rd ed. Washington, 1837. Contains some primary sources, but is inaccurate.

Sparks, Jared, ed., *The Works of Benjamin Franklin* . . . , 10 vols. Boston, 1836-1840.

State of Facts. Showing the Right of Certain Companies to the Lands Lately Purchased by them from the State of Georgia. Boston, 1795. An anonymous pamphlet.

Thomas, E. S., *Reminiscences of the Last Sixty-five Years* . . . . also, *Sketches of His Own Life and Times,* 2 vols. Hartford, 1840.

Wilson, Caroline Price, comp., *Annals of Georgia* . . . . , 3 vols. New York, and Savannah, 1928-1933. Important early records. The first volume has State Revolutionary Payroll, etc. The third volume contains mortuary records for Chatham County.

3. *Newspapers*
Augusta Chronicle and Gazette of the State, 1789-1807.
Augusta Herald, 1800.

Bibliography

City Gazette and Daily Advertiser (Charleston), 1795, 1796. Library of Congress.
Columbian Museum and Savannah Advertiser, 1796-1806. Emory University.
Federal Gazette and Baltimore Daily Advertiser, 1796.
Gazette of the State of Georgia (Savannah), 1787, 1788.
Georgia Gazette (Savannah), 1788-1802.
Georgia Republican and State Intelligencer (Savannah), 1803-1806.
Georgia State Gazette or Independent Register (Augusta), 1788.
National Intelligencer and Washington Advertiser, 1801-1806.
North Carolina Minerva (Fayetteville), 1796. University of North Carolina.
South Carolina Weekly Gazette (Charleston), 1785.

II. SECONDARY SOURCES

A. GENERAL HISTORIES

Adams, Henry, *History of the United States of America During the Administrations of Jefferson and Madison,* 9 vols. New York, 1889-1891.
Fortescue, J. W., *A History of the British Army,* 10 vols. London, 1910-1935.
Hildreth, Richard, *The History of the United States of America,* 6 vols. Revised ed. New York, [c. 1853-1880].
McMaster, John Bach, *A History of the People of the United States, from the Revolution to the Civil War,* 5 vols. New York, 1892-1900.
Morse, Jedidiah, *The American Gazetteer, . . . on the American Continent, . . . with a Particular Description of the Georgia Western Territory.* Boston, 1797.
Nevins, Allan, *The American States During and After the Revolution; 1775-1789.* New York, 1924.
Phillips, Ulrich Bonnell, *The Course of the South to Secession,* edited by Coulter, E. Merton. New York and London, [c. 1939].
Stedman, C., *The History of the Origin, Progress, and Termination of the American War,* 2 vols. London, 1794.
Tarleton, Lieutenant-Colonel [Sir Banastre], *A History of the Campaigns of 1780 and 1781, in the Southern Provinces of North America.* London, 1787.

B. STATE HISTORIES

Chappell, Absalom H., *Miscellanies of Georgia, Historical, Biographical, Descriptive . . . ,* three parts in one volume. Atlanta, 1874.

Cooper, Walter G., *The Story of Georgia*, 4 vols. New York, 1938. The fourth volume is biographical in character.

Coulter, E. Merton, *A Short History of Georgia*. Chapel Hill, 1933.

Georgia. A Guide to its Towns and Countryside. (Federal Writers Project). Athens, 1940.

Johnson, Amanda, *Georgia as Colony and State*. Atlanta, 1938.

Jones, Charles C., Jr., *The History of Georgia*, 2 vols. Boston and New York, 1883. The most comprehensive of nineteenth century histories of Georgia. Based on original sources.

Knight, Lucian Lamar, *Georgia's Landmarks, Memorials and Legends*, 2 vols. Atlanta, 1914.

McCrady, Edward, *The History of South Carolina in the Revolution, 1775-1780*. New York and London, 1901.

McCrady, Edward, *The History of South Carolina in the Revolution, 1780-1783*. New York and London, 1902.

Miller, Stephen F., *The Bench and Bar of Georgia: Memoirs and Sketches . . . , a Court Roll from 1790 to 1857, . . .* , 2 vols. Philadelphia, 1858.

Northen, William J., ed., *Men of Mark in Georgia . . .* , 7 vols. Atlanta, 1907-1912.

Park, Orville A., *The History of Georgia in the Eighteenth Century as Recorded in the Reports of the Georgia Bar Association.* [Probably Macon, 1921].

Phillips, Ulrich Bonnell, *Georgia and State Rights. A Study of the Political History of Georgia from the Revolution to the Civil War, with Particular Regard to Federal Relations.* Washington, 1902. Good background study of politics during the period of this study.

Pickett, Albert James, *History of Alabama, and incidentally of Georgia and Mississippi, from the Earliest Period*, 2 vols. Charleston, 1851.

Ramsay, David, *The History of South Carolina, from its First Settlement in 1670, to the Year 1808*, 2 vols. Charleston, 1809.

Ramsay, David, *The History of the Revolution of South Carolina, from a British Province to an Independent State*, 2 vols. Trenton, 1785.

Stevens, William Bacon, *A History of Georgia, from its First Discovery by Europeans to the Adoption of the Present Constitution in MDCCXCVIII*, 2 vols. Philadelphia, 1859. Based on widely selected primary sources. One of the best of the early writers on Georgia history.

Wheeler, John H., *Historical Sketches of North Carolina, . . .* , 2 vols. Philadelphia, 1851.

White, George, *Historical Collections of Georgia . . . .* New York,

1855. While serving as librarian in Charleston, Savannah, Milledgeville, and New York, White secured transcripts of colonial documents from London, Paris, and Madrid. He drew much on Sherwood and did not always make acknowledgment. Contains county history and short biographies based on original sources. Chiefly secondary.

White, George, *Statistics of the State of Georgia* . . . . Savannah, 1849. No publisher. Variously paged. Both primary and secondary sources of value.

C. County and City Histories

Lee, F. D., and Agnew, J. L., *Historical Record of the City of Savannah*. Savannah, 1869.

Wilson, Adelaide, *Historic and Picturesque Savannah*. Boston, 1889.

D. Monographs and Special Articles

Adams, Samuel B., "The Yazoo Fraud," *Georgia Historical Quarterly*, VII (1923), 155-65.

"Bethesda Crisis in 1791 . . . . Disaster to Whitefield's House of Mercy Averted," editorial, *Georgia Historical Quarterly*, I (1917), 108-34.

Bowers, Claude Gernade, *Jefferson and Hamilton. The Struggle for Democracy in America*. Boston and New York, [c. 1925].

Bowers, Claude Gernade, *Jefferson in Power. The Death Struggle of the Federalists*. Boston, [c. 1936].

Charlton, Walter G., "Button Gwinnett," *Georgia Historical Quarterly*, VIII (1924), 150-57.

Clarke, M. St. Clair, comp., *Cases of Contested Elections in Congress from the Year 1789 to 1834, Inclusive*. Washington, 1834.

Clarke, William Bordley, *Early and Historic Freemasonry of Georgia* . . . . Savannah, [c. 1924].

Courtenay, William A., *Proceedings at the Unveiling of the Battle Monument in . . . Commemoration of the Centennial of the Battle of Cowpens*. Charleston, 1896.

Cunningham, T. M., "The Constitution of Georgia," *Georgia Historical Quarterly*, XXI (1937), 92-99.

Downs, Randolph C., "Creek-American Relations 1782-1790," *Georgia Historical Quarterly*, XXI (1937), 142-84.

Foster, Sophia Lee, comp., *Revolutionary Reader. Reminiscenses and Indian Legends*. Atlanta, 1913. Chiefly secondary.

Gamble, Thomas, *Annals of Savannah: Savannah Duels and Duellists, 1773-1877*. Savannah, [c. 1923].

Gamble, Thomas, "Georgia's First Contested Election; Jackson ousted Wayne from Congress," *Savannah Morning News*, February 23, 1930.

Gamble, Thomas, "Mad Anthony Wayne as Planter," *Savannah Morning News*, December 8, 1929.

Gamble, Thomas, "When James Jackson and Thos. Gibbons First Met Here on the Field of Honor," *Savannah Morning News*, January 19, 1930.

Green, Fletcher M., *Constitutional Development in the South Atlantic States, 1776-1860, a Study in the Evolution of Democracy.* Chapel Hill, 1930.

Grice, Warren, "Georgia Appointments by President Washington," *Georgia Historical Quarterly*, VII (1923), 181-212.

Harden, William, "A Neglected Period of Georgia History by the Editor," *Georgia Historical Quarterly*, II (1918), 198-224.

Haskins, Charles H., *The Yazoo Land Companies*. New York, 1891. The best study on the Yazoo question. Documented.

Heath, William Estill, "The Yazoo Land Fraud," *Georgia Historical Quarterly*, XVI (1932), 274-91.

Lossing, Benson J., *The Pictorial Field-Book of the Revolution; ...*, 2 vols. New York, 1851, 1852.

Mackall, Leonard L., "Edward Langworthy and the First Attempt to Write a Separate History of Georgia, With Selections from the Long-Lost Langworthy Papers," *Georgia Historical Quarterly*, VII (1923), 1-17.

McElreath, Walter, *A Treatise on the Constitution of Georgia*. Atlanta, 1912.

McLendon, S. G., *History of the Public Domain of Georgia*. Atlanta, [c. 1924].

Manual of the University of Georgia. Atlanta, 1890.

Murray, Paul, "The Whig Party in Georgia, 1825-1853." An unpublished Doctoral Dissertation, 1940. University of North Carolina.

Rabun, James W., "Georgia and the Creek Indians." An unpublished Master of Arts thesis, 1937. University of North Carolina.

Sakolski, A. M., *The Great American Land Bubble* .... New York and London, 1932.

Tittamin, William, "Forts Jackson, Lee, and Barton." Savannah, 1944. A typed MS. of 10 pages. Georgia Historical Society Library, Savannah.

Treat, Payson Jackson, *The National Land System, 1785-1820*. New York, 1910.

E. BIOGRAPHIES

Beveridge, Albert J., *The Life of John Marshall*, 4 vols. Boston, 1917, 1929.

Boyd, Thomas, *Mad Anthony Wayne*. New York and London, 1929.

Caughey, John Walton, *McGillivray of the Creeks*. Norman, 1938.

Charlton, Thomas U. P., *The Life of Major General James Jackson*, Part I. Augusta, 1809. Reprinted, Atlanta, [1897]. Part I ends with Jackson's refusal of the governorship in 1788; Part II was never written. The reprint has an appendix, pages 57-215, which contains Charlton's "Eulogium," several biographical sketches of Jackson by other writers, and a collection of thirty-five of Jackson's letters. All references to Charlton's *Life* in this work are to the reprint. Copies of the original may be seen at the University of Georgia, the Charleston Library Society, and the Library of the Boston Athenaeum.

Elliott, Mamie McRee, "A Sketch of the Life of James Jackson (1757-1806)." An unpublished Master of Arts thesis, 1939. University of Georgia.

Garland, Hugh A., *The Life of John Randolph of Roanoke*, 2 vols. New York, 1851.

[Gilmer, George Rockingham], *Sketches of Some of the First Settlers of Upper Georgia, of the Cherokees, and the Author*. New York and London, 1855. Contains some original documents.

Graham, James, comp., *The Life of General Daniel Morgan of the Virginia Line of the Army of the United States*. New York and Cincinnati, 1856.

Harden, Edward J., *The Life of George M. Troup*, Savannah, 1859.

Hays, Louise Frederick, *Hero of Hornet's Nest, A Biography of Elijah Clark, 1733-1799*. New York, 1946.

"Jackson, James," *Biographical Directory of the American Congress, 1774-1927*, 1142, 1143. Washington, 1928.

"Jackson, James," *The New International Encyclopedia*, edited by Daniel Cort Gilman, *et al.*, XII, 516. New York, 1933.

"Jackson, Joseph Webber," *Biographical Directory of the American Congress, 1774-1927*, 1143. Washington, 1928.

Jenkins, Charles Francis, *Button Gwinnett, Signer of the Declaration of Independence*. Garden City, N. Y., 1926.

Johnson, William, comp., *Sketches of the Life and Correspondence of Nathanael Greene . . .*, 2 vols. Charleston, 1822.

Jones, Charles C., Jr., *The Life and Services of the Honorable Maj. Gen. Samuel Elbert of Georgia*. Cambridge, 1887.

Knight, Lucian Lamar, "Genealogy of the Knight, Walton, Cobb, . . . Jackson, Grant and other Georgia Families." N. p., no date. This typed bound volume may be seen at the Library of Congress.

Pickens, Andrew Lee, *Skyagunsta, the Border Wizard Owl. Major General Andrew Pickens (1739-1817)*. Greenville, S. C., [c. 1934].

Preston, John Hyde, *A Gentleman Rebel, Mad Anthony Wayne*. New York, [c. 1930].

"Wereat, John," *The National Cyclopaedia of American Biography* ..., I, 493.

Whitaker, Arthur P., "Jackson, James," *Dictionary of American Biography*, edited by Allen Johnson and Dumas Malone, IX, 544, 545.

Wildes, Harry Emerson, *Anthony Wayne, Trouble Shooter of the American Revolution*. New York [c. 1941].

INDEX

Adams, John, 55, 105, 144, 146, 149, 158, 161, 164, 168, 175, 178, 181, 187, 188, 189, 191; federal appointments in Georgia, 169; and the Judiciary Act, 172-74
Adams, John Quincy, 140; writes of Jackson, 140, 183
Alien and Sedition Acts, 164-65; 188
Allen, Isaac, at Long Cane Creek, 8
Allison Henry, captain, 16; candidate for Congress, 69
Ames, Fisher, 71, 76, 77
Augusta, Battle of, 14-15, 186
Augusta, state government at, 6, 65, 67
Augusta, Treaty of, with Creek Indians, 46
Augusta Chronicle, 110 132
Aurora (Philadelphia), 119, 120

Bacon, Nathaniel, 141
Baker, Col. John, 4, 14
Baldwin, Abraham, 139, 146, 147, 165, 166, 168, 184; congressman, 69, 86; and the Wayne-Jackson controversy, 94-95, 97, 100; challenged by Gunn, 123-24; commissioner in Yazoo cession, 137; president *pro tempore* of Senate, 170
Barnard, Timothy, Indian agent, 40
Barnwell, Major Robert, 21
Bassett, Richard, 173
Bell, Jeff, 93, 97
Benton, Thomas Hart, on the death of Jackson, 183
Bethesda Orphanage, 62-63
Bigby, Tom, 120
Big Warrior, chief at Coleraine conference, 52

Bishop, Abraham, writes on Yazoo speculations, 135, 140
Blackstock, Battle of, 7, 186
Blount, Lt. Stephen, 16
Boudinot, Elias, 64, 75
Bowles, William Augustus, 163
Bradley, Stephen R., 170
Brailsford v. Georgia, 64
Briggs, Isaac, candidate for Congress, 69
British, Georgia breaks with, 2-3; attacked in Savannah harbor, 3; attacked at Savannah 4-5; in battle of Cowpens, 9-10; North Carolina campaign of, 12-14; battle for Augusta, 14-15; at battle of Ogeechee, 19-20; lose Savannah, 22-23, 59; restitution of confiscated lands, 158-59
Brown, Thomas, Georgia Tory, 14; surrenders at Fort Grierson, 15; at battle of Ogeechee, 23
Brown, William, 165
Brownsboro Plan, 25-26
Brownson, Nathan, 20; plot against, 17
Bryan, John, 33
Bryan, Jonathan, 3
Bryan, Joseph, 138
Bugg, Sherwood, 16
Bulloch, Archibald, president of Council of Safety, 2, 3
Bulloch, William, 165
Burke, Dr. Michael, 155
Burnett, Charles, 32
Burrows, John, attacks Jackson, 94, 96

Campbell, Archibald, British officer, 4, 19, 20
Candler, William, 33
Carey, Mathew, 7

213

Carleton, Sir Guy, orders evacuation of Savannah, 23
Carnes, Richard, legislator, 142; judge, 155
Caswell, Richard, governor of North Carolina, 40
Charlton, Thomas U. P., 13, 145; eulogium on Jackson, 184-85
Chatham County, 59, 61, 67; Academy and Bethesda Orphanage, 62-63; and removal of state papers, 65-66; and Yazoo Act, 109-10
Cherokee Indians, in the American Revolution, 22-23, 50; cede land to Georgia, 143; on Georgia frontier, 150; removal of, 188. See Indians
Chickasaw Indians, and Yazoo lands, 111-12. See Indians
Chisholm v. Georgia, 64
Choctaw Indians, and Yazoo lands, 111-112. See Indians
Christ Episcopal Church, 29
Chronicle (Savannah), 54, 120, 126
Church, Alonzo, 147
Clarke, Alured, British general, 17; arouses Indians, 22
Clarke, Elijah, and American Revolution, 7, 8, 14, 15, 33, 39, 40, 49, 50
Clarke, Elijah, the Younger, in Yazoo land companies, 144; student at Yale, 146
Clarke, John, in Yazoo land companies, 144; appointed to University Board, 147
Clay, Joseph, candidate for Congress, 69
Clay, Joseph, Jr., lawyer, 104
Clymer, George, and Coleraine conference, 51
Cobb, John, Governor Mathews' secretary, 40
Coleraine, Treaty of, 126, 138, 162
Collier, Thomas, 129
Columbian Museum (Savannah), supports Jackson, 119, 120, 160, 165; newspaper war on Yazoo lands, 124-26, 129; attacks Jackson, 170-72
Constitution of 1777, 60, 65; of 1798, 89, 101, 128, 147, 152
Corbett, William, reports on Jackson controversy, 153-54
Cornwallis, General Charles, and American Revolution, 8, 10, 13-14
Council of Safety, appointed, 2, 3
Cowpens, Battle of, 8-10; 186

Cox, Zachariah, and Yazoo lands, 139, 141
Coxe, Tenche, 161
Crawford, William H., Jackson protege, 145, 146
Creek Indians, 73, 87, 150; in American Revolution, 22, 23; Treaty of Galphinton, 36-37; give trouble after Revolution, 38-42, 43-46; make Treaty of New York, 46-48; renew attacks, 48-51; Coleraine conference and treaty with, 51-54; land cessions of, 137, 141-42, 162-64. See Indians
Cunningham, Major John, 11
Cuthbert, Major Seth John, 30

Dallas and Ingersoll, law firm, 26, 159
Daughters of the American Revolution, 186
Davidson, William, heads North Carolina militia, 13
Davis, David, reveals plot against Jackson, 17-18
Dayton, Jonathan, 177
d'Estaing, Count, in American Revolution, 5
de Grasse, Count, in appreciation of, 103
Devaux, Major Peter, 5, 66
Digest, official, controversy over, 128-29, 166
Dill, James, 31
Duane, William, editor, 119
Dwight, Thomas, 71, 77

East Florida, invaded, 3-4; Indian troubles with, 48; refuge for slaves, 151, 162
Ebenezer, legislature at, 59
Eigle, John, 93
Emmanuel, David, 114; governor, 167
Excise tax, Jackson opposes, 77-78

Farley, Samuel, close friend of Jackson, 2, 28, 184
Federalist (Washington), 166, 169
Federal Gazette, 89
Ferguson, Patrick, at King's Mountain, 8
Ferrand, Marie Louis, 181
Few, Benjamin, defeated at Long Cane Creek, 8
Few, William, and Indian problems, 36, 46; as a conservative, 67; candidate for Congress, 69; defeated for

Index   215

Senate, 101; and Yazoo lands, 107, 114, 124; judge, 134
Fishdam Ford, engagement at, 7
Fletcher v. Peck, 143
Fort Arthur, 158
Fort Grierson, siege of, 14-15
Fort Jackson, 3, 186
Fort Ninety-Six, 8, 14, 15
France, and Louisiana Purchase, 179-80; naval war with, 149-51; and Santo Domingo trade, 181-82
Franklin, Benjamin, 89, 158, 159
Franklin, George, 114
Frelinghuysen, Frederick, 124

Gallatin, Albert, 54, 103, 137, 176
Galphinton Treaty, with Indians, 36-37, 53, 55
Genet, Edmond, 50 102
Gentleman's Gazette (London), 90
Georgia, breaks with Britain, 2-3; revolutionists attack in Savannah harbor, 3; attack on Savannah, 4-5; militia at Cowpens, 8-11; militia in North Carolina campaign, 12-13; siege of Augusta, 14-15; battle of Ogeechee Ferry, 19-20; capture of Savannah, 21-23; resents Treaty of New York, 47; protests actions of Coleraine conference, 53-55; Washington visits, 55-56; economic plight of, 63-64; state sovereignty cases against, 64-65; political situation 1781 to 1797, 67-68; and National Bank, 85; Wayne-Jackson contested election, 90-91; and Yazoo land sale, 105-09; annulling of Yazoo sale, 109-13; Rescinding Act of, 114-22; Yazoo land cession in, 136-39; foreign relations of, 149-53; foreign slave trade, 152-53; restitution of confiscated lands in, 162-64
Georgia Gazette (Savannah), 41, 90, 92; publishes Jackson's essays, 110; controversy with Jackson, 153-55
Georgia Republican and State Intelligencer, 119
Georgia State Gazette or Independent Register, 31
Gershal, Archibald, 142
Gibbons, Thomas, 60, 63, 69; duels of, 29-31, 101; and 1791 contested election, 93, 98, 99; opposed for judgeship, 169
Gibbons, William, in Yazoo land fraud, 107

Gibbons, William, Jr., 66
Giles, Major Edward, 11
Giles, William Branch, opposes National Bank, 84; and Wayne-Jackson controversy, 100
Gillis, Sheriff R., 149
Glascock, James, and Yazoo fraud, 128
Glascock, Thomas, and relations with Indians, 36, 49
Glass, John, 109
Glen, Major John, 152
Glenn, John, on Council of Safety, 2
Goodgame, John, 18
Granger, Gideon, Postmaster-General, 140, 174-75
Graves, John, candidate for Congress, 69
Greene, Nathanael, 61, 66, 186; in American Revolution, 8-9, 11, 12-13, 15-16, 20, 21; retirement and death, 37-38
Greene, Mrs. Nathanael, 157
Greene, Lt. William, 20
Gresham, Davis, senator, 142
Grierson, Colonel, Tory, captured and shot, 15
Griffin, Cyrus, Indian commissioner, 45
Gunn, James, 55, 165; in American Revolution, 13, 14; and Indian troubles, 40, 49; challenges to duel, 37, 123-24; U. S. senator, 101, 102; and Yazoo lands, 107, 109, 115, 126, 128, 133, 142; duels with Jackson, 126-27
Gunn, Mrs. James, 133
Gwinnett, Button, 67

Habersham, James, 22; and Bethesda Orphanage, 63
Habersham, John, in American Revolution, 23; collector of customs, 151
Habersham, Joseph, 3, 66, 67, 104
Hall, Gov. Lyman, 64
Hamilton, Alexander, Federalist, 70, 71, 151, 161, 188; policies of, 75-83
Hammond, Colonel Leroy, 15
Hammond, Samuel, in American Revolution, 7, 11, 14
Hampton, Wade, 21
Handley, Gov. George, deals with Indian problem, 41-42
Hanson, John, 64
Harper, Robert Goodloe, 54
Harvey, Lt. Benjamin, 16
Hastings, Madame Selina, and Bethesda Orphanage, 62-63
Hastings, Theophilus, 62

Hawkins, Benjamin, in American Revolution, 61; and Indian relations, 53, 162-63
Heard, Stephen, justice of peace, 142
Hendrix, James, at Coleraine conference, 51, 52, 54
Hillegar, Baptist, candidate for Congress, 69
Hooe, J. P., 174
Hopewell treaties, 111
Houstoun, Sir George, and Bethesda Orphanage, 63
Houstoun, John, governor, 33; plantation attacked, 42; Revolutionary radical, 67; candidate for Senate, 101
Houstoun, William, candidate for Congress, 69
Houstoun County, organized, 106
Howard, Col. John Eager, in American Revolution, 9, 10, 11
Howe, General Robert, 4
Howley, Richard, sent to Congress, 6
Hudson, Nathaniel, and the Wayne-Jackson controversy, 93, 97, 98
Humphreys, David, Indian commissioner, 45

Inman, Joshua, 11
Inverness, American vessel, 3
Irwin, Jared, governor, 33, 58, 105; and Indian relations, 51, 52, 58; and Yazoo lands, 114, 117

Jackson, Abraham, brother of James, 154
Jackson, Andrew, 145, 165
Jackson, Henry, brother of James, 32
Jackson, Jabez Young, son of James, 29
Jackson, James, the elder, 1
Jackson, James, birth, 1; comes to America, 1-2; holds offices under Council of Safety, 2; in first violences against Britain, 1, 2-3; Major in attack on Savannah, 4-5; duels with George Wells, 5-6; at Fishdam Ford engagement, 6-8; urges history of Georgia be written, 12; and Battle of Cowpens, 8-12; with Greene in North Carolina, 12-13; at siege of Augusta, 14-15; marches to relief of Ninety-Six, 15-16; commander of Georgia State Legion, 16-17; Tory plot against, 17-18; captures Ebenezer, 18; relates hardships of his troops, 18-19; fails to take Ogeechee Ferry, 19; attacks at Butler house, 19-20; and the capture of Savannah, 22-23; presented house in Savannah, 24; enters law practice, 25-26; marriage, 27-28; family life of, 28-29; personal characteristics, 31, 191-192; planter, 31-34; 187; as a Mason, 35; educational and literary interests of, 35; duels with Gibbons, 29-31; financial status of, 34-35; honorary member of Society of Cincinnati, 36; given highest Georgia military honor, 36; delivers challenge to Gen. Greene, 37; makes military arrangements for funeral of Gen. Greene, 38; takes measures against runaway slaves, 39-40, 42; supports bills for Indian control, 39; frontier service against Indians, 40-42; troops of mutiny, 42-43; enters Congress, 43; and the Indian problem, 43-45, 46, 48-51, 187; opposes Treaty of New York, 47-48; elected to U. S. Senate, 50; and the Coleraine conference, 51-55; greets Washington, 55-56; petitions legislature for pay for Revolutionary services, 56-58; last military services of, 58; elections to legislature, 59-60; leniency of toward Tories, 60-61; conservative in state financial policies, 61; and University of Georgia, 61-62, 146-47; trustee for Chatham Academy and Bethesda Orphanage, 62-63; and Georgia economic problems, 63-64; and state sovereignty, 64-65; on state military service, 65; and separation of state and church, 65; in controversy over removal of state papers, 65-66; refuses governorship, 66; ends legislative career, 67; and Constitution of 1798, 67; presidential elector, 1788, 67; elected governor, 66, 67, 68; political support of, 67-68; enters lower house of First Congress, 69-72; on president's power of removal, 72-73; advocate of states' rights and democracy, 73-75, 89; on Hamilton's financial plan, 75-83, 84-85, 89; opposes lower federal courts, 78-79, 89; on location of capital, 83-84; and naturalization bill, 84; views on military affairs, 85-86; and salaries of federal officials, 86; and the question of slavery, 86-89; election controversy with Anthony Wayne, 90-101; second duel with Gibbons, 101; elected to U. S. Senate, 101; and Jay's Treaty, 101-103; on military affairs, 103; op-

Index

poses excise tax, 104; urges federal civil appointments for Georgians, 104; resigns from Senate, 104; and the Yazoo land sale, 105-109; runs for legislature, 109-10; essays of published, 110-13; and rescinding of Yazoo sales, 113-18, 189-90; and destruction of Yazoo documents, 118-22; attacks on after Yazoo annulment, 123-24, 124-26, 132-33, 135; fights duels over Yazoo affair, 126-30; controversy with Waldburger, 130-32; attacks James Gunn in a letter, 133; controversy with George Walton, 133-35; and cession of Yazoo lands, 136-39; on adjusting Yazoo claims, 139-43; leader of Jeffersonian party in Georgia, 144-46; elected governor, 146; and Constitution of 1798, 147-48; urges salary increase for state officials, 148-49; and state tax system, 149; foreign affairs during governorship of, 149-53; controversy with *Southern Sentinel*, 153-55; attempts to check disease, 155; and development of cotton gin, 156-58; and restitution of confiscated lands, 158-59; reelected governor, 159; controversy over 1800 legislative message, 160-62; and Indian relations, 162-64; and public education 164; criticizes Alien and Sedition laws, 164, 188; elected to U. S. Senate, 165; honored at banquet, 165-66; summary of governorship of, 167; enters U. S. Senate, 168; and the patronage question, 168-70; refuses office of president *pro tempore*, 170; press attacks on, 170-72; favors repeal of Judiciary Act, 172-74, 188; and extending mail transportation, 174-75; regard for Jefferson, 175-76, 187-88; chairman of military committee, 176; favors repeal of excise tax, 176; and small states vs. large states, 176-77; and the Louisiana Purchase, 176-80, 188; opposes removal of capital, 180-81; on the embargo against Santo Domingo, 181-82; death of, 182-85; will of, 185; evaluation of as a public figure, 185, 186-91; memorials to, 186
Jackson, James, Jr., 29, 147
Jackson, James, grandson, 29
Jackson, John, son, 29
Jackson, Joseph Webber, son, 29
Jackson, Mary Charlotte Young (Mrs. James), 27-29, 109, 168, 185

Jackson, William Henry, son, 29, 147
Jay, John, 102, 109, 158
Jay's Treaty, 102-103, 109, 151
Jefferson, Thomas, 105, 145, 146, 164, 168, 169, 170, 172, 177; quoted, 19, 87; and Hamilton's policies, 70, 71, 83; and Yazoo lands, 137, 138; Jackson's regard for, 103, 175, 187, 188, 191
Jeffersonian Aurora (Philadelphia), 119
Johnson, Rev. John, 63
Johnson, Joseph, 7
Jones, George, at 1798 Constitution Convention, 147
Jones, James, on Yazoo investigation commission, 114; on Indian Commission, 137; at 1798 Constitution Convention, 147
Jones, Seaborn, 92-132
Judiciary Act of 1801, repeal of, 172-74, 188

Kincaid, George, confiscated lands of, 32-33
Kincaid, Mrs. George, restitution of lands of, 158
King, John, Indian commissioner, 36; elected to legislature, 142; and Spanish border troubles, 163
King's Mountain, Battle of, 8
Knox, Henry, and Treaty of New York, 46

Lacy, Col. Edward, 7
Langworthy, Edward, 7, 12, 18, 109
Lanier, Lemuel, 33
Leclerc, Victor, 181
Lee, Harry, at capture of Augusta, 14, 15
Lewis, Attorney-General, 96, 98, 99, 100
Lincoln, Benjamin, Continental Southern commander, 5; Indian commissioner, 45, 104
Lincoln, Levi, 137
London, John, 93
Long Cane Creek, engagement at, 8
Longstreet, William, 115
Louisiana Purchase, 176-80, 188
Louisville, Georgia capital, 59, 113
Louisville Gazette and Trumpet, 154
Lowden, William, 109
Lyons, John, 16

Mackay, Archibald, witnesses Jackson's will, 185

Maclay, William, Senator, opposes Hamilton's plans, 70, 71
Macon, Nathaniel, 54
Madison, James, 45, 71, 72, 73, 74, 100, 104, 105, 124, 137, 138, 145, 168-69, 172, 174; and Hamilton's policies, 75-83
Maien, John, paints Jackson portrait, 186
Mann, Luke, Georgia senator, 115, 142
Marbury v. Madison, 174
Marbury, William, 174
Marion, General Francis, 8
Marshall, John, 143
Martin, John, governor, 21
Masonic Lodge, 35, 183, 184, 185
Mathews, Gov. George, and Georgia land speculations, 33; deals with Indian ravages, 39-40; praises Jackson, 41, 51; elected to Congress, 69; on militia committee, 85; and Yazoo land bill, 105, 107, 116, 123, 141
Maxwell, Benjamin, and bribes offered Jackson, 26, 125
McAllister, Jackson overseer, 34
McCall, Col. James, at Battle of Cowpens, 9
McDowell, Col. Charles, 11
McGillivray, Alexander, 40, 43, 52, 82; incites hostilities, 38, 41; at Rock Landing conference, 42; Jackson hostile toward, 44-45; and the Treaty of New York, 46, 47
McGillivray, John, 31
McHenry, James, Secretary of War, 148, 162
McIntosh, Lachlan, 17, 142
McIntosh, Capt. William, 30
McMillan, Alexander, controversy with Jackson, 153-55
McNeil, editor of *Chronicle*, and Indian problems, 48, 54
Meigs, Josiah, and University of Georgia, 146, 147
Mein, William, confiscated lands of, 26, 158
Midway Congregational Church, 4
Millar, Nicholas, 16
Milledge, John, 35, 48, 57, 101, 102, 103, 121, 127, 153, 168, 185; in American Revolution, 3, 5; as governor, 58, 105, 184; and Yazoo lands, 133, 137, 139; on University Board, 147
Milledge, Mrs. John, 168
Milledgeville, capital, 59

Miller, Daniel, 97
Miller, Phineas, and the cotton gin, 157-58, 161
Milton, John, Georgia Secretary of State, 65, 66
Mississippi Territory, organized, 106,136
Mitchell, David B., and Yazoo Rescinding Act, 114, 125; lawyer, 146; appointed Federal district attorney, 169; and death of Jackson, 184
Mitchell, John, 34
Monroe, James, 105, 145, 151, 178
Moore, John, 93; on rescinding committee, 114
Moreton-Hamstead, Devonshire, 1
Morgan, Daniel, in the American Revolution, 8, 9-10, 11, 12, 186
Morris, Gouverneur, 102, 172, 173
Morrison, Captain John, 16
Morse, Rev. Jedidiah, *Geography*, 78; and the Rescinding Act, 121
Mossman, James, 158
Mounger, Edwin, state treasurer, 155
Murphy, Daniel, Georgia superintendant of Indian affairs, 38

Napoleon, 179
National Bank, established, 84-85
National Intelligencer, 119, 139, 185
New York, Treaty of, with Creek Indians, 46-48, 138, 149, 152, 162
Niles Register, 67

Oconee Section, lands, 51, 54, 55
Ogeechee, Battle of, 19-20
Osborne, Henry, candidate for Congress, 69; contested election, 1791, 91-94, 97, 98, 100, 101
Oswald, Richard, 159

Palmer, Thomas, 109
Pearre, James, Jr., 65
Pendleton, Nathanael, and Yazoo land fraud, 107, 142
Penn, William, 187
Pickens, Col. Andrew, commander in American Revolution, 8-10, 11-12, 13, 14, 15, 16, 186; and Coleraine conference, 51, 53
Pickering, Timothy, 104, 136, 175
Pickett, A. J., duel with Jackson, 126
Pierce, William, candidate for Congress, 69
Pinckney, Thomas, 54, 146, 151
Philips, Captain Ralph Spence, 129

Index

Phillips, Ulrich Bonnell, evaluates Jackson, 185
Porcupine's Gazete, 132
Porcupine's Works, 154
Prevost, Major General Augustin, 4
Prevost, L. Col. Mark, 4
Provincial Congress in Georgia, 12, 27

"Quids," 138, 188

Randolph, John, 138, 143, 184, 188
Rawdon, Lord, British officer, 15, 16
Rescinding Act, of Yazoo lands sales, 115-18
Richmond Academy, 45
Ross, James, 177
Ross, Capt. William, leader in mutiny of Jackson's troops, 42

Salter, John, 155-56
San Lorenzo, Treaty of, 151
Savannah, in American Revolution, 1-4; destroyed by fire, 58; capital, 59, 65, 67; at the death of Jackson, 186
Savannah Hibernian Fusileers, 168
Scarborough, British vessel, 3
Schriver, J. M., candidate for Congress, 69
Scott, John M., surgeon, 98
Screven, General James, 4
Seagrove, James, Federal Indian agent, 48, 49, 50, 52; duel with Jackson, 126; and the Waldburger controversy, 132
Sevier, John, 56
Shaffer, Balthaser, 109
Shoulderbone, Treaty of, 53-54
Simmons, William, leader in plot against Jackson, 18
Simms, James, and the Coleraine conference, 51, 54
Sitgreaves, Samuel, 136
Skidaway Island, last Revolutionary fighting on Georgia soil, 23
Slavery, debated in First Congress, 86-89; controlling trade in, 151, 152-53, 162; importation of, 180, 181; holdings of Jackson, 191
Smith, John Car., 109
Smith, Samuel, 93, 98
Smith, S. C., 71
Society of the Cincinnati, 36
South Carolina Yazoo Company, 107
Spain, forts of on Georgia territory, 48; relations with Georgia, 151-52, 162, 163; and the Louisiana Purchase, 177-80
Stafford, John R., 30
Stallings, Lt. Ezekiel, 16
Stallings, Capt. James, 16
Stark, Ebenezer, 185
State of Franklin (Tennessee), promises aid against Indians, 40
Stedman, C., *History of the Origin, Progress, and Termination of the American War,* 19
Stephens, William, attorney-general for Council of Safety, 2; grandmaster of Masonic Lodge, 35; and removal of Georgia state papers, 65; federal district judge, 169
Stevens, William B., 119
Stirk, Samuel, 14, 66
Stith, Judge, and Yazoo land fraud, 107, 169
Strong, Caleb, governor of Massachusetts, 109
Sturges, Daniel, Georgia's surveyor-general, 32, 57, 139, 171
Suchens, Moultrie, 106
Sumner, Job, candidate for Congress, 69
Sumter, Col. Thomas, 7, 44

Taliaferro, Benjamin, Indian commissioner, 48, 137; Georgia senator, 52
Tallassee, County of, ceded to Georgia, 37, 45; returned to Indians, 46-47; disputed, 51, 54, 55, 137, 162
Tammany Society of Savannah, 185
Tariff, Jackson on, 175-77
Tarleton, Lt. Col. Banastre, and the American Revolution, 6, 8-10, 13
Tattnall, John Mulrine, 31, 91; Indian commissioner, 48; citizenship restored, 60
Tattnall, Josiah, 146, 147, 165
Telfair, Gov. Edward, and Indian troubles, 36, 48, 49; in controversy over removal of state papers, 65-66; candidate for Congress, 69; calls special election, 1792, 100, 101; and Yazoo lands, 107, 124
Tennessee Yazoo Company, 107
Thomas, E. S., 120
Thomas, Robards, 123
Torrent's Tavern, engagement at, 13
Treutlen, Gov. John Adams, 12
Troup, George M., governor, 105; Jackson's protege, 145; party leader, 146

Trumbull, Jonathan, Speaker of the House, 100
Twiggs, John, in American Revolution, 7, 18, 19; and Indian relations, 39, 48, 49 50; and Yazoo fraud, 107, 124, 126; on University Board, 147
Tybee Island, attacked, 3

University of Georgia, 61-62, 147

Virginia Gazette, 87
Virginia Yazoo Company, 107
Von Vattel, Emmerich, 141

Waldburger, Jacob, clerk to Jackson, 26; and Osborne impeachment trial, 91; controversy with Jackson, 130-32
Walker, George, 169
Walsh, Thomas, land speculator, 106, 107
Walton, George, in American Revolution, 1, 3, 11; head of radical patriot government, 6, 67; judge, 12, 25; governor, 33, 42, 43, 105; controversy with Jackson, 125, 133-35
Washington, George, 8, 37, 71, 72, 73, 102, 151, 178, 187; and Indian problems, 43, 46-47, 48, 49, 51; visits Georgia, 55-56, 90, 91; Jay's Treaty, 103-104; and Yazoo lands, 108, 142
Washington, Major Thomas, 16
Washington, Col. William, 9, 10
Washington Advertiser, 119
Watkins, George, 52, and the Yazoo transactions, 115, 126; *Digest* of, 128, 129, 166
Watkins, Col. Robert, fights and duels with Jackson, 127-30; *Digest* of, 128, 129, 166
Wayne, Anthony, in American Revolution in Georgia, 21, 23, 170, 186; at death of Gen. Greene, 37, 38; Congressional candidate, 67-68; contested election of 1791, 90-101; county named for, 139
Webber, Mary, mother of James Jackson, 1
Wells, George, duels with Jackson, 6; radical patriot, 67
Wereat, John, close friend of Jackson, 2, 6, 184; in conservative patriot group, 6, 67; and Yazoo lands sale, 107, 112, 124
Wereat, Nancy, 27
Wesley, John, 62

West, Samuel, 20
Whiskey Insurrection, 11
White, Col. Anthony Walton, 21
White, George, 58
White, Dr. James, Indian agent, 39
White, Samuel, Federalist, 176, 177, 179
Whitefield, Rev. George, and Bethesda Orphanage, 62, 63
Whitefield, George, ward of Jackson, 185
Whitefield, Thomas, ward of Jackson, 185
Whitefield, William, ward of Jackson, 185
Whitney, Eli, and the cotton gin, 157-58, 161
Wildes, H. E., 92
Williams, Hezekiah, British officer, 21
Williams, Roger, 187
Wilson, James, and Yazoo land sale, 107, 141, 142
Winn, Col. Richard, at Fishdam Ford engagement, 7
Wolcott, Oliver, commissioner on Yazoo land titles, 136
Wright, Sir James, royal governor of Georgia, 2, 6, 18, 21, 23, 27, 32
Wright, Robert, 176
Wright, Major Samuel, 151
Wylly, Alex, 158
Wylly, Richard, 65, 104

Yazoo lands, sale of, 105-07; Jackson opposes sale, 12, 68, 104, 108-10; Jackson's essays on, 110-13; rescinding of Yazoo Act, 113-17, 189-90; Rescinding Act included in new Constitution, 117-18; documents burned, 118-22; newspapers attack Jackson for stand on, 124-26, 132-33, 135; Jackson duels fought over, 126-30; Jackson-Waldburger controversy over, 130-32; Jackson-Walton controversy over, 133-35; ceded to United States, 136-39, 148; claims adjusted, 139-43
Yorktown, surrender at, 14
Young, James Box, 185
Young, Mary Charlotte, marries Jackson, 27-28
Young, Mrs. Sophia, 185
Young, Thomas, 26, 27
Young, William, Jackson's father-in-law, 185

Zubly's Ferry, 1

www.ingramcontent.com/pod-product-compliance
Lightning Source LLC
Chambersburg PA
CBHW020946230426
43666CB00005B/195